D1255927

The Thane of Cawdor Comes to Bauxite

THE THANE OF CAWDOR COMES TO BAUXITE

and Other Whimsy and Wisdom

From the Pen of **Mike Trimble**

BUTLER CENTER BOOKS

LITTLE ROCK, ARKANSAS

The Butler Center for Arkansas Studies
Central Arkansas Library System
100 Rock Street
Little Rock, Arkansas 72201
www.robertslibrary.org

ISBN (Hardcover): 978-1-945624-27-8

Editor: Ernie Dumas
Cover illustrations and design: David Malcolm Rose
Book design: H. K. Stewart

The Butler Center is grateful to the *Arkansas Democrat-Gazette*, *Arkansas
Times*, and *Denton Record-Chronicle* for permission to reprint Mike Trimble's
writings in these pages.

Library of Congress Cataloging-in-Publication Data

Names: Trimble, Mike, 1943-2021, author.
Title: The Thane of Cawdor comes to Bauxite and other whimsy and wisdom /
    from the pen of Mike Trimble.
Description: Little Rock, Arkansas : Butler Center Books, [2023] | Includes
    index. | Summary: ""Although of a relatively scarce breed," the Arkansas
    Times observed in the obituary of the itinerant writer it had once
    employed, "Mike Trimble was Arkansas's and perhaps the country's
    greatest self-deprecating journalist." Readers will find in the
    following selections from Trimble's fifty-year inventory of wit and
    wisdom all the vindication they might seek for that quaint judgment-the
    rare humble author"-- Provided by publisher.
Identifiers: LCCN 2023002056 | ISBN 9781945624278 (cloth)
Subjects: LCSH: Journalism--Arkansas. | Arkansas--Social life and customs.
Classification: LCC PN4725 .T75 2023 | DDC 818/.5409--dc23/eng/20230309
LC record available at https://lccn.loc.gov/2023002056

Printed in the United States of America.
This book is printed on archival-quality paper that meets requirements of the
American National Standard for Information Sciences, Permanence of Paper,
Printed Library Materials, ANSI Z39.48-1984.

Butler Center Books, the publishing division of the Butler Center
for Arkansas Studies, was made possible by the generosity of Dora
Johnson Ragsdale and John G. Ragsdale Jr.

"There live not three good men unhanged in England, and one of them is fat."

— Shakespeare, *King Henry I*

Contents

Foreword

"ALTHOUGH of a relatively scarce breed," the *Arkansas Times* observed in the obituary of the itinerant writer it had once employed, "Mike Trimble was Arkansas's and perhaps the country's greatest self-deprecating journalist." Readers will find in the following selections from Trimble's fifty-year inventory of wit and wisdom all the vindication they might seek for that quaint judgment—the rare humble author. Whether he was chronicling rising political worthies like the far-into-the-future governors Asa Hutchinson and Mike Beebe, or, more often, the ordinary and feckless people that he encountered every day, befriended, and spent most of his career writing about, Trimble usually found a way, subtly or artlessly, to bring up his own failings, such as identifying the wrong person as the dead woman in an obituary he had written in his earliest days for his first employer, the *Texarkana Gazette*. Like the yokels in the vaudeville duos Laurel and Hardy, Abbott and Costello, Rowan and Martin, and Fey and Poehler, Trimble's confessed bumblings were purposeful and studied instruments of his humor, but a narrative of Trimble's career, which will follow in a moment, suggests that the overweening modesty may also have been a genuine emotional release. Readers can decide such matters for themselves.

Like his friend Charles Portis, who wrote five marvelous novels about the adventures of quaint Southern characters, Trimble would scoff at being compared to Mark Twain, as in "the Mark

Twain of the twentieth century," which was an occasional refrain about Buddy Portis. It is, however, an apt analogy for both men. Critics likened Portis's early novels about the odysseys of eccentrics like Norwood Pratt, Mattie Ross, and Ray Midge to Twain's *The Adventures of Huckleberry Finn* and *The Adventures of Tom Sawyer*. All three men started their writing careers as journalists before drifting into humor—Twain and Portis most famously as novelists, Twain and Trimble as authors of varieties of non-fiction humor built upon the vicissitudes of the social order and of life itself.

Both Portis and Trimble, who died eighteen months apart in 2020 and 2021, were sons of schoolteachers and grew up in small south Arkansas towns, steeped in the swagger, name-calling, lingo, and imaginative metaphors of boys and laboring men. The idiomatic style, expressed best in the dialogue of all their works, would come to define the style and art of both men, as well as of a third contemporary journalist, humorist, and friend of both men, Bob Lancaster of Sheridan, whose departing essay about his friend who was taking over his column begins this collection. Lancaster published a picaresque novel (*Southern Strategy*) and several collections of equally picaresque accounts of men who dotted and disturbed Arkansas and regional history from Hernando de Soto to Tommy Robinson, most notably *The Jungles of Arkansas* and *Judgment Day*. All three started their careers as Men of Letters in the 1960s and 1970s as journalists, writing one of the two daily humor columns in the *Arkansas Gazette*, "The Arkansas Traveler" and "Our Town."

In 1965, when Portis, who had graduated from the *Gazette* to *The New York Herald Tribune* in London, was quitting journalism and coming home first to the Ozarks woods and then to Little Rock to try his hand at fiction, Trimble was joining the *Gazette* staff as a reporter. By 1970, when Portis had already published two of his five novels, *Norwood* and *True Grit*, Trimble's editors decided that his gifts were not straight reporting but features. Unlike other reporters, he tended to insist on using the mannered grammar and dialect of the people he wrote about and quoting it "straight," rather than converting it to the King's English—as the paper's owner and editor for the better part of a century, John Netherland Heiskell, strongly preferred. Trimble would write, for example, while quoting a riverboat queen on a swampy stretch of the White River: "I done some work on a house for a lady, and I took a couple of rooms off it she didn't need and hauled 'em over here." Sometimes copy editors brought his sentences into compliance with Heiskell and *Gazette* style; sometimes they didn't. As a feature writer and roving columnist whose job was to give readers some relief from the depressing realities of the news with small doses of the mundane joys of life around the countryside, Trimble was free to do exactly what he did best, and he did.

All his columns and lengthy features—such as classic pieces on the Little Rock hellraiser Robert "Say" McIntosh and the reclusive hillbilly letter writer H. E. Harvey, both republished in this volume—recorded what they said exactly as they said it, and how they said it. Like the dialogue in Portis's masterpieces and Lancaster's, they manifested no judgment about the character, ignorance, or even the ill manners of the men and women who spoke the words; rather, they were merely a true measure of the feelings and expression of the authors' subjects.

Like Portis, Trimble found humor everywhere, in mundane events, casual dialogue, facial expressions, even in the stiff repartee of a federal courtroom, and, again like Portis, he recorded it all deadpan. Manifested in all the humor and irony was the artist's striving, as Joseph Conrad once described it, to capture some truth about the world, if not a moral one then the beauty, joy and disappointments of human and animal relationships. His best actual reporting was from the courtroom of U.S. District Judge J. Smith

Henley, who presided over the famous long-running trials in the 1970s over Arkansas's famously primitive jails and prisons. What other reporters dismissed as irrelevancies Trimble gave life to, such as the judge's long and careful examination of a worm and two odd leaves that a persecuted prisoner found in his turnip greens at lunch in his cellblock. The reporter's relationship with the dour old judge was sometimes strained. When Trimble, awakening in his car by dawn's birdsong after a night of partying, rushed into the courtroom during a trial still wearing a Superman sweatshirt, Henley halted the trial and had the bailiff remove the reporter until he could return with a tie and jacket. The judge once summoned Trimble to his chambers to ask if it was true that the reporter had named his cat "Smith Henley" and why. Trimble had made the mistake of mentioning his cat's name to a law clerk. The cat was crabby, but Trimble explained to the judge that it was an unusually dignified feline.

The problem for Mike Trimble was not the manners of the people he wrote about or what he wrote (although that sometimes disrupted his career), but rather his success. Except for the columnist's occasional drift into pure whimsy, nearly all his reporting and writing unearthed irony, pathos, and usually humor in the events of the day, which made for the same pleasurable reading that all of us find in good fiction. After leaving serious reportage for column writing and features, he always developed fanatical followings that he could never quite understand. It happened wherever he went, and the burden of high expectations and low self-confidence that he could meet them was more than he could bear. He nearly always moved to something else and started over.

In his last job, as an editorial writer for the *Denton* (Texas) *Record-Chronicle* in 2006, Trimble received an award from the American Society of Newspaper Editors for writing the best editorials in the nation the previous year. Six years later, he got himself fired when he refused to start writing even occasional editorials that followed the publisher's right-wing bent. Three years earlier, ironically, Trimble had received an award from the conservative chamber of commerce, which earned him a unanimous resolution of praise from the Texas House of Representatives, proclaiming that Trimble's "ability to inform, entertain and engage his readers … has gained the lasting respect and admiration of his readers and colleagues alike."

Travis Mac Trimble was born November 3, 1943, to Edgar Mac Trimble and Frances Trim Trimble, schoolteachers who had moved to Arkansas from Louisiana and had settled at Bauxite. His mother taught English—both Mike and his sister, Pat, were her students—but his father got a better-paying job as the personnel and safety director at Alcoa, which had opened a big aluminum-production plant at Bauxite at the start of World War II and owned the town. Mike was the center and linebacker for the Bauxite Miners, in those days a magically successful small-town football team that produced college stars like the 'forties Arkansas Razorback legend Leon "Muscles" Campbell, who got his nickname by bending a railroad spike with his hands. Trimble's experience along with those of his teammates and Bauxite townspeople like Muscles and his luckless old man would become the subjects of legendary articles in the *Arkansas Times* magazine that Trimble aficionados clipped, saved, and read aloud at parties (and which are reprinted here).

One piece, which was a deep account of the success of a Bauxite English teacher in turning Bud, the leading jock on the Miners team, into a Shakespeare muse, recounted in detail how the teacher, Trimble's mother, assigned Bud to play Macbeth and infected him with the tragic psychological dilemmas of the mad king.

Another long magazine piece was about the Bauxite Miner football team of 1959, the camaraderie, and the enduring effect of the team's loss to its chief rival, the pathetic Bryant Hornets.

"Most of us are doing pretty well, I guess," begins Trimble's classic memoir about the ultimate humiliation of male adolescence—getting trounced by a second-rate football squad. "Salty Crowson is selling insurance and raising a short ton of kids over in Conway, and Jonesy is a college professor with a highly praised book under his belt. Satchelbutt Wilmoth married his high school sweetheart; ditto Bud Richards, who, last I heard, was running a very used car lot out on the highway and serving on the Bauxite School Board. I earn three squares a day just sitting in a chair, typing."

"I don't hear much from the members of the 1960 Bauxite Miner football team—except for Salty, who handles my insurance, and always calls around my birthday to remind me that I am one year closer to dying. But every year around this time I start thinking about them—Salty and Satchel and Bud and Rolleigh and Harold Selby and Dan Reed and the rest—and I wonder if they are still as embarrassed as I am at getting beat by Bryant."

Trimble deprecated his own talents and role on the team. His article reported that on a critical play that cost the Miners a game he tried to block a Bryant defender along the sideline to free his teammate for a touchdown and instead wound up mauling Bauxite's prettiest cheerleader, the girlfriend of his star—and infuriated—teammate.

After two years at the University of Arkansas at Fayetteville, Trimble went to work as a reporter for the *Texarkana Gazette*, where his friend Jimmy Jones from nearby Hope worked. Jones went to work for the *Arkansas Gazette* in Little Rock. At a party at Jones's apartment in Little Rock, another *Gazette* reporter met Trimble, liked him and said he should come to work for the Little Rock paper. Trimble said he didn't have the ability. The *Gazette* reporter sent a memo to the managing editor, Arla Reed Nelson, saying that he feared that Gene Foreman—a former *Gazette* writer and editor who had become the managing editor at the *Pine Bluff Commercial* (and later, *The Philadelphia Inquirer*) and, to Nelson's chagrin, had hired away a *Gazette* copy editor—was going to hire a brilliant Texarkana reporter, Trimble. Nelson called Trimble and hired him.

His news stories and features always picked up observations that other reporters would miss. Writing about a fancy event at the Little Rock Country Club honoring an early civic and civil rights leader, Trimble's news article noted that the steaks were "as big as saddle blankets" and that the honoree was the only Black person in the big crowd who didn't wear the white jacket of a servant. The publisher of his paper, who helped arrange the event, was irked by Trimble's observation but didn't fire him.

Finally, the editor assigned him to write one of the two famous daily columns in the *Gazette*—"Our Town" and "The Arkansas Traveler"—that had been or would be written by such legends as Portis, Lancaster, Ernie Deane, Charles Allbright, or Richard Allin. Trimble felt inadequate but soon had a rabid following, especially in the newspaper corps. One especially memorable column, mournful but also funny, was about Trimble's burial of Red, his incorrigible Irish setter and faithful friend.

The expectation that every column had to achieve some majesty was more than Trimble could bear. He went back to reporting and soon quit.

One of his last articles for the *Gazette* was a long Sunday feature about Murry's, a famous catfish restaurant on the White River at DeValls Bluff run by Olden Murry, a Black man who had once worked on riverboats on the Mississippi River until he was injured. It followed a Trimble feature about Fisher's Bar-B-Q in Little Rock, a little joint that allowed white customers like Trimble in a shabby back room. Trimble proclaimed Fisher's the best restaurant in Arkansas and its barbecue the best food in the state. His article about Murry's at DeValls Bluff recounted a typical day in the life of the aging Murry, scurrying around on the south bank of the White

River preparing for the big crowds that crammed his ramshackle café, which was made from remnants of old railroad cars. The Monday after the article appeared, Trimble got a call from his old deskmate at the *Gazette*, William Shadle, who had given up reporting and gone to work for the Social Security disability office. He congratulated Trimble on a fascinating article about Murry's hard work but then said the only trouble was that Murry had been drawing 100 percent total and permanent federal disability benefits for twenty years. Shadle undertook every job with utmost fidelity. The agency went after Murry for recovery of the benefits. Trimble was horrified at what he had done and the dilemma he had created for both men. Murry hired one of his regular customers, Bobby Fussell, a former U.S. prosecutor and later the federal bankruptcy judge for Arkansas, to defend him. Fussell eventually told the government that Murry couldn't repay the benefits, so it needed to take ownership of the catfish house. The government relented and dropped the case. To celebrate, Fussell rented a bus and invited Trimble and his friends, who included the then-presiding U.S. attorney, Paula Casey, to ride to DeValls Bluff for a free catfish dinner with trimmings. Late in the feast, Murry brought out a platter of fried crappie and dumped several hunks of the steaming fish on Trimble's plate. Someone noted that it was illegal to harvest crappie commercially. It was agreed, for the sake of the horrified prosecutor, who thought she was involved in a felony, that probably no crime had occurred because a friend of Murry had caught the crappie gratis and the meal was free.

Trimble went to work for the *Arkansas Times*, a monthly magazine and later a weekly paper, where he wrote such pieces as his Bauxite memories, but even there the high expectations every month or week were more than he could stand. The end came when he wrote about the big new national headquarters building of Dillard's department stores on Cantrell Road, a would-be fluff piece in which he said the structure looked like a mausoleum with a clock. Dillard's was, until then, a big advertiser in the *Times*. Dillard's ads didn't return to the *Times*, and neither did Trimble.

Trimble then applied for a vacancy at the *Pine Bluff Commercial* covering several outlying towns. He listed me as a reference. The Pine Bluff executive editor, Jane Ann Ramos, the former editor of the *Fort Smith Times-Record*, telephoned me, and I told her about Trimble's brilliance. Yes, she said, she had read some of his clippings and was impressed, but why in the world was such a gifted man applying for the *Commercial*'s lowest reporting job? Because he needs a job, I told her. "Hire him. You'll love the guy." A few months later, they were married and she had to fire him because the company had a nepotism policy.

Trimble went to work for the *Arkansas Democrat-Gazette* as a state-desk reporter and commuted to Little Rock. Soon, Jane Trimble was named publisher of the daily *Weatherford Democrat* west of Fort Worth, and she and her husband moved to Weatherford, where Mike devoted himself to serious journalism and opinion sharing and to the lives of his daughter, Erin Gray, and her children, Camryn and Turner. Mike went to work as a copy editor, reporter, and finally as the editorial writer for the Denton daily newspaper northeast of Weatherford, and three years later Jane joined him there, first as a city-hall reporter and then as managing editor. She left the Denton paper to join the editorial staff of the *Star Telegram* in nearby Fort Worth. The publisher of the Denton newspaper fired him in 2014 for refusing to write more conservative pieces. It was his last job. He died of liver cancer November 20, 2021.

—*Ernie Dumas*

Acknowledgments

IF MIKE TRIMBLE were still in circulation, he would modestly protest the publication of a collection of his stuff. It doesn't rise, he would say, to that level of distinction. He would, nevertheless, want to thank the people who made those memorable articles possible, starting with all the creatures of the Animal Kingdom that were the subjects of the pieces he wrote and that are included in this compendium—the noble dogs Pearl and Red and creatures of the wild as well as the humans whom he found so much pleasure in writing about: his buddies and family members at Bauxite and, well, practically a whole generation of residents of that company town as well as others whom he would encounter and publicize during a long journalistic career. So, Acknowledgments must include the whole index at the back of this book. Trimble might make an exception for President Richard M. Nixon and Vice President Spiro T. Agnew.

As for the actual publication, recognition should start with Guy Lancaster, the eminent historian of Arkansas and the editor of the *Encyclopedia of Arkansas History and Culture*, who upon reading Trimble's obituary in November 2021 suggested this book. Mike's sister, Pat Patterson, his daughter, Erin Gray, his niece, Julia Taylor, and his brother-in-law, Carrick Patterson, heard similar suggestions and helped reclaim from musty boxes Trimble pieces that were published in the *Arkansas Gazette* forty to fifty years ago. Max Brantley, a colleague at the *Gazette*, remembered favorite pieces that absolutely had to be found. Donna Fielder, a friend and colleague of Trimble at the Denton paper and an accomplished author herself, chronicled his exploits at the superb little daily and provided the editorials that won him a national award for writing the best editorials in the United States.

Bob Lancaster, who sort of launched Trimble's literary career by handing off the Arkansas Traveler column to him in 1973 and was his lifelong friend, had suggestions. Lancaster had forgotten his last Traveler column formally introducing *Gazette* readers to Trimble, which appears in the next few pages.

The 200-year-old *Gazette* has never been fully indexed, but the staff at the Butler Center for Arkansas Studies at the Central Arkansas Library System helped scan microfilm of the newspapers for more than a decade. Alan Leveritt, the founder and publisher of the *Arkansas Times*, and the staff there helped locate and scan many of Trimble's profiles and stories from its first magazine era. Kara Cravens of the *Arkansas Democrat-Gazette* library retrieved from the archives Trimble pieces that had begun to seem to the editor to be only imaginary. The newspaper's publisher, Walter Hussman Jr., along with Leveritt at the *Arkansas Times* and Bill Patterson, publisher of the Denton, Texas, *Record-Chronicle*, eagerly consented to the republication of Trimble's long-ago work for their journals. Christopher Dumas, the world's fussiest editor, refined the whole volume to see that it met *Gazette* editor John Netherland Heiskell's goal that everything would be exemplars of the King's English, while also preserving Trimble's and his characters' rustic diction. David Malcolm Rose, whose "Lost Highway" models are among Arkansas's premier artistic collections and who is himself a humorist of rare talent, restored the distinction of some of the original publications of Trimble's pieces that were resurrected from musty archives or boxes. He also designed the book's cover from an early Trimble pose of Rembrandt's Renaissance painting *Aristotle Contemplating the Bust of Homer*, as Trimble might have modeled Aristotle's pose today for the great Macbeth story in this volume.

Passing the Traveler Baton

By Bob Lancaster
Arkansas Gazette
1973

THIS IS MY LAST column as the *Gazette*'s Arkansas Traveler. Against the advice of everybody I know who has good sense, I've accepted a call to become a journalistic missionary in the Pennsylvania Heart of Darkness [*The Philadelphia Inquirer*].

That was no easy decision, but there are millions upon millions of people up there who've never heard of git-fiddling, trotline-fishing, or Woo Pig Sooey, and somebody had to enlighten them sooner or later, so I volunteered.

The real beneficiaries of my departure, though, are the readers of this column. Because hereafter it will be written by a veteran *Gazette* reporter named Mike Trimble. He's a good guy and a funny guy and an uncommonly talented writer—all of which you'll discover in short order by watching this space.

There are many things about Trimble that are best left unsaid. His negotiations with the Health Department over the condition of his apartment, for example. And how he abandoned the last car he owned when it got to be more trouble than he thought it was worth. And his earnest, pitiable efforts to house-break his dog, Pearl.

But by way of introduction I'll tell you a few of the saner, more credible things I know about Trimble.

He's twenty-nine years old, a bachelor, and has trouble with his spelling. He had a cat that was run over by a car last year. He bought a motorcycle in North Little Rock once and learned to ride it on the trip back home. His father, Mac Trimble, is a retired safety director at the Alcoa plant at Benton. His mother, Frances Trimble, is a retired high-school English teacher.

He was born and reared in Bauxite and still thinks it's the greatest place in the world despite the fact that it no longer exists. Kids growing up in Bauxite in that era didn't have much to do except go over to Benton because the nearest jukebox and drive-in restaurant were over there. So Trimble went to Benton a lot.

I first met Trimble in 1959 or 1960 in a high school football game. He was a noseman for the Bauxite Miners and I was right offensive end for the Sheridan Yellowjackets. The Miners were a scruffy, dirty-looking team in gray-and-black uniforms and Trimble fit right in.

Even then, Trimble knew he wasn't cut out for football, but the Miners had to use whatever came along. I didn't know him at the time, but in retrospect I'm sure Trimble was the one who kept shouting from the bottom of every pileup: "Help! Help!"

Both the Miners and Yellowjackets were so inferior that year—and so bunged-up and demoralized from earlier encounters from the District 5A stud teams from Magnet Cove and England—that we made a gentleman's agreement before the kickoff to go easy on one another. Trimble sought to sabotage the pact by trying to bite a plug out of the calf of our best halfback in a first-quarter pileup, but he inadvertently gnawed down on the wrong leg and hobbled one of his teammates—an all-district safety man—for the remainder of the season.

That didn't enhance his gridiron career, but it impressed a visiting scout from a pro-rassling outfit in Tulsa. The scout offered to put Trimble into a hooded duo of tag-team villains that was one member short on account of one of the team having resigned to marry a strait-laced dwarf.

Instead, Trimble went off to college at the University of Arkansas. He aspired to become a professional news photographer, but the only pictures he ever submitted in his photojournalism class were artistic snapshots of dandelions. He wasn't interested in going on television to endorse gubernatorial candidates, so he was never elected student-body president.

Trimble was a young man with a sense of humor and a lively interest in matters pertaining to the real world, so his stay at the university was abbreviated. He did endure formal education a year longer than I did, though, for what that's worth.

He took subsequent refuge (in 1963) in the newspaper business, working for a spell at the *Texarkana Gazette*, where he won distinction for his exposé of the song "Them Old Cottonfields Back Home." (He proved in that exposé that it was a geographical impossibility for a Louisiana cotton patch to be located a mere mile from the Texas–Arkansas border city.)

Then he Gomered his way through several years of semi-honorable service with the Army Reserve and the Arkansas National Guard.

He was recruited into the Guard by his brother-in-law, who got a five-dollar bounty for persuading him to enlist but who later, in a fit of conscience, offered to give Trimble $2.50 of the blood money. Trimble took it. At one Fort Chaffee encampment, Trimble spent a week sleeping on the ground because he forgot to bring his cot.

His service in the Reserve was with the 343rd Public Information Detachment, whose motto was cribbed from a character in *Catch-22*: "I don't want to make sacrifices. I want to make dough."

Trimble came to work at the *Arkansas Gazette* in 1966 and has been a police reporter, general-assignment reporter, and federal-court reporter. He wrote on the Other Achievements section of his resumé: "I am the sole support of a Triumph motorcycle and a 1962 Porsche that needs a ring job. I am fat, because I eat and drink too much, and I never seem to have any money. I could have been a famous hillbilly singing star."

He has retained his interest in music while here, and is given to delivering one-line conversational reviews, as when he told my wife, a Billy Preston freak, "Billy P. is not fit to carry Aretha Franklin's wig."

1.

MINER CHRONICLES

Memoirs of a Miner

Arkansas Times
1985

MOST OF US are doing pretty well, I guess. Salty Crowson is selling insurance and raising a short ton of kids over in Conway, and Jonesy is a college professor with a highly praised book under his belt. Satchelbutt Wilmoth married his high school sweetheart; ditto Bud Richards, who, last I heard, was running a very used car lot out on the highway and serving on the Bauxite School Board. I earn three squares a day just sitting in a chair, typing.

I don't hear much from the members of the 1960 Bauxite Miner football team, except for Salty, who handles my insurance, and always calls around my birthday to remind me that I am one year closer to dying. But every year around this time I start thinking about them—Salty and Satchel and Bud and Rolleigh and Harold Selby and Dan Reed and the rest—and I wonder if they are still as embarrassed as I am at getting beat by Bryant.

I don't mean getting beat by Bryant last year, or even the year before; Bryant doesn't even play Bauxite in football anymore, having outgrown any semblance of athletic parity with the Miners since becoming a landing field for Little Rock's white flight about ten years ago. I mean getting beat by Bryant in 1960, the year that Rolleigh and Dan Reed and Bud Richards and Jimmy Birmingham and Bill Ramsey and Jonesy and Johnny Holland and Paul Mansfield and I were seniors.

I am getting embarrassed right now, just thinking about it. My God! Bryant! Until 1960, Bryant had *never* beaten the Bauxite Miners, ever! They had seldom even scored. Until 1960, the Bryant game was the annual slaughter, always played at home because Bryant didn't have its own field; it was always played against a bunch of skinny, inept players whose uniforms didn't even match. I remember lining up as an eighth grader against a Bryant tight end who played in cowboy boots.

We had started the 1960 season as the undefeated District 5-A champions. In 1959, the mighty Black and Gray had roared through the schedule like a turpentined kitty. We had rocked 'em, we had socked 'em. We had Kicked Butt. Now, only a few months later, it was ashes, all ashes. *Sic transit gloria mundi!* The Bryant Hornets had beaten the Bauxite Miners, and before the season was over, so had just about everybody else. The center had not held, and I was the center.

Huckledy-buck.

Football was serious business in Bauxite when I grew up there. We had basketball mainly so the coaches could make sure that the football players didn't get too fat or have too much fun during the off-season. The student body went to basketball games so they could meet up with the boyfriends or girlfriends and hold hands, and some parents went to make sure that's all they did, but it was football that everybody cared about. Photographs of past Miner teams were enshrined by Ed Ricketts in his barbershop, in the glass display cases that held the Wildroot Cream Oil and the Lucky Tiger Hair Tonic.

They were formidable-looking, those old timers in the pictures; they looked like men. R. M. Frey, the other barber, assured us they WERE men—men to conjure on, men to be reckoned with. There, in one cracked and faded picture, holding one of those old-timey fat footballs and looking grim as a pallbearer, was George Cole. He had gone off to the University of Arkansas and had played football there, winning fame as a dropkicker. Now he was a Razorback assistant coach. And in another picture, a more recent one, was Moose Mize, who had terrorized enemy running backs and who, not even half-trying, the story went, because it wasn't even football, had gone to the state track meet as Bauxite's only representative and had won the whole blessed thing—by himself!

And in still another photo, there was Muscles Campbell, the ultimate Miner hero, unequaled all-around athlete and the most punishing straight-ahead runner the Arkansas Razorbacks ever had. Denied lasting stardom with the Chicago Bears only because of crippling knee injuries, Muscles was the epitome of what it meant to be a Miner. When he got married while still in college, the *Pick and Shovel* ran two photographs side by side—one of the newly married couple walking down the aisle and the other of Muscles hitting a home run for Bauxite's entry in the Central Amateur Baseball League. The caption was: "A Bat in his Hands; a Girl on his Arm." *The Pick and Shovel* was our newspaper. It was a monthly.

Those pictures were our icons. As little boys, when we played sandlot football on neighborhood teams (there were two: the Holly Street Hoodlums and the Norton Town Nightmares—I was a Nightmare), we not only assumed the identities of the well-known Razorback stars of the day—the Carpenter brothers, Lamar McHan, Dave Hanner, Billy Ray Smith (the elder) and Bud Brooks—but those in our local pantheon as well: Moose Mize, Muscles Campbell, his younger brother Pug, Knob Grimmett, Pedro Williams, and 'Tater Sweeten. (We were referring to Little 'Tater, of course, not Big 'Tater. Big 'Tater did not play football, as far as I know. Little 'Tater won a football scholarship to the University of Houston. He got his picture in the *Pick and Shovel* for attending school for twelve years without ever being absent, or even tardy.)

Some of you may think I am making these names up, but I'm not, as anyone who grew up in Saline County can tell you. If there was one thing the town of Bauxite could do better than produce football heroes, it was think up nicknames for its male citizens, athletes or not. Everyone knew Buckethead Stiles, and Sourgut Green became so used to his moniker that he adopted it officially after dropping the slightly less-than-genteel "gut," even running successfully for Saline County judge with "Sour Green" imprinted on the ballot. We also had Chigger Chase (small but tough), Beaver Williams (overbite), Duroc Stuckey (red hair), Hollywood Duvall (moved in from California), and his cousin Paddlefoot (yes, very). Satchel Wilmoth's brother was called Shorty, and their daddy was called Bottle. There were Sonny Bono (before the no-talent singer), Jiggs Bono, Goober Hamilton (before the TV show), Chago Dial, Hooty Hodge, Slick Parsons, Hick'rynut Williams, and Doughnut McKelvy. These are just off the top of my head. I could think for a while and get as many more, but you get the idea.

As we played our sandlot games on autumn afternoons—all us Hootys and Jiggses and Goobers and Chagos—we dreamed of wearing the Black and Gray, of one day being enshrined in the barbershop display case, next to the butch wax. What would Frey the barber say about us to that next generation of little boys as they gazed at the gallery of immortals? It was a question of some gravity, and even at the age of nine or ten, we were preparing to assume the mantle of Miners by assuming in play the names and jargon of our heroes. The coach of the Bauxite Miners of that era was an ebullient man named Bob Banks, whose trademark was a nonsense word he'd use to pep his boys up in practice or in games. "Huckledy-buck!" Coach Banks would shout. "Huckledy-buck!" the little boys would scream as they rolled about on their backyard gridiron.

Huckledy-buck.

The years dragged rapidly by in that contradictory way that years pass in a country town. There was junior high football, in tattered hand-me-down uniforms and equipment, and finally, in the ninth grade, I became a Miner.

But only barely. I spent my ninth-grade season trying to stay alive in practice. Physically a late bloomer, I was counting on puberty to transform me at any moment into a tall, well-muscled young athlete like the teammates who trounced me regularly in practice scrimmages. On game nights, I was on the bench and secretly glad to be there.

My neighbor on the bench was Wop Ware, but he was not as content with his lot as I. Wop was a ninth-grader too, but was about eighteen years old, having pursued learning at his own leisurely pace. Wop smoked, drank beer when he could get it, and had a girlfriend over at Benton who worked in a dime store. I was a pudgy bookworm who wore thick glasses. I do not know, even to this day, what made us soulmates, but that is what we were. Wop had gone out for football to impress his girl, but he hadn't considered the possibility that his physical limitations might keep him from the starting lineup. For one thing, he was so bowlegged that he could hardly run. "That boy couldn't stop a pig in a two-foot alley," Frey the barber once remarked as Wop left the shop after a trim. The smokes and the beer probably didn't help either.

"This is embarrassing," Wop complained to me on the bench during the first game. "Betty's getting more exercise than I am just going to get a cold drink at the concession stand!"

Having nothing better to do, I addressed the problem, and by the third quarter, I had a solution. Having learned from Wop that Betty knew next to nothing about football, I suggested that he tell her to show up on Wednesday nights, when we played our B-team games, and simply let her believe she was watching a varsity contest. The ruse apparently worked: Wop told me happily the next Thursday that Betty's only comment was that the crowd had certainly dwindled since the last game.

The rest of my freshman year was generally spent shining the lettermen's football shoes, packing their gear for road trips, and periodically checking for the appearance of body hair. On road trips, I would make sure I got a seat on the bus right behind Don Morrison, a huge but gentle farm boy who would spend the road trip talking with an assistant coach about animal husbandry.

Until then, most of my information about sex had come from a couple of impromptu backyard lectures from Gerald Magby, and while Gerald's information ultimately proved to be pretty accurate, I thought it too fantastic at the time to give it any credence. The lore imparted by Don Morrison, on the other hand, had the ring of authenticity about it, dealing as it did with the real, honest-to-gosh world of bulls and cows, boars and sows. This wasn't theory; this was fact, and I stored away as much information as I could. It was to cause several very embarrassing moments a few years later.

The summer after my ninth grade year was spent in heavy thought. Puberty had finally arrived, but it hadn't wrought the miracle I had expected. I looked a little better in gym shorts, but the muscular body I had ordered had apparently been out of stock, and I was sent instead an oddly shaped model that was mostly legs. I looked like a pair of pliers. Running summertime wind sprints with my teammates, I would make the same marvelous up-and-down pumping motions with my arms and legs as they, only to see their backs get smaller as they left me in the dust. Clearly, if I was going to see any action as a sophomore, I would have to rely on my brains, not on my athletic ability.

My plan was to pick out some specialty and become proficient enough at it to guarantee some playing time. The specialty had to be easy—I knew my athletic limitations—and it had to be something nobody else wanted to do, because if they did, they could surely beat me out. I toyed with the idea of placekicking, but gave it up quickly. I could get no distance, and besides, there were others interested in the job. Same with holding for the placekicker; for some reason, that job seemed unofficially reserved for the quarterbacks, sort of like the Jewish seat on the Supreme Court. Finally, I hit upon it: I would become a snapper; that is, I would center the ball for punts and kicks.

It was an inspired choice. Nobody was interested in making long snaps. First of all, a snapper looked undignified, all scrunched down with his head between his legs, looking at the world upside-down. Secondly, anyone assuming that position was extremely vulnerable to getting his can knocked off by a vicious noseguard or a blitzing linebacker. No doubt about it, the job was mine if I wanted it. Moreover, sheer repetition could assure a modicum of proficiency. With no competition, I'd be in like Flynn. I wouldn't be a starter, but I would be getting into the game before the outcome was decided, maybe even getting my jersey a little dirty.

It worked. I never got very good at snapping—about one in four attempts would soar over the punter's head and into the end zone—but no one else had thought to practice at all, since they didn't want the job, and I was the best of a bad lot. Before the first game of my sophomore year, the coach announced that I would snap for punts.

Huckledy-buck!

I guess it is time to introduce you to my coach. Bob Banks, the Miner coach of my childhood and the inventor of huckledy-buck, had quit to take a job at one of the aluminum plants. (He stayed in the game, though, as a referee. He officiated at many Miner games, and will appear at other places in this narrative, as sort of a Greek chorus.) My coach was a short, muscular man named Dan Bass and, true to the tradition of the town, he had a nickname. It was Tick.

There is a lot of dissatisfaction among my friends over football coaches, and it is a dissatisfaction I share. The macho image, the teaching of sport-as-warfare, the idea that coaching somehow provides the best training for school administrators—all of that disturbs me. Coach Bass was different, but he wasn't different in ways that would be evident to most of my friends. His habits were traditionally masculine. He used a paddle liberally, and his favorite way of greeting one of his players was to hit him—*hard*—on the upper arm. Yes, he taught civics, and yes, he later became an administrator, and yes, he wanted very badly to win football games.

And he could lose his temper. His trademark was placekicking the team medicine kit after a particularly inept play on the part of his charges. The kit would fly open, and the team managers would scurry about gathering up the tape, scissors, Ace bandages, Firm-Grip, and analgesic balm before they rolled out onto the field of play. On the surface, he would not appear to fit your average liberal's idea of an enlightened educator.

There was an important distinction, however, though a subtle one, and not subject to easy analysis. It was, I think, a sense of fun, a realization that we were playing a game, and that although part of his job was to make sure we played it hard and well, the larger part was to preserve that fun, for his players and for himself.

There was also—he would poke me on the arm really hard for saying this—a gentleness that manifested itself when it was needed. Nothing gushy, just an awareness of when to turn the volume down.

I first became witness to that during my sophomore year. For some reason that defies analysis to this day, Coach Bass had filled an open date by scheduling a road game with the Warren Lumberjacks. The Lumberjacks were out of our classification to begin with, and that year they were riding high under coach Mickey O'Quinn. There probably weren't a handful of teams in the state outside what was then known as the Big Eight that could have stayed on the field with them.

It was a slaughter. I was getting in the game only when we punted, and it seemed that I was logging as much playing time as anyone on the team. They'd score in two plays; we'd run three more plays and punt.

Finesse was not the strong point of the Lumberjacks; they simply beat you into the ground. For a while there, the contest resembled one of those games in an animated cartoon, with platoons of stretcher-bearers carting off the wounded in an unending procession.

At one point, when another woozy Miner was being helped off the field after emerging from a pileup looking through the earhole of his helmet, Coach Bass signaled for a replacement. The candidate for duty, whom I will refrain from identifying, looked down at Coach Bass, then over to where Howard Page was lying on a stretcher, his leg bent all funny.

"If it's all the same to you, Coach," said the reluctant gladiator, "I'd just as soon not."

This exchange took place near the end of the bench, where I was taking a blow between punts, and I was probably the only person other than the two principals who heard it. I was amazed at my teammate's action—I did not yet know wisdom when I saw it—and waited for the explosion. It didn't come. Coach just said, very gently, "Okay, son. Just go on over there and sit back down." He even gave the player a reassuring pat on the arm as he walked away.

Huckledy-buck.

The Lumberjacks blew us out 50–8, but nobody else did, and behind the passing of Buddy Harp and the defense of Terry Allen, we won the district championship by beating the Magnet Cove Panthers in the last game of the season. My shuttle-diplomacy-style specialty had earned me a letter, if not sports immortality.

That summer, our team picture went up in a place of honor in Ed Rickett's hair-tonic case.

In 1959, nobody even touched us. Jimmy Davies, looking like a mole as he squinted around his contact lenses, bowled over defenders like ninepins, and Jimmy Birmingham just blew right past them, behind the blocking of Ragon Don Kinney, Jiggs Bono, and Goober Hamilton. We hardly ever had to punt, but we were so far ahead so much of the time that I logged a lot of playing time as a second-teamer. The last game was against Magnet Cove, and it was a romp in a driving rainstorm. After the game, we took our sodden, mud-covered uniforms and threw them around the dressing room with glee. On the Monday after the game, Pete Hopper, the principal, solemnly called all the football players out of class and led us to the gym, where he pointed out the ravaged locker room. The floors were covered with a thick coating of dried mud. The walls were covered with a thick coating of dried mud. Even the ceiling, fifteen feet high, was covered with a thick coating of dried mud.

"Boys," Mr. Hopper intoned, "I am real proud of you, winning the championship and all, and I'm not even going to make a big fuss about this mess. I just want to know one thing. How in the world did you do it?"

That next summer was a time for more figuring. I was tired of spending my athletic career looking at an upside-down punter. I had had enough of being a face on the team picture; I was ready to be singled out to young boys by Frey the barber; I was ready to hear the roar of the crowd.

I figured my chances were good. I had more experience at center and linebacker than any other of the returning players. I wasn't very good, but the experience alone should give me an edge. Besides, I was a senior, a two-year letterman. Bauxite was a United Steelworkers town, and seniority should count for something.

We reported to two-a-days ready to romp and stomp again. We were the undefeated Miners, and we aimed to stay that way. We should have known something was up by the cautious tenor of Coach Bass's opening chalk talk. The year before, he had laid it on the line: "Boys, I really don't see how anyone on our schedule can beat us." This year, he said: "Boys, we can win again," but he didn't say how many.

Well, we won three, right off the bat, probably from sheer momentum and the intimidating effect that we had striding into opponents' gyms wearing our "Undefeated District 5-A Champion" jackets.

Then we journeyed to Lonoke County for a game with England, and the roof fell in. They were big and they were fast, and they weren't scared by our uniforms. In short, they were a pretty good football team. By the middle of the second quarter, it was 25 to 0, and their subs were starting to come into the game.

We had started bickering among ourselves.

"My man? My man? What act of Congress made him my man all of a sudden? He was your man till he knocked you on your butt three plays ago!"

"If you can't hold him out, Trimble, at least wave at him as he goes by."

Only Bud Richards kept his cool. He was off by himself, giggling. I inquired as to the reason for his high good humor in light of the fact that we were getting our clocks cleaned.

"I'm gettin' 'em," Bud chortled. "I'm gettin' 'em. I'm pulling their leg hair in the pileups!"

About that time Rolleigh stormed up in high dudgeon. "Some sumbitch is pulling my leg hair in the pileups," he roared.

Bud looked shocked. "They shouldn't oughtta do that," he said indignantly, and he trotted off to get in position for the next play.

We held them to 25–0, partly because they played a lot of subs and partly because Rolleigh played like a madman for the rest of the game. Bud and I decided on the bus trip home to continue the hair-pulling ploy for the rest of the season. "It sure got ol' Rolleigh fired up right enough," Bud reasoned.

Three more drubbings followed, at the hands of Cabot, Gurdon, and Sylvan Hills. The word was out now: the Miners could be had. One of the games was in a cold rainstorm, and, for the first time, I felt some sympathy for those Magnet Cove players we had beaten in the rain the year before. When you're winning, playing in the rain is fun; when you're losing—no; when you're getting slaughtered—it is miserable. Your fingers are so cold that you can't bend them, and your knuckles get scraped, and they burn with an icy fire. There is no warmth on the field; there is no warmth on the bench. The only warmth is in the mud, and when you're lying there at the bottom of a pileup, you mutter under your breath to the others: "Get up slow! Get up slow!"

Huckledy-buck.

About this time, I discovered an interesting phenomenon. Always before, when the Miners had won, I would go home and dream about the game all night, tossing and punching the pillow, replaying each block, each tackle, each long snap to the punter. With that first loss, I quit dreaming. I would fall into bed and sleep the sleep of the dead until morning. Never have I have slept so soundly.

Things were getting grim, both in practice and around town. Coach Bass complained that we were entirely too jocular for a team that played as badly as we did. He made Bud Richards remove his flame job and pin-striping from his helmet, and threatened extra wind sprints.

Townsmen were beginning to grumble. Frey the barber somehow linked our misfortune to the general moral decay of Western civilization.

"I just can't figure out what's the matter with you boys," he complained from under his green plastic eyeshade as he scraped the back of my neck with a straight razor. "It's … Well, it's somethin', but I can't figure out what it is. I'll tell you one thing, though." Now he was gesturing with the lather- and neck-hair-covered razor. "You wouldn't catch Moose Mize layin' flat on his back gettin' run over by no Gurdon Go-devil."

He pronounced "Go-devil" as though it meant "pansy."

"I think you boys have had it too easy, is what I think. Them big ol' silver helmets! George Cole didn't wear no silver helmet. He didn't wear a helmet at all, silver or another kind. You got pads on your knees and pads on your shoulders. You even got fancy pads. You can't tell me Satchelbutt Wilmoth needs no fancy pads. I don't know what's the matter with you boys. You be needing any butch wax today?"

It was much the same elsewhere about town. Charlie Gibbs quit giving us free orange soda-pops on Saturday mornings at his café in Swamp Poodle. "I don't back no losers, boys," he said.

Our only ally, it seemed, was Henry Henning, the custodian of the Community Hall. For those familiar with the writing of Larry McMurtry, Henry can be described as our Sam the Lion: wise, caring, never condescending, a counselor with a push broom and a big ring of keys.

"What them old boys don't tell you," Henry mused as he lit a Lucky and leaned on his broom, "is that them teams with Moose Mize and 'Tater Sweeten on 'em didn't win all their games neither. Not even Muscles' team won 'em all. Some of them teams didn't win hardly any. Them old boys don't tell you that 'cause they don't really remember it theirselves. What they remember is 'Tater and Moose and Muscles and how good they was, and how much fun it was to watch 'em play, even when they got beat."

"'Course," Henry added, giving his soothing logic that ironic Henry Henning twist that we had come to expect, "you boys ain't all that much fun to watch."

We took all this in silence, we bearers of the Miners flame, partly because there wasn't much we could say in rebuttal and partly because we knew help was on the way in the form of the Bryant Hornets. We might be bad—hell, we *were* bad—but at least we weren't Bryant. The hapless Hornets carried the effluvia of defeat about them wherever they went; it was as much a part of them as their ragged blue uniforms. The worst insult any Bauxite football player could be subjected to was still "You looked like Bryant out there." (We had begun to hear that some.)

Well, the Hornets were coming to town, and woe unto them! Huckledy-buck!

It started out quite well, really. We took the opening kickoff and moved the ball easily, mostly on a couple of long runs by Jimmy Birmingham and Bud Richards, some up-the-middle plowing passes by Johnny Holland, and some short passes from Salty Crowson to Chris Brazil and Harold Selby. Bud and I got in some good leg-hair pulling, too. Salty took it in for a score not five minutes into the game, and we lined up for the kickoff with smirks on our faces.

They did not stay there long. On the second play of the series, I blitzed between the center and guard and put a monstro hit on the Hornet quarterback for a sizable loss. I was laughing from the sheer pleasure of it all when I suddenly realized that the guy I had creamed was laughing, too.

He was laughing because he didn't have the ball. I looked up just in time to see a blue jersey recede toward the horizon at an unbelievable pace. (It was years before I saw anything move that fast again: it was in the movie "Star Trek," when the Enterprise went into warp drive.)

His name was Louis Besancon, and he was a west wind that played football. We had heard of him, of course: the *Benton Courier* had carried a story about him the spring before when he set some records at a track meet. But good grief, that was track! What did track have to do with anything? More specifically, what did track have to do with football?

Plenty, as it turned out. To make it mercifully short, Louis Besancon ate our chili. He scored on long runs and short runs, dump passes and long bombs, around end and up the middle. We did not score again. When the final horn sounded, and the visitors' stands erupted into a miniature V-J Day of screaming, dancing, hugging, and kissing, we slunk to our dressing room.

"This one's going to be pretty hard to explain," Rolleigh muttered.

Huckledy-buck.

I have never quite forgiven my parents for making me get a haircut on the Saturday after the Bryant game.

"Pitiful!" said Frey the barber. "Pitiful!" He stopped hard on the first syllable each time, and punctuated the accents with a none-too-gentle swish of his razor on the back of my already crimson neck. "You boys were PIT(swish)iful out there."

There was no refuge anywhere. Henry Henning stood on the steps of the Community Hall and surveyed us with sad, reproachful eyes.

"Bryant." He sounded like the voice of doom. "Pitiful."

"If we're so all-fired pitiful," said Rolleigh, "seems like somebody would take pity on us."

But no one did, except Coach Bass. Maybe he figured we were hopeless, that no amount of cajoling and medicine-kit kicking would get the job done. Or maybe it was relief. Maybe he figured that if he hadn't been fired or lynched after the Bryant game, he'd never be fired or lynched for anything. At any rate, he lightened up. He started joking around in practice again and returned to his howdy-doo pops to the arm. In one game—another blowout—I was being beaten to death by a maniacal middle linebacker who lined up right in front of me and pumped his arms furiously until the ball was snapped.

"Why's he doing that, Coach?" I asked during a time-out.

Coach gazed at me intently before answering. "He's trying to tire himself out so he'll get his second wind quicker."

Huckledy-buck.

Have I by any chance left the impression that the Bryant game was the low point of the year, the final and complete humiliation, the absolute depths of the slough of despond? If so, let me make haste to correct it. What I meant to say was that the Bryant game was our lowest point as a team. I, myself, still had pages to write in the annals of athletic shame.

It was at Lonoke, and we were taking our by-now familiar drubbing. By some unusual circumstance, the Jackrabbits were forced to punt—their third team must have been in—and Jimmy Birmingham, our speedster, fielded the ball near the sideline on about the 20.

He crossed the field toward the Bauxite stands, and as sometimes happens on such plays, a lane suddenly opened for him. All at once I realized that Jimmy could go all the way if he got only one block, and I realized, too, that I was in the perfect position to make it. The only man with a shot at Birmingham was skulking along the sideline in front of our bench, watching the progress of the ball carrier. I had the perfect angle on him. I would spring Birmingham loose for a touchdown and at last—at last!—hear the approving roar of the crowd that had occupied my dreams since childhood. There was no way I could miss; the poor chump was so intent on Jimmy that he didn't even notice that I was about to knock his block off.

I didn't realize anything was wrong when I felt the satisfying "thunk" of the hit. I didn't realize anything was wrong when I was suddenly enveloped in darkness. I finally realized something was wrong when I reached to pull a few obligatory leg hairs and touched smooth, hairless skin.

44

That's when I realized I had cold-cocked a cheerleader.

I was no stranger to embarrassing moments; no one on that Miner team was. I had made a fairly regular thing of sailing the ball over the punter's head in my three years as a snapper, and I once had retreated from my linebacker's position to field a short punt only to have the ball strike me squarely on the top of my helmet. But this was different. With one ill-timed leap, I had opened up a heretofore undiscovered vista of football buffoonery. Worse, the thing was somehow connected to the dark and mysterious world of sex: I had boldly gone where no man had gone before, but I had done it in a clown suit, before an audience of angry and derisive critics. It seemed to be a terrifying Freudian dream, but it was real.

All of that flashed through my mind in an instant, to be replaced by a more practical and immediate dilemma: how in the hell was I going to get out of there?

Careful not to touch anything, I backed out from under the voluminous skirt to determine whom I had hit. It was Myrtle Baxley, the homecoming queen and Bud Richards's main squeeze. I turned around in terror. There was nowhere to go.

The roar of the crowd? Yes, there was some roaring, all right. Birmingham, who had been clobbered by the lone defender, was roaring. Myrtle's momma was roaring. And above it all, I heard a shrill voice shout, "Congratulations, Trimble, you finally hit somebody!"

It is amazing the number of different thoughts one can entertain in times of panic. I thought of my father: he would be mortified by the bonehead play. I thought of my mother: she would be incensed that I had forgotten my manners and hadn't even helped Myrtle to her feet. I thought of Bud Richards: he would kill me if I had harmed his beloved Myrtle, and he wasn't going to be too happy about where I had ended up, either. I would have thought some more, but about that time, Coach Bass kicked the medicine kit.

Impartial observers said later that it was the best medicine-kit kick of Coach's career. It tore the top clean off the hinges and sent Band-Aids fluttering like confetti. I didn't actually see it—my back was to the bench—but almost immediately after I heard the sound of the impact, I saw a fat roll of adhesive tape roll rapidly past me and toward the spot where my team was gathering for the huddle.

I know it does not make any sense now, but I somehow became convinced that I had to beat that roll of tape back to the huddle. If I did not, I might as well keep on running clear out into the wilds of Lonoke County to wander forever among the soybean fields. I began to run. I had never run so hard. There was fire in my lungs and a lump of ice in my soul. I caught the tape about five yards from the huddle and pulled up, panting, in front of my teammates, who were looking at me as though I were a crazy man. The tape rolled to a stop, and a referee picked it up and put it in his pocket. Then the referee looked at me and winked.

"Huckledy-buck," said Bob Banks.

Huckledy-buck.

Myrtle was not injured; thus I was saved from an untimely death at the hands of Bud Richards, though once more before the season was over, I was to wish that Bud had gone ahead and done the deed.

Have I by any chance left the impression that the Lonoke game was my own personal low point of the season, the night of my greatest humiliation? If so, let me hasten to correct it. What I meant to say was that the Lonoke game was the night of my greatest public humiliation. There was one more, a private humiliation—shame might be a better word—that I have not shared with anyone until this very day.

It was the last game of the season, at Magnet Cove. The Panthers had had their season finale spoiled for two straight years by the Bauxite Miners; now they were ready for revenge.

I do not recall whether Magnet Cove had a particularly good team that year. I do know that they had Randy Stewart; they couldn't have needed much else.

Many of you will remember Randy Stewart. He made all-Southwest Conference as a center for the Arkansas Razorbacks about 1965, and I understand he's now some kind of corporate face card for Exxon down around Midland, Texas. In 1960, Randy Stewart was a center and linebacker for the Magnet Cove Panthers, and he was of a type not often seen in the backwaters of Arkansas football: legs like tree trunks; a torso like a sack of wrecking balls, and a neck as big around as a sewer pipe. For that last game of the season, for my farewell to football, my final chance to salvage some respectability, Randy Stewart was—to use a term so loosely as to be ridiculous—"my man."

Huckledy-buck.

I have played in football games in which I feared we would lose. I have played in games in which I feared we would be disgraced. The 1960 Bauxite Miner–Magnet Cove Panther game was the only game in which I feared I would be killed. This was not an irrational fear that began the week of the game and built slowly, irreversibly, as the day of the contest neared; this was a fear that manifested itself—unexpectedly but fully supported by the empirical evidence—about the second play of the game when Randy Stewart tore the helmet from my head with a forearm shot, wrenched both of my arms from their sockets with a double flat-handed shiver to the shoulders, and tromped the length of my now-supine form into our backfield to all but decapitate Salty Crowson, who had stopped in the middle of a roll-out to gape at the carnage, as people sometimes will be reflexively struck dead in their tracks when they come upon a particularly bloody car wreck.

"Punt!" I begged in the huddle.

Salty shook his head in the negative.

"Why not?" I whined.

"It's second down. We can't punt on second down!"

"Why not?" I croaked again. "It ain't gonna get any better."

Salty shook his head again. I looked over at Rolleigh, the right guard and the strongest man on our team. "I sure could use some help."

Rolleigh gazed for a moment across the line, where Randy Stewart was standing under a cloud of steam that made him look like a volcano about to erupt.

"I'm a little tied up right now," Rolleigh said. "Why don't you try me again tomorrow at the barber shop?"

I looked around the huddle at my other teammates. All of them remained in their hands-on-knees huddle stance, staring silently and intently at their shoelaces.

"Thanks, men." I had meant it to sound sarcastic, but the tremor in my voice spoiled the effect.

We finally did punt, but, as had become a pattern in our games, the Panthers scored in about three plays, and we were again on what must laughingly be called the offensive. Three more running plays and a punt resulted in my getting a chipped tooth, a bloody nose, and a mouse the size of a golf ball under my left eye. By the end of the first half, it was all I could do to drag myself to the visitor's locker room. I lay on the floor, a wet towel on my head, as Coach Bass made his traditional rounds around the room, speaking encouragement to each player in a quiet voice and giving a critique of the first half of play. When he got to me, he said softly, "Protect yourself, son," and then moved on.

On our first possession of the second half, Randy Stewart slammed me so hard on the helmet that the suspension webbing broke, leaving my head to rattle around like a baseball in a bucket. I was on my third helmet of the night, and the end wasn't yet in sight. That's when the primal instinct for survival took over; that's when I inflicted upon myself the final and complete humiliation.

That's when I tried to make a deal with Randy Stewart.

I have forgotten or repressed the actual words I used to put forth the proposition, but the gist of it, delivered through the ear-hole of his helmet as he lay atop me in a pileup, one arm around my neck and the other around the ball carrier, was that what the hell, this was the last game of the season and they were going to win big anyway, and I'd do everything possible to stay out of his way, even tip him off to the flow of the play before the snap if he wanted me to, if only he would lighten up and let me survive. He did not say anything when he let me up; he just smiled.

I was hopeful. A smile is a smile, right? The next play was to be a sweep around right end, and true to my end of what I hoped was our bargain, I indicated the direction of the play with a none-too-subtle rolling of the eyes.

As soon as I snapped the ball, I headed to the left, opposite the flow of the play. I looked over my shoulder, and my heart stopped. Randy Stewart was not moving with the ball. Randy Stewart was not even looking at the ball, and it was clear that he was not even going to try to make the tackle. Randy Stewart was heading right for me, and I knew I was a dead man. The words that sprung to my lips just before the impact were a lie, an outrageous and despicable lie that came not from my brain but from some deeply buried survival gland wherein dwelt the hope that a man of principle might also be moved to pity.

"My sister has polio!" I yelled.

I was sitting up; I could tell that much. I could see the toes of my shoes in front of me, pointing up, but I couldn't ascertain at what point my body was making contact with the ground. I seemed to be floating. Hazy figures moved in and out of my field of vision. Someone seemed to be holding up some fingers, and asking me how many I saw. I thought for a moment that I was in jail: black bars ran up and down in front of my eyes. Then the floating sensation gradually subsided, and the jailhouse bars became the black stripes on the shirt of a football game official. Again he asked me about fingers. I replied, apparently correctly. The official grinned at me and winked.

"Huckledy-buck," said Bob Banks.

Huckledy-buck.

The barber shop at Bauxite has been torn down for years, and while I mourn the passing of a landmark of my youth, sometimes I think it is for the best. If the barber shop were still there, where would the picture of the 1960 Bauxite Miners be? In the restroom? Or would it be in the hair-tonic case, but pasted on backward, with its public side saying only "A Kodak Paper"? Or worst of all, would the picture be displayed normally, with one face inked out, one ignoble and undeserving gladiator consigned to nonpersondom by the ballpoint of Frey the barber? I do not know.

There is another thing I do not know. As I recall the defeats and the long bus trips home that followed, the split lips and the pratfalls, the busted medicine kits and the knocking of cheerleaders on their megaphones, I do not know why I loved it so, or why I love it still.

Perhaps it was the insularity of it all. We were very small frogs, but we performed in a pond commensurate with our size. Our world was bounded by Pine Haven on the east, Swamp Poodle to the west, Crumby Town to the south, and the Baptist Church to the north; it was so familiar to us that we did not so much live in it as wear it, like an old, comfortable suit of clothes. Or perhaps a security blanket.

I have said that football was important to the town, and it was, but it was important as football, nothing else. Schoolchildren in Bauxite were seen as children, not as representatives of the town as a whole, or as surrogates for the thwarted ambitions of grownups, or as metaphors for the political or spiritual state of the country,

Frey the barber's plaints notwithstanding. Nobody ever accused us of being anything but bad football players.

And so we were free to play, and it was play, and it was fun. Grantland Rice was wrong. It is not how you play the game that counts; it is that the game is played.

I have seen the big-time high schools play. Sometimes they do it on Astro-Turf, and their coaches wear those fancy headsets just like the one Freddie Akers wears. Their players are big and fast and marvelously talented, some of them, and they have my respect and my good wishes, but I cannot give them my heart. My heart is with the slow and gawky country boys, as they take to the dusty, dim-lit fields on starry autumn nights.

Joe Broadway and Mr. Nixon

Arkansas Gazette
November 1973

WELL, PRESIDENT NIXON says that the tapes that weren't going to be surrendered and then were going to be surrendered now won't be surrendered because they don't exist, and for some reason the whole thing has started me to thinking about Joe Broadway.

As you may or may not recall from reading the papers over the years, Joe constituted the only crime wave my hometown of Bauxite ever had. All of the activities revolved around the Bauxite branch of the Benton State Bank, which he burglarized once and robbed at gunpoint three times.

Joe was born and reared at Bauxite, so there wasn't much question of mistaken identification each time he struck. The bank management, which maintained a surprising sense of humor throughout the whole thing, finally tore down the old branch office and replaced it with a bulletproof drive-up window—and an armed guard.

Joe pleaded guilty to all the charges against him, and when the federal judge at Little Rock inquired if Joe had anything against the bank, Joe said no, it was just easy to rob.

Which brings us to why the president's latest revelation made me think of Joe Broadway. I wonder if Joe, as he waited outside that federal courtroom after the fourth robbery, ever considered stepping up to the judge and saying, "Judge, I have never set foot in the Bauxite Bank in my life."

As I said, Joe's activities were just about the only instances of bona-fide crime in the history of Bauxite, unless you want to count stuff like the time Duroc Stuckey got his hand stuck in the Coke machine at Earl Lindsey's filling station about midnight one night and was discovered when Earl opened up the next morning. Even that incident sort of ties in, because Duroc knew better than to whine about how he had just been trying to recover a lost nickel.

Scraping the bottom of the barrel in the Bauxite crime annals, we come to Slick Parsons and the Great Watermelon Raid of 1959. This is a caper I took part in myself, so there will be no distortions caused by second- or third-hand information.

The Raid was carried out by certain members of the Bauxite Miner football team one hot August afternoon after one of those debilitating two-a-day practice sessions. The getaway vehicle was an old panel truck used by the school to take home the footballers who lived out in the country. The raiding party having arrived at the patch, Slick Parsons was designated as the lookout while the raiders went about their work. Unfortunately, a warning procedure wasn't established.

As luck and justice would have it, the owner of the patch drove up, and while the raiders were able to conceal themselves in the watermelon foliage, Slick was left perched atop the panel truck and was forced to acknowledge the farmer's presence. The farmer, apparently not too suspicious at this point because he had not seen the rest of us, amiably inquired about Slick's identity and his reason for sitting atop a panel truck in the middle of a private road.

Unruffled, Slick replied with a grin, "I am Leroy Parsons and we are stealing watermelons, and I am the lookout."

I am not absolutely sure what all this has to do with anything, other than that the people who grew up in Bauxite pretty well knew when the jig was up.

There also may be a question of comparative honesty involved in it somewhere, but it is either too obscure or too obvious for me to get a real handle on. About as far as I can get with it is that, although I don't know the whereabouts of Slick Parsons or Duroc Stuckey, I know where Mr. Nixon is, and I know where Joe Broadway is. One is in the White House and the other is in jail.

Bud Richards and the Scottish Play

Arkansas Times
1985

IT WAS ONE of those conversations that friends of long standing have, the kind in which we recall how silly we were in our college days in the vain hope of proving to ourselves that we are not nearly so silly today.

"Can you believe," she said, "that we once sat down and seriously discussed whether or not Ray Charles was a genius?" I immediately cast doubt on my own intellectual progress by responding that there didn't seem to me to be any doubt, then or now, that Ray Charles was indeed a genius, but that I was still willing to discuss it seriously—up to and including the use of dueling pistols—with any tin-eared, gourd-headed sucker who wished to argue in the negative.

She gave me a look. It was the same sad, affectionate look she had given me many years before when, as a college freshman, I had proposed marriage to her five minutes into our first date. (It never came to anything. She immersed herself in the world of art. I dropped out of school to become a Grub Street hack, trying to buff a literary sheen onto newspaper accounts of car wrecks and quorum-court meetings. We keep in touch, though.)

"Have you ever seen a genius?" she asked in that way of hers that says she already knows the answer, and it doesn't help my argument any.

"I cannot say definitely that I have seen a genius," I said huffily, not willing to concede the point entirely. "But I have seen genius. Without the 'a'."

"Tell me about it," she said.

So I told her about Bud Richards and Macbeth.

It was 1961, and the senior class of Bauxite High School—all thirty-one of us—were suffering senior English under the watchful eye of a teacher referred to as Miz Trimble in my hearing and Old Lady Trimble when I was out of earshot. She was my mother. Still is.

The psychological dynamics of having one's mother for a high school teacher—or, for that matter, having one's son for a pupil— is a neglected area of scientific research. The whole thing was a familial and social minefield, to be navigated by intuition alone. For instance, I knew instinctively that no matter what else I let slide, I would get my English homework in on time and in good order. For her part, my mother understood and accepted that I would occasionally attempt to disrupt class decorum as a way of proving that, while I might be the teacher's son, I was not the teacher's pet. I, once again in my turn, expected—actually counted on—the disciplinary hammer to fall as hard on me as on my class-mates. Maybe harder.

And so the ball bounced back and forth: a compromise here, a non-negotiable position there, a liberty taken here, the con-sequence of that liberty there. It was as complicated as any Middle East ceasefire ever negotiated, and it was made even more remarkable by the fact that never a word passed between us about it. I still count it as a miracle that it never broke down completely.

It came close once, but that was nobody's fault. It was on one of those sultry early-September afternoons at the first of the school year, when my mother had given us some time at the end of the period to get ahead on our homework, work on extra-credit book reports, or stare slackjawed out the window, as we saw fit. All of a sudden, my mother interrupted the reverie to make an announcement.

"Look, class," she said. "Isn't this strange? I've got this cramp in my hand from holding a pencil too long. It doesn't hurt, but I can't move any of my fingers. I can't figure out why they cramped in that position."

She showed us the offended right hand. It was indeed cramped, all the fingers curled tightly into a fist.

All but one.

"Isn't that something," all right. It was something that my mother—raised in polite New Orleans society, schooled in the classics at Louisiana State University, and married to a man so gentle that the word "damn" never passed his lips in my presence, let alone hers—did not even know existed.

"Would you just look at that!" my mother said. And everyone did—everyone except me. I simply lowered my face into my hands as pandemonium took over. Pleased and surprised at the uproarious reaction—she was never opposed to laughter in the classroom, only anarchy—my mother continued to gesture toward the farthest corners of the room, unknowingly fulfilling the secret yearning of God knows how many longsuffering teachers and causing me to try to disappear beneath my desk, certain that our fragile alliance had been shattered to smithereens.

Somehow, it had not. I survived the mortification of the day (yes, to my shame, I was mortified more by my mother than for her, something I felt guilty about for years until I became a parent myself and learned that mortifying one's children is more than inevitable, it's practically one's duty), and I did not mention the incident to her that evening. I have never mentioned it to her, as a matter of fact, and when she reads of it (she checks this stuff out carefully for errors in grammar and syntax), somebody is going to have to explain it to her. It is not going to be me.

Well, where were we? Oh, yes, it was 1961, we were seniors in a tiny Arkansas high school, and we were about to wrestle with William Shakespeare. It was not our first encounter. We had tackled *Julius Caesar* two years earlier, and it had not been a pretty sight. The eleventh grade had been given over to American literature, thus we had been given a year to rest up.

This year's assault was to be on *Macbeth*, and my mother created a small stir in class when she announced that we would give a readers' theater presentation of the play—no sets, costumes, or stage action, just the "actors" reading their roles from their desks. Shakespeare can seem dull and impenetrable just squatting there on the page, she said, but the words would come alive when spoken aloud, even without sets or props. An advantage of the readers' theater format would be that we could pause anywhere we wished to discuss the action, examine the characters' motives, or look up "bodkin" in the dictionary.

We were skeptical but curious. Roles were assigned, and the reader-actors were advised to read ahead as much as possible to avoid complete bumfuzzlement upon encountering such words as "benison" or "thither." I was cast as Duncan. It was, it seems to me now, another of those silent compromises between my mother and me. It was an important role in the play, but not a dominant one; I would be killed early in the second act. Those of my classmates for whom being chosen for such a thing was anathema would not be able to say that I had got out of it by virtue of being the teacher's son; those for whom being chosen was a big deal wouldn't be able to say I got a fat part for the same reason.

The role of Macbeth went to Bud Richards.

Bud's first name was Ralph, but everyone save a few teachers— my mother among them—called him Bud. My mother was no stuffed shirt in the classroom, but she believed in a certain amount of formality between teacher and student. She would no more call Harvey Hamilton "Goober" than she would allow him to call her "Frannie." (The only exception I can recall her making was for Jiggs Bono. I don't know what Jiggs's first name was, and maybe my mother didn't either. I wouldn't be surprised if Jiggs's parents didn't know what his first name was. He had been called Jiggs since the day he was born.)

Bud lived in West Bauxite, also known as Swamp Poodle, or sometimes just Poodle. Bauxite proper was a company town. All the houses, the general store, the picture show, the hospital—everything—was owned by Alcoa, which maintained the town in order to staff its bauxite mines and refining plants. I guess you could call it corporate communism. West Bauxite was, by comparison, a tiny spot of free enterprise on this socialistic landscape. People there owned their own houses, or rented from someone who did, and there were privately owned businesses: Putty Hendrix's grocery; Charlie's Café; Earl Lindsey's Esso station, and Elmer Sheaf's Thrifty Store. An informal subdivision within Swamp Poodle we called Stuckeyville, because many members of that family had begun houses there, although none had ever finished one.

A few town people looked down their noses at Swamp Poodle, but none of us kids did. If anything, we probably considered it the best part of town, or at least the most interesting. You could win real money on the pinball machines down at Earl Lindsey's Esso, and it was said that a grown-up could even place a bet on a horse race there during the Oaklawn season. Charlie Gibbs cooked up fine cheeseburgers in his café, and he would let us young bloods hang around and curse, as long as no ladies were present. We thought Swamp Poodle was a fine place, and Bud Richards was proud to live there.

It might not be accurate to say that Bud Richards was the most "popular" kid in school, because even back then and even in so small a place, the word "popular" toted a lot of phony baggage around with it—things like looks, social standing, the ability to throw or catch a football. It is more accurate to say that Bud was probably the best-liked kid in school. Honest, open, and possessed of a perpetually sunny disposition, Bud was universally liked, even by those teachers who sometimes became frustrated with his casual outlook on life and on secondary education.

This is not to say that Bud Richards was not intelligent; he was. But he channeled his intelligence into the pursuits he considered most important: fixing up old cars, making beautiful and substantial furniture in the school shop, and deciphering the dirty parts of "Be-Bop-a-Lula."

Bud was never a rebellious or impertinent student. He realized that his teachers had a job to do, and, being a naturally helpful kid, he was anxious to help them do it.

One day in civics class Coach Bass was drilling us on one of those long lists of dull facts that everybody has to learn in civics but nobody remembers. Coach was going down the roll asking questions. "What is the compensation for work?" he would ask. (The correct answer was "wages.")

It was Bud's turn.

"Bud, what is the compensation for shelter?" Coach asked. (The answer was "rent.")

Bud scrootched up his face. He wanted to help Coach by answering the question. He liked Coach Bass. Coach Bass liked Bud; Bud was a good halfback. Bud thought some more.

"You mean shelter like a tent, Coach?"

"No, Bud, like where you stay."

"You mean like where I live?"

"Right, Bud! Where you live. Now where do you live, Bud?"

"Swamp Poodle, Coach."

"Your house, Bud! Your house! What does your daddy give for that house y'all live in?"

That cleared it up. You could almost see the light bulb click on over Bud's head. He broke into a big grin, obviously pleased that he was going to be able to help Coach Bass do his job.

"Forty-five dollars a month, Coach!"

I do not keep up with the world of classical literature, but it is my dimly held impression that *Macbeth* has only lately been rehabilitated by scholars to its former status as one of Shakespeare's finest plays, maybe even the finest. For a while there, if memory serves, *Macbeth* was given the sort of second-string status that serious critics sometimes reserve for works of art so glorious that their appeal extends beyond the insular confines of academia and into the world at large. As I said, I am not sure about that, but I do know that a longstanding superstition in the theatrical world is that the play is unlucky, and that many actors refuse to speak the play's name in a theater. They call it "the Scottish Play." I once asked an actor acquaintance of mine about the origins of the superstition, and he didn't know much more about it than I did. There were stories of actors dying violent, untimely deaths while involved in productions of *Macbeth*, he said, and he had also heard that, in Shakespeare's time, many people thought that the verses uttered by Hecate and the three witches were authentic incantations, therefore tainting the whole play with evil.

One thing for sure, he said: the superstition was still alive, and a lot of people were deadly serious about it.

"I was out of town doing a play," he recalled, "and we were sitting in the theater just talking when I happened to refer to *Macbeth*. The director jumped all over me. I thought she was joking at first, but she was serious. And this wasn't some far-out person; this was a woman whose work I really respect."

So Bud Richards was to be our Macbeth. The happiest, most contented, and most guileless of us all was to portray the tortured, ambitious nobleman in a play so shrouded in moody lore that those most closely associated with it dared not speak its name.

It took us about three days to complete our reading of *Macbeth*, what with all the pauses for recapitulating the action, interpreting obscure passages, and quelling the general hilarity when Lady Macbeth uttered the word "nipple." At first, Bud seemed to consider the whole thing a lark, and my mother had to reprimand him a couple of times for acting silly as he read his lines.

But it was not long before something about the play seemed to seep into Bud's consciousness, and all of us could tell that it began to matter to him. He had jokingly adlibbed a few lines early on, stringing hithers and thithers into amusing nonsense phrases only to be brought up short by my mother. Later on, he was to depart from the script again, but these were not the improvisations of a young man playing the fool; they were the missteps of an actor so deeply immersed in his role that he momentarily forgets what is real and what is theater.

After being exhorted by Lady Macbeth to screw his courage to the sticking place and do the murder that will make him king, Bud responded, "Good grief, woman!" The rest of us immediately looked toward my mother, waiting for her to pounce on Bud again, but she did nothing. I guess she was the only one—except for Bud—who realized what was going on, that "Good grief, woman!", while it might not be what Shakespeare wrote, was certainly what he had in mind.

Later, when Banquo's ghost appeared to reproach Macbeth for his latest murderous episode, Bud rose unbidden from his desk, pointed a trembling finger at Banquo across the room, and shouted: "Oh, Lordy. You can't say I done it! Don't wave those gory locks at me!"

As Macbeth had come alive earlier for Bud Richards, it came alive at that moment for me. All the evil, all the false courage summoned to commit a cowardly deed in the name of ambition, all the guilt and fear coming home to roost, suddenly became clear to me, and compelling. And it wasn't Shakespeare's "gory locks" that did it; it was Bud Richards's "Oh Lordy!" I have since seen actors who got money for it do that scene as written; they did not move me half so much.

On the last day of our reading, Bud was subdued as we filed into the room at English period. He had obviously read ahead; he knew he was a goner. Malcolm and Donalbain had finally got their act together and, under the able generalship of Macduff, Macbeth's former buddy, were coming to claim their birthright. The witches had screwed up Macbeth with trick prophecies; the insurgents had carried bushes in front of them; and Macduff's mama had given birth in the Hollywood Way. The jig was up, and Bud knew it. As Macduff, played by a skinny, timorous young man named Turkey Ridling, issued the final demand for surrender—"Yield thee, coward!"—Bud slowly rose from his seat, his book in one hand and his pencil in the other, gripped as though it were a sword. This time, he read his lines just as the man wrote them.

"I will not kiss the ground before young Malcolm's feet," Bud roared.

"And to be baited with the rabble's curse.

"Though Birnam Wood be come to Dunsinane,

"And thou opposed, being of no woman born,

"Yet I will try the last. Before my body

"I throw my warlike shield; Lay on, Macduff,

"And damn'd be him that first cries 'Hold, enough!'"

The room was dead silent. Bud dropped his book on the floor and glared across the room at Turkey Ridling, who appeared terrified. Bud sneered, and his lips silently formed the words, "C'mon, sumbitch."

Turkey blanched and shook his head. You couldn't have got him out of that chair with a hand grenade.

I looked quickly toward my mother, to see if she had caught Bud's unauthorized profanity. She could not have missed it; she was looking right at him, but she said nothing.

So Macbeth was slain, the scene changed, and within a minute's time, the surviving players had figuratively exeunted to catch the coronation over at Scone. The Scottish Play was over.

And that, I told her, was the time I had seen genius. Not "a" genius, unless you want to count Shakespeare himself, but the quality of genius. It was all over the place in that classroom for three days. First of all, there was the genius—quite possibly accidental— of some forgotten, faceless bureaucrat in the state Education Department who had seen fit to put *Macbeth* in the hands of teenage savages. While it is a play whose murky depths are still being explored by heavy hitters in English departments everywhere, it is also a thumping good story, as replete with action, intrigue, and gore as any modern-day splatter flick. I can't imagine any red-blooded American youth not taking to *Macbeth* if he or she gives it half a chance. To while away the time until the magic takes hold, young scholars can keep their eyes open for the crude jokes about booze, urine, and impotence, in the same way they look (or used to look) for bare-breasted natives in the *National Geographic*.

And what of Bud Richards's performance as Macbeth? Dare I say it was a work of genius? I will go this far: I will say that it was touched by genius; Bud's, Shakespeare's, Earl Lindsey's (Earl wrote poetry, did I tell you that?), somebody's. I was mesmerized by his reading; we all were, even my mother. Genius at work? Maybe not, but something, something good.

(Here's something else good to think about. Bud still lives in the Bauxite school district: he has a grandbaby now. One of these days—you can count on it—some beehive-hairdoed mama is going to raise unshirted hell at a school board meeting about teaching that filthy Shakespeare to her innocent young'uns. Bud Richards is going to be there, and he's going to listen quietly for a while, and then he's going to stand up and say, "Wait a dadblamed minute, lady ..." It is a comforting scenario.)

Finally, I must make bold to put in a word for my mother, a teacher of English and literature. I would guess that most teachers, when adding up their accomplishments, tend to remember best those students who went on to do great things. I do not know if Bud Richards has done great things, but I consider him a triumph of the art and science of teaching, and I hope my mother does, too. She lured Bud into the world of great literature, if only for three days, and gave him his creative head once he got there. Even more important, she somehow knew the role that he should play. When we looked at Bud, we saw a kid who put pinstripes and a flame job on his football helmet and did a startlingly accurate imitation of a chicken. My mother looked and saw the Thane of Cawdor.

"Like Michelangelo," my friend interrupted. "He looked into the stone and saw an angel."

Exactly, I said. Exactly.

The Great Bauxite
Outhouse Explosion

Arkansas Times
April 1989

ONE OF THE PROBLEMS with writing about the time Jack Campbell's outhouse blew up in my hometown of Bauxite is that the story seems to those of us who've heard it for all these years pretty much a one-liner by this time. We'll be sitting around and someone will say, "Remember the time Jack Campbell's outhouse blew up?" and everybody will laugh, and that will be that, sort of like the old story about the prison inmates who recounted familiar jokes by shouting out a number.

Another problem—a bigger one—is that a small but persuasive contingent contends that the story isn't funny or that if it is told in such a way as to *seem* funny, then something is wrong with the sensibilities of the teller, or with those of the listener who laughs at it. Jack Campbell certainly didn't think it was funny. The explosion damn near killed him, for one thing, and for another, Jack became, once he had recovered, the object of occasional joshing about the incident until the day he died. He took the wooling around stoically because, as a merciless josher himself, he knew he had to be able to take it as well as he could dish it out. But he was a proud man, and he did not particularly enjoy being the object of a privy joke. He never lost his cool and took the bullyraggers to fist city, where he no doubt could have ended all discussion quickly and painfully—but he probably wanted to, and he never got to where he could laugh about the explosion himself.

His widow still feels much the same way, and adds that not only was it in pretty bad taste to make fun of a near-fatal accident in the first place, it got worse as the years wore on and free-lance wags started embellishing the story for comedic effect to the extent that a lot of the popular versions of the story that continue to float around Saline County barbershops and deer camps bear little, if any, resemblance to the truth. She certainly has a point.

Wouldn't you know it, though: Here comes another free-lance wag—the most reprehensible of the lot, probably, because he's doing it for the money—to give this tasteless story even wider circulation after first presenting a convincing argument against it. Why would anybody do that?

It's hard to say. I'm afraid that getting too deep into the thing is going to result in some kind of side-pocket dissertation on original sin, but let's have a go at it and see if we can manage to keep away from the theological shoals.

To take the easiest point first, there is in Arkansas a rich if lamentable tradition of backhouse humor that abides to this day, due in no small part to the fact that most Arkansawyers still had outhouses when the rest of the country was sitting pretty. I am not going to defend it, at least not here, but it exists, whether we like it or not—witness folklorist Vance Randolph's highly regarded collection of sexual and scatological jokes and folk tales called *Pissing in the Snow*. We may deny it, and we may even manage to disguise it if we have enough city polish and aplomb, but the fact is that about eight of ten of us are going to succumb to a snicker at the first unexpected blast of a whoopee cushion. It is not an easy thing for the eight of us to live with, but there you are.

A sad and terrible thing, but I cannot think of it even for a moment without laughing. I thought of it at my own father's funeral as I sat beside the open grave, and when I recalled my father's joy in the telling of the story, I erupted in a muffled spasm of mirth and grief that I must hope was interpreted only as the latter by my dad's friends and relatives.

So I am going to try to tell about Jack Campbell and the Great Bauxite Outhouse Explosion, but in deference to the reservations about it that have been outlined here, I figure that the least I can do is try to get it right, without any of the fictive embellishments that have become encrusted to the story over the years. To that end, I have conducted exhaustive interviews with the only eyewitness to the incident. He lives in Benton, his name is Leon Campbell, and he is Jack Campbell's son.

Leon Campbell is better known to many Arkansawyers as "Muscles." He is sixty-one now, and the nickname still fits him as comfortably as it did during the Forties and Fifties, when he lugged a football for, respectively, the Bauxite Miners, the University of Arkansas Razorbacks, and the Chicago Bears. Muscles grew up in Bauxite with three brothers and two sisters in the days when Bauxite was a thriving company town, owned lock, stock, and company store by the Aluminum Company of America, which built it to support its bauxite-mining operations in Saline County.

Jack Campbell was the company's head carpenter in Bauxite and was a master craftsman. Muscles says he has seen his father look at a set of house plans, pre-order the lumber, and have one two-by-four left over when the job was done. He was a stocky, powerfully built man, and was rough in his speech and manner.

"He was a good daddy, and he loved us all," Muscles says, "but he would hit us boys if we did something wrong, or if he *thought* we did something wrong. He would flat whale the tar out of us."

The four Campbell boys—Elmer, Leon, Charles, and Larry—all survived the whalings well enough to become superb athletes. *Arkansas Gazette* sports editor Orville Henry once referred to them collectively as "the rock-built Campbell clan." They also seemed to inherit from their father a rough-hewn self-confidence that sounds like simple braggadocio in the retelling but was actually sort of ingratiating, because there was never any meanness in it. Larry, for instance, at about the age of nine, came into possession of a beat-up old bicycle. The thing wouldn't even run—it had no chain, seat, or tires—but Larry proudly pushed it everywhere he went. Once, as he puffed his way up Hospital Hill with the inoperative bike, a couple of old gaffers on the barbershop porch inquired with heavy sarcasm as to why anyone—even a fool kid—would push a busted bicycle all over town. Larry never missed a step. "It beats walkin'," he said.

In 1939, the year of the Great Outhouse Explosion, Bauxite was a busy town, although not as busy as it would get later on, when the Second World War would suck up all the aluminum the country could produce and push the population of the little town to an all-time high of nearly ten thousand.

Like many company towns, Bauxite was an odd mixture of the rural and the industrial. There was a cadre of professional people—engineers, geologists, accountants, and such—most of whom had come to Bauxite from more urbane or even exotic climes. (A few of the geologists and mining engineers had logged jungle duty in the bauxite mines near Paramarimbo, in Suriname.) They lived in a section of town sometimes called Silk Stocking Row by those not quite so high on the corporate ladder. Houses on Silk Stocking Row had gas heat and indoor plumbing. Other houses, those on Sand Hill or Chestnut Street or in Crumby Town or Peaceful Valley, did not. The dwellers were families of miners, teamsters, dragline operators, painters, grease monkeys, plant laborers, and carpenters.

It was before the days of open-pit mining, and miners ventured each day into deep shafts to blast the low-grade bauxite ore from the bowels of the earth. The mines were named for the wives of the company foremen—Maude, Bertha, Prudence, et cetera— and it was considered quite sophisticated and worldly for a Bauxite kid to hear the rumble of faraway dynamite, check the direction whence it came, and announce with a smirk: "Sounds like they're stripping Bertha again." Deep in the underground, miners loaded tramcars with the rubble from the blasts, their way lit by fiercely bright lamps attached to their caps. In those days, batteries powerful enough to produce such a light would have to have been bigger than a man could carry, so the miners' lamps were not electric.

They were carbide lamps.

Calcium carbide is a granular, grayish-black substance that's made by mixing quicklime and simple carbon—called coke—and baking them in an electric furnace. Chemically speaking, calcium carbide is an organic compound, CaC_2, meaning that an atom of calcium and two atoms of carbon make up one molecule of calcium carbide. Because calcium has a relatively higher atomic number than carbon (the atomic number, if you must know, is the number of protons in the nucleus of an atom), the two form a rather uneasy alliance in combination. Calcium carbide is what chemists call an active compound, meaning it will fly apart and become something else at the drop of a hat. Add water (H_2O) to calcium carbide, for instance, and the calcium atom sashays off with part of the water molecule to form calcium hydroxide—$Ca(OH)_2$—a highly toxic substance that's also called slaked lime. The carbon, meantime, unites with the hydrogen atoms in the water to produce acetylene (C_2H_2), an invisible, garlicky-smelling gas that burns like forty-seven houses afire. Because it burns so hot—6,000 degrees Fahrenheit—acetylene gas is used to fuel cutting torches. Because it burns with such a fiercely bright white light, it was used in miners' lamps in the days before tungsten lamps or tiny, powerful batteries.

A miner's lamp consisted of a reservoir for the calcium carbide fuel, a tiny stopcock and nozzle to regulate and concentrate the flow of acetylene, and a small, polished reflector set behind the nozzle. The granulated carbide was poured into the reservoir, sort of like pouring peppercorns into a pepper mill, and a measured amount of water was added before the top was screwed on tightly. The water and the carbide percolated to produce the acetylene gas, which became compressed as it filled up the open space of the small reservoir. When a miner needed light, he opened the stopcock a little, allowing the pressurized gas to start hissing out through the nozzle. He'd strike a match to the nozzle, and—voila!—a long ferocious white light shooting from middle of a round reflector and blinding anything in its path.

Jack Campbell wasn't a miner, but he, like everybody else in a mining town, knew about carbide lamps. He had one himself that he used when he was gigging frogs at night on the Saline River. As a matter of fact, Muscles recalls, Jack was wearing his carbide head-light on the night of the Great Saline River Water Moccasin Massacre and Boat Disaster.

"My job was to paddle the boat while Daddy stood up in the front and gigged frogs. The boat was his pride and joy. He had made it himself out of cypress, and the bottom was a solid piece of wood, not a seam in it.

"I was paddling in close to the bank, where you have to be to get the frogs, and we got into some tree limbs that was hanging over the water. I was reaching up with my oar to get the limbs out of Daddy's way when I heard something go kathwump! into the middle of the boat. I got a bad feeling about it right away, and I said, "Daddy, what's in the boat?"

"Daddy turned around to look, and right there in the beam of that lamp was a water moccasin as big around as my arm. Daddy dropped his gig and reached down in the bottom of the boat and picked up the old twelve-gauge double-barreled shotgun he always carried into the woods. I hollered at him to hold up, but before I could get it out, he had blowed a hole the size of a dinner plate in the bottom of that cypress boat. The water come up like a fountain in the middle of that boat, and we started to sink, real nice and easy. As soon as the water got up over the oarlocks, that old snake swam off just as calm as you please, and my daddy started cussing me for causing him to ruin his boat. When the boat finally settled on the bottom, we was standing in water up to our chins, and Daddy was still cussing."

By now, you are probably way ahead of me, so I had best get on to the detailed account of the Great Bauxite Outhouse Explosion. It was a pleasant afternoon in 1939, and Muscles Campbell, then a lad of only ten or so, was playing in the backyard with two pet squirrels that had been banished from the house after eating the lapels off Jack Campbell's Sunday go-to-meeting suit. Young Muscles was absorbed in his play, but, like most intelligent young boys, he was a keen observer of the adult activities that went on around him, so he noticed when Jack Campbell came through the backyard and headed toward the outhouse, a wide-mouthed glass jar held in the crook of one arm.

Muscles remembers noting with no particular interest that the jar was filled with carbide.

Jack stayed in the outhouse only a second or two, just long enough to drop the jar down the hole. Then he came through the backyard and into the house.

Muscles has thought about this a lot over the years. His daddy knew how a carbide lamp worked, knew that the stuff was dangerous when it got wet. The only thing that Muscles can figure out is that Jack made at least one, and maybe two, terribly wrong assumptions. The first wrong assumption, seeing as how Jack obviously thought the carbide was stale and needed throwing away, would have been that the stuff had lost its chemical vigor. The second might have been the assumption that he had closed the top of the jar tightly enough to prevent the leakage of any gas.

Nothing much happened for about forty minutes. Young Muscles Campbell continued to play idly with his two pet fox squirrels, and the sounds of routine kitchen activity occasionally drifted through the back screen door of the Campbell house on Chestnut Street. Finally, though, the screen door banged open, and out came Jack Campbell, heading for the outhouse with a purposeful stride. He entered the small structure, let the door close behind him, and—we can only assume this—practiced a time-honored personal ritual by flipping his hand-rolled Prince Albert cigarette butt through one of the openings in the two-hole facility and into the volatile abyss.

Muscles Campbell will remember it in minute detail for the rest of his days.

"There was this unbelievable explosion—louder than anything I ever heard in the mines—and then that shithouse just *disappeared*! Some people that wasn't there like to tell it that the roof flew up in the air and the four walls just fell down one at a time, like it was a Three Stooges comedy or something, but it wasn't like that. It blowed that outhouse clean to bits. The one-by-twelves and the one-by-sixes were flying through the air like airplanes. I could hear 'em hum when they came past my head."

Lumber wasn't the only thing flying.

"It was a mess," Muscles recalls. "It was like somebody had climbed down there and filled up a gunnysack with that stuff and then cut out one corner of the sack and commenced to swing it around over their head. I could hear it hit the side of the house: THOPA-THOPA-THOPA-THOPA-THOP!"

"Then I looked up to where the outhouse was, and there was this massive ball of flame and white smoke, and right out of the middle of it staggered my daddy! His clothes were smoking, and he didn't have an eyebrow left on his head. We got him up to the little old hospital up there and they wrapped him up in sheets coated with Vaseline. He liked to have died, but he finally turned out okay except for some old burn tissue on his eyebrows and some scarring around his ears."

And so ends the first published eyewitness account of the Great Bauxite Outhouse Explosion. There isn't much to say in the way of a postscript, except to recount a part of the folklore surrounding the incident, a story that Muscles Campbell can't confirm. A few years after the explosion, the story goes, when the company spread the amenities theretofore available only on Silk Stocking Row to other parts of town, Jack Campbell's house on Chestnut Street was the first one to get indoor plumbing. I do not know if that is true or not and, if it is true, I do not know if was done at Jack Campbell's request or as still another sly joke at his expense. There is probably no truth to it at all, but it is a good way to wrap things up, and every good story needs at least one stretcher in it just to keep the readers on their toes.

2.

MOVERS, SHAKERS, AND CHARACTERS

The Right-hand Man

Arkansas Times
April 1986

FOR A FIRST-TIME political candidate, there probably isn't anything that can match Announcement Day, that morning when the inchoate leader strides to a bank of microphones and tosses his or her Stetson—or, as a Fayetteville rip-and-misread radio newsman once called it, "stepson"—into the ring. Nothing will be quite that fine again. Campaign schedules will get fouled up; reporters' questions will get tougher; contributors will scale down their pledges or renege on them entirely; the candidate will endure the humiliation of having a handshake spurned by some steely-eyed, snuff-dipping old gaffer in overalls and a gimme cap for reasons that might have to do with political philosophy or that might be dictated by nothing more significant than the cut of the candidate's suit, or the length of his hair.

But not on Announcement Day. Announcement Day belongs to the candidate. The polls haven't solidified; the fatigue hasn't set in. The audience is vociferously and unanimously supportive, unless the candidate has been so unwise as to offend Say McIntosh at some point in the past, and reporters who ask hard questions can be assured in all honesty that "those issues will be addressed in detail as the campaign develops." Announcement Day is the reward we give our candidates for all the bad food, bad coffee, bad advice, and bad company they'll have to put up with for the next

77

few months. It is a day—perhaps the only day—during which the candidate won't wonder if it is all worth it.

Asa Hutchinson had his Announcement Day on January 13, a Monday, and from all indications, it was a successful one. There was no element of surprise, but political announcements aren't meant to be surprises any more; they're ceremonies that confirm what everyone has known for months, and aside from giving the candidate a trouble-free day in the sun, they serve mainly to allow headline writers to use Stock Head Number 564: "(Name of Candidate) Makes it Official; To Run for (Name of Office)."

First in his hometown of Bentonville; then in Fort Smith, where he had cracked the statewide media as a federal prosecutor; then in the rotunda of the state Capitol at Little Rock; and at airport press conferences in Jonesboro and Texarkana—Asa Hutchinson announced that he would run for the United States Senate, as a Republican, against the incumbent Democrat Dale Bumpers, a man who had himself come out of relative obscurity more than fifteen years ago to make a name for himself in Arkansas politics.

The rite had all the required trappings: Tim Hutchinson, the candidate's brother and a Republican state representative, spoke, as did former congressman Ed Bethune, his sailboat tan only slightly yellowed by the Arkansas winter. The family—a smiling, attractive wife and four of the cleanest children in Arkansas—were attired in outfits featuring plenty of Razorback red.

Hutchinson himself wore touches of scarlet—his tie was of red silk, tied in a military knot, and two peaks of a carefully folded red handkerchief peeped from the breast pocket of his suit coat. The remainder of his ensemble was almost funereal: dark-blue suit, black perforated wing-tips, white broadcloth dress shirt. A wrist-watch and a wedding band were his only ornamentations. The outfit, together with his youthful visage, gave Hutchinson the appearance of a high school senior delivering a valedictory address wearing the practical, serviceable suit his parents had insisted upon, but asserting his own taste with the gaudy accessories of a timid but hopeful young blade.

In his prepared announcement, Hutchinson followed what has become the traditional line for Republicans running in a state where a lot of voters still have a hard time voting for a Republican even when they agree with him. He barely mentioned the Republican Party, instead emphasizing his allegiance to "conservative policies," "traditional values," "a strong defense," and his opposition to "excessive taxes and government controls."

Asa Hutchinson

"I'm not going to go around the state talking about Republicanism," he said a little later in response to a reporter's question on why his chosen political party had got such short shrift. "I'm going to be talking about responsible government and representing the people of Arkansas."

His supporters in the audience, a diverse group that ranged from loyal Republican moderates from the Winthrop Rockefeller days to zealous members of the Family, Life, America, God organization, cheered with genuine enthusiasm. The press obligingly refrained from throwing any knucklers, although the Little Rock contingent did get a little bumptious when the candidate tried to put off their question-and-answer session for a few minutes in order to shake some hands. In all, it was a fine Announcement Day.

Real life—*real* political life—began to intrude the next day, with the newspaper accounts of Hutchinson's appearances. On the night before, the radio and television accounts had pretty much confined themselves to the candidate's prepared statements; the print people went into much more detail. The newspaper accounts noted that Hutchinson's four children were enrolled in a private, sectarian school in Fort Smith; that he had attended Bob Jones University, a fundamentalist college with an unsavory reputation for racism and the dogmatic, ultraconservative politics of its founder and eponym; that his audience of supporters at Little Rock included not only members of FLAG and pro-life groups, but relatives of Justice Jim Johnson, whose political career had been forged early on in the fires of racial hatred. Hutchinson's brief appearance a few days later at a pro-life rally at the state Capitol got a lot of play in the papers, too. Hutchinson couldn't have been too surprised at the coverage, but it was no doubt a matter of concern to a man who was describing himself as a moderate, a "forward-looking conservative who is not afraid of change."

On a less ideological note, the Hutchinson camp hardly had time to fully savor the unanimous cheers of the Announcement Day crowds before it faced the prospect of a party primary battle against a surprising and formidable foe. In the space of three days, Little Rock financier Jackson T. Stephens became the best-known mystery man in the state—everybody knew his name; nobody knew much about him except that he had three more dollars than Oliver Warbucks and was supremely ticked off at Dale Bumpers, who a few days earlier had made a flippant remark to his brother Witt at a private lunch in the Stephens, Inc., dining room implying that the old oligarch was senile when he resurrected the legal battles back in the 'Fifties between the young lawyer and the gas baron over severance rights in the rich gas basin around Fort Smith and Charleston.

As Stephens played Howard Hughes with the press—certainly a novelty in Arkansas politics but not all that unusual for a man who's used to manipulating a financial empire from behind board-room doors—Hutchinson's stock as a viable candidate dropped, or seemed to, which is probably the same thing. He had been considered an underdog against Bumpers from the beginning, of course; he had acknowledged as much, and even seemed to relish the role. Now, though, nobody was talking about him very much. The talk was of a Bumpers–Stephens race, and if there is anything worse for a politician than being vilified, it is being ignored. There was little consolation in the fact that Stephens had nothing but good things to say about Hutchinson; it seemed only that he regarded him as so small an obstacle to the Republican nomination that he could afford to be charitable. For his part, Hutchinson couldn't afford to say much about Stephens, either, as long as there was a chance that he might reconsider and back out of the race. No sense in baiting the bear.

A Little Rock reporter was pondering these developments as he drove to meet Hutchinson for an interview about a week after Announcement Day. The reporter had made one call to Hutchinson's campaign headquarters to request the interview and had been a little surprised when the candidate had called back himself to set the thing up. He would be in Little Rock a couple of days hence, Hutchinson said over the telephone, and while he had a busy schedule, he could spare an early-morning hour over breakfast at the Legacy Hotel, where he was staying. The slow-starting reporter stumbled into the lobby a few minutes early, one shoe untied and his necktie still slung over the rearview mirror of his car out in the parking lot. Hutchinson came downstairs on the dot of seven-thirty, dressed once again in dark suit, white shirt, red tie and hankie. After ordering and eating a Junior Samples–sized breakfast—"I didn't get a chance to eat any supper last night"—Hutchinson leaned back in his chair and began to answer questions.

After more than twenty years of interviewing political candidates, the reporter had learned that there is little chance of getting any true insight into a politician during a face-to-face interview. A lot of reporters pride themselves on their ability to ask probing questions, and a few of them really do, but the reporter had long since conceded to himself that he wasn't one of them, and that, if the truth were known, there were very few questions that any candidate worth his filing fee hasn't already anticipated, and prepared for. Most of the interview bore out the reporter's experience, with Hutchinson reasonably but predictably stating that yes, his religious faith was important to him, but he was running his campaign on political issues, not moral or spiritual ones, and that Jack Stephens's possible candidacy was "exciting" and yet another manifestation of the general discontent over the record of Dale Bumpers.

But there was one moment that was different, a moment that ran against the low-key, almost tentative Announcement Day delivery. It came in response to a meatball, Barbara Walters–type question about what the candidate perceived to be his greatest strengths and weaknesses while serving as United States attorney for the Western District of Arkansas. Hutchinson related his perceived strengths in a predictable way: tenacity, organizational ability, and a "knack for getting to the heart of a criminal case." Then he considered his weaknesses, and his pale blue eyes narrowed as he leaned across the ruins of his breakfast.

"As for a weakness," he said, "there seems to be something in the way I meet people for the first time that makes them under-estimate me."

It was not the answer that startled the reporter so much as the manner in which it was delivered. Hutchinson's somewhat tentative oratorical style at the announcement had reminded the reporter of a high-school student thanking the local Legion post for sending him to Boys' State, and the reporter had wondered how in the world the new senatorial candidate had ever got all those crooks thrown in the can. Now he knew, or at least he suspected that he knew: there was an edge in Asa Hutchinson's voice that said a lot more than his words. Jack Stephens isn't doodly-squat, it said, and if I have to whip him to get to Dale Bumpers, then that's exactly what I'll do.

Hutchinson is a native of Gravette, in the heart of northwest Arkansas's chickenland. His parents, Mr. and Mrs. John Hutchinson, raised poultry and kids: there are six Hutchinson children; Asa, at thirty-five, is the youngest. The children are widely spaced in years, and the youngest Hutchinson spent most of his childhood time with his brother Tim, the state representative, who is a year older.

"We did just about everything together," Hutchinson said of himself and his brother, "a lot of it in friendly competition—running, wrestling, playing backyard football, that kind of thing. Tim was usually the leader, and he was the leader in getting interested in politics. I can remember us both getting excited about Goldwater."

That would have been in 1964, when Asa Hutchinson was about fourteen.

Hutchinson attended grade school at Gravette, but the family moved to Springdale when he was young, and he attended high school there, sacking groceries after school and playing football for the Bulldogs, though not, he says, with much distinction.

"We had some great teams when I played," Hutchinson recalled, "but I wasn't one of the reasons. I guess my greatest claim to fame is that I played behind some real good football players."

Partly because of his religious background and partly because "it had a good accounting department," Hutchinson went to college at Bob Jones University, a church school in Greenville, South Carolina. Even in 1968, when Hutchinson enrolled, the school had a national reputation for religious fundamentalism, political conservatism, and social puritanism. School officials at Bob Jones have never seemed too interested in refuting those charges, but they've tried, without much success, to refute claims of another institutional ism: racism. Hutchinson says now that he did not agree with the school policy that prohibited interracial dating, but that as a respecter of authority and a recipient of the college's educational benefits, he abided by the rules.

Hutchinson didn't know he wanted to be a lawyer when he enrolled at Bob Jones University; he wasn't even sure he wanted to be an accountant: "I sometimes tell people I chose accounting as a major because when you look through the college catalogs, it's always near the top of the list."

But he became involved in formal debate activities while an undergraduate, and the hours spent in research in the school library preparing for debates fascinated him. Before his senior year was up, he had decided to go to law school. He enrolled in the University of Arkansas Law School at Fayetteville upon earning his diploma from Bob Jones University in 1972, and, upon receiving his law degree in 1975, he went into private practice in Bentonville.

He also entered politics, as a Republican, serving first on the county GOP committee and later as its chairman. He served as Bentonville's city attorney, a part-time, nonpartisan post, and ran unsuccessfully for prosecuting attorney on the Republican ticket. He also founded a radio station, KBCV-FM. It is a religious-format station, the only one in the area, and while Hutchinson says "you don't get rich with a religious-format station in a small market," he also says that it's in the black.

When the post of United States attorney for the Western District of Arkansas came open late in 1981, Hutchinson decided to try for it. Several lawyers applied to Congressman John Paul Hammerschmidt for the patronage position, but Hutchinson's labors in the party vineyards stood him in good stead.

"I was able to muster a great deal of support for my appointment," Hutchinson said, "and in December of '81, I think it was, Congressman Hammerschmidt told me he was going to submit my name to the President."

In March, 1982, President Reagan named Hutchinson to the post. At thirty-one, he was the youngest United States attorney in the country.

Lawyers in the Western District differ over some aspects of Hutchinson's tenure as U.S. attorney, but they all seem to agree that he hit the ground running.

"I don't think there's any doubt that he increased the caseload," one lawyer said. "He really cranked up the machinery."

Hutchinson got in on the ongoing prosecution of a goodly number of Arkansas's county judges, who were accused of taking kickbacks from purveyors of sewer pipe and hot-mix asphalt and such. His office went out after Searcy County Sheriff Loren Reeves and succeeded where other agencies had failed, nailing the high sheriff on charges of selling marijuana to an undercover agent. In another celebrated drug case, he busted the brother of the governor and extracted a plea from the young man, who then provided evidence against Hot Springs lawyer Sam Anderson, who was subsequently charged with trafficking in cocaine. (Hutchinson got a conviction, but at this writing, the case is on appeal.) In the wake of the Gordon Kahl shootout, it was Hutchinson who successfully prosecuted those accused of harboring the right-wing tax protester. And then there was the case of the Covenant, Sword, and Arm of the Lord, with Hutchinson on national television wearing an FBI flak jacket, negotiating with the right-wing zealots and finally obtaining guilty pleas on a slew of federal weapons charges.

Pretty heady stuff, but Hutchinson was not without his detractors. Some lawyers, admittedly some of them Democrats and admittedly some of them defense attorneys who butted heads with the U. S. attorney's office in court, say that in his zeal to prosecute, Hutchinson sometimes got the traditional priorities of his agency reversed.

"Asa gambled," one Arkansas lawyer said. "He'd get his indictment; then he'd make his case. I don't think that's a very smart way to build a case, but he got away with it a lot of the time."

Another defense lawyer went further: "It's not just risky," he said, "it's wrong. It's very easy for a prosecutor to get an indictment from a grand jury. The U. S. attorney is in almost complete control of what a grand jury sees and hears. He doesn't have to present a case in chief [including all the evidence]; in effect, just about all he has to do is say, 'Trust me; I think this is a bad guy.' Sometimes it is a bad guy, but sometimes that bad guy isn't guilty of the crime that's presented to the grand jury. Even worse, sometimes it isn't a bad guy. Sometimes the indictment is obtained on wrong information. The defendant is able to prove that in his trial, but by that time, he's already been put through the humiliation and expense of indictment and trial; there's a stigma there that can't be erased."

Hutchinson's critics cite some of his more celebrated cases to bolster their contention. The Sam Anderson case, for one: Roger Clinton was hauled in and indicted, and with the prospect of a conviction staring him in the face, he pleaded guilty and testified against Anderson. "Anderson's case is on appeal right now," one lawyer commented, "and the fact that the Court of Appeals has set him free while the appeal is pending tells me that they think he has a good chance of winning."

"That CSA thing was nothing but a fishing expedition," says another lawyer. "What did he have as his authority to go in there in the first place? One fugitive warrant?"

(Hutchinson has said much the same thing in recounting the CSA episode to appreciative audiences on the campaign trail: "I remember thinking, 'What if we go in and don't find anything?'")

Even Hutchinson's admirers concede there is something to the detractors' arguments, but they deny that justice was ill-served by the way Hutchinson went about his business. Ron Fields is the prosecuting attorney in Fort Smith—the state prosecuting attorney—and while he takes great pains as an elected official to emphasize that he's speaking of Asa Hutchinson only as a federal prosecutor, not as a potential United States senator, it's clear he likes the cut of Hutchinson's prosecutorial jib.

"Okay," Fields said, "I'll admit that at the federal level, it's been traditional for the FBI to handle the investigation, and then hand the complete case over to the U. S. attorney, who then presents it to the grand jury. But as a practical matter, there are times when the law-enforcement agency doesn't know everything that a prosecutor needs to make his case. Just because an arrest is made doesn't mean that you quit building your case. Asa ran his office more like we do at the state level; that is, there were times when he used his office as an investigative agency. If it puts criminals behind bars, I don't see anything wrong with that."

It isn't known how the federal law-enforcement people—the FBI; the Alcohol, Tobacco, and Firearms division of the Treasury Department; the Drug Enforcement Administration—felt privately about Hutchinson's methods, but after the fugitive warrant was served on CSA leader James Ellison, and after thirteen CSA members copped pleas on federal weapons charges, the young prosecutor received a citation from the FBI and the Director's Award from Treasury. Although there is disagreement on whether his conviction rate matched that of his predecessor, there was no doubt that Hutchinson kept things jumping.

Says Fields: "He flat revolutionized the role of the U. S. attorney in the Western District."

As Asa Hutchinson tells it, the more he read the papers, the more he felt that things were out of whack. There was Ronald

Reagan, who had got the support of Arkansas's electorate in two presidential elections, going about the process of setting the country right, and he kept reading in the *Washington Post* about "the liberal senator from Arkansas, Dale Bumpers."

"It just didn't make sense," Hutchinson said. "Here were the people of Arkansas, overwhelmingly supporting the policies of President Reagan, while their senior senator voted with Teddy Kennedy 84 per cent of the time."

Find six things wrong with this picture and win a Swell New Air Rifle.

Hutchinson concluded that Dale Bumpers needed to be unseated, that he *could* be unseated, and that Asa Hutchinson was the man who could kick the legs out from under the chair.

There was one thing wrong with that scenario—or there was *at least* one thing wrong—and it was that Congressman Ed Bethune of Searcy had tried the exact same strategy two years before against David Pryor and had been trounced like a yard dog for his trouble.

Not the same thing, says Hutchinson, and he has a point. Pryor is the quintessential candidate, a man who sometimes seems as though he would rather run than serve. Although Bumpers is a tireless and skillful campaigner—one of the few public servants who can walk into a room full of hostile Kiwanians and leave having won, if not the hearts and minds of his entire audience, at least a grudging respect for his point of view, and maybe a convert or two—Pryor is possessed of a gift that simply makes most people like him a whole lot. Hutchinson is betting that a lot of people don't like Dale Bumpers nearly as much.

The Jack Stephens factor took care of itself on Saint Valentine's Day, when the industrialist news-released his intention to stay out of the race. For tax purposes, Stephens had moved his voting residence from Little Rock to Florida, which had no income tax, so he seemed ineligible to run for office in Arkansas. That little tactical problem didn't surface and Stephens certainly wasn't going to mention it, or take questions. Hutchinson could breathe a little easier—Stephens had looked to be his only GOP primary opponent, and none other has emerged as of this writing—and he also could look forward to the financial largesse of his one-time potential opponent. There is no law that says Stephens has to contribute to Asa Hutchinson's campaign, of course, but he already has committed himself to knocking off Dale Bumpers, and, as April Fool's Day approaches, Hutchinson seems to be the only other dog in the hunt.

There is going to be another factor in this race, too, and it will be interesting, if painful, to see it develop. It is, simply, the fact that Hutchinson is, if not officially running as, a bona-fide member of the religious right, and it is hard to figure out just how much this will count for or against him. It is doubtful that Bumpers, always in the past a high-minded campaigner, will openly make an issue of this, but then, he won't have to; it is already out there on the record: the fundamentalist religious affiliation; the Bob Jones connection; the children in the church school; the support of the Jim Johnson clan; the anti-abortion, pro-school prayer stance; and a propensity during his tenure as U. S. attorney to couch his law-enforcement efforts as a holy crusade to a degree that startled and alarmed even the law-and-order-minded federal agents who worked with him.

For his part, Hutchinson is fighting the image as strongly as he can. In his favor is the prosecution of the far-right CSA. He brings it up in every speech, and reminds his listeners that the CSA was a group that "would tread on the rights of minority groups through intimidation and violence." He studiously avoids religious references in his speeches. In a February appearance before law students in Little Rock, he made an offhand reference to an illegal alien apprehended on the Mexican border with no possessions save "a little red Bible" and then seemed consciously to haul himself up, assuring the students that "my only point is that she came into this country with virtually nothing but the promise of a better life." To a man with religious convictions as deep as Hutchinson's it must seem ironic, if not downright unfair, to have to be so careful about references to the Deity.

"Yes," he said in an interview, "my religious faith is the most important thing in the world to me. It affects everything I do, and it should. But I do not ask anyone to share my religious beliefs. My campaign will stand on the governmental and political issues. It will appeal to a broad range of voters." (Indeed, there are a few surprises, though not many, as Hutchinson answers questions about potential issues. For example, despite the orthodoxy of the right, and despite the fact that his children attend a secular private school, Hutchinson says he is opposed to tuition tax credits for private education. "I'm against it both philosophically and on the basis of economics," he said. "I am firmly committed to public education. As a parent, I simply wanted my children to have a Christian education, and I think I have that right. I am running on basic political issues, not theology.")

Others, of course, don't agree. "Sure, he'll talk about defense and the deficit," one political observer said, "but he'll be running on abortion and busing."

Put another way—maybe a fairer way, maybe not—Hutchinson won't *have* to mention abortion, or busing, or school prayer, at least not too much. He's already got the vote of every rightwinger to the left of the CSA, and he's already lost the votes of everyone even slightly to the left of the old Win Rockefeller Republicans. What he hopes to salvage now are the votes of those on the cusp of conservatism, the voters who don't like Dale Bumpers' voting record, but who are put off by what they see as the religiosity of the evangelistic right. Those are the people who are going to have to ask themselves some hard questions in the voting booth. The certified lefties will be able to vote against Asa Hutchinson with a clear conscience—his strictly political positions will dictate that—but there are some thoughtful conservatives who are going to have to grapple with the possibility that they may be voting against Hutchinson because they don't agree with his religious beliefs.

No one likes to think of himself or herself as intolerant, and Hutchinson has crafted his campaign so as to put people on the defensive as they argue with themselves. Although the religious right has pushed itself into the political arena and thereby made itself fair game for political debate in the eyes of a lot of people, others still feel uneasy about questioning someone's faith. Hutchinson is in a good position to exploit this uneasiness. He mentions his religion only when asked about it; any other discussion comes from the media, not from him or from his campaign organization. Since he already has the votes of the religious right in his pocket, he needs to make no more appeals in that direction. Instead, he can concentrate on those less-than-liberal voters who still try to separate religion from politics.

The big question is whether there are enough of them to make a difference, and whether Hutchinson can bring them into his camp if there are.

[**Editor's Note:** Dale Bumpers defeated Asa Hutchinson in the general election, 433,122 to 262,313, a significantly larger margin than David Pryor's victory over Ed Bethune in 1984. Hutchinson subsequently lost a race for attorney general in 1990 and a race for governor in 2006 and was elected to the U.S. House of Representatives in 1996. As the congressman from northwest Arkansas and a member of the House Judiciary Committee, he prosecuted President Bill Clinton in Republican-led impeachment proceedings in the House in 1998 and the trial in the Senate to remove him from office. Hutchinson contended that Clinton's failure to be completely candid about his amorous dealings with a female White House staffer amounted to perjury and obstruction of justice. His brother, Senator Tim Hutchinson, was one of the jurors and voted to convict the president on both charges and remove him from office. Bumpers, who had defeated Hutchinson in 1986, gave the closing argument in Clinton's defense, ridiculing Hutchinson's allegations of criminal misconduct. The Senate, with a few votes from Republicans, acquitted Clinton on both charges. Hutchinson many years later said he had prosecuted Clinton reluctantly and that he had done so only "to help our country go through a difficult time." In 2014, Hutchinson was elected governor and re-elected in 2018. In 2022, he began planning a race for president in 2024, setting up a potential race against former president Donald Trump, who he insisted had never done anything deserving of impeachment or removal from office. Trump is the only president to have been impeached twice.]

Shadow Boxer

The Life and Times of
Robert (Say) McIntosh

Arkansas Times
June 1989

EARLY ON an April morning, Robert (Say) McIntosh was on the campus of Little Rock Central High School, his stated objective being to clean up the school—not figuratively, as in Cleaning Up Dodge City, although that was on his agenda, too, but literally. He had been hanging around the campus for several weeks, planting flowers (many of which had succumbed to a late cold snap), raking leaves, and picking up trash. He was also haranguing students and other passersby who were watching but not helping.

A slow-moving car filled with young people cruised down Park Street in front of the school, radio blaring, and a couple of soft-drink cups flew out the car window and landed near McIntosh's feet. Quick as a snake, he scooped them up and threw them back toward the open window. They didn't go in, but somebody apparently got splashed. Curses rang out from inside the car, and it slowed momentarily, though it didn't stop.

"Aren't you shamed?" McIntosh shouted at the retreating car. "You're living like pigs!"

Making people uncomfortable is what Robert McIntosh does best, and he may do it better than anyone else in the world. Not just high-school students, either, but teachers and preachers and mayors and newspaper editors and judges and legislators and governors and United States senators and—well, *everybody*. Black, white, rich, poor, male, female—it doesn't matter; Say McIntosh is an equal-opportunity scold. He is a Black man who once threw a barbecue for the Ku Klux Klan. He is a successful restaurateur who constantly gives away money but who can't seem to pay his bills. He is a man who says all he wants is to be like Jesus—he once tied himself on a cross to protest something or other—but who has shot a man in the butt, turned over a desk on a prosecuting attorney, and duked it out with an off-duty policeman. He has no constituency, no base of political power except his ability to wart anyone he deems worthy of warting, yet one of the more popular political rumors last year was that he was primarily responsible for keeping Bill Clinton out of the 1988 race for the presidency. It sometimes seems as though McIntosh has devoted his life and fortune to what writer Terry Southern once called "Making it Hot for Them."

After his cleanup efforts at Central on that April morning, McIntosh repaired to his nearby take-out restaurant on Fourteenth Street to get ready for his busy day. A couple of employees were already at work: a pot of black-eyed peas bubbled on a stovetop; lemonade stood in translucent plastic buckets; and a dozen sweet-potato pies were arrayed on a counter in the front of the cramped restaurant's work area.

Despite the earlier incident with the kids in the car, McIntosh was elated. That morning, a letter to the editor had appeared in the *Arkansas Gazette* praising McIntosh for his Central High cleanup campaign. What made the letter special to McIntosh was that it was written by a white Central High student who had written an earlier letter to the same paper doubting the restaurateur's sincerity and inviting him to put his trash bag where his mouth was. McIntosh had proceeded to do just that, the second letter admitted, and was due some credit for it. The letter's author took some credit for spurring McIntosh into action, but McIntosh said that was okay by him.

"I don't care if the boy says I took his advice," McIntosh said as he walked around stirring peas and sampling lemonade. "I'm

Say McIntosh

just proud of him because he had guts enough to write in and say he had changed his mind. He thought I wasn't doing nothing but jiving at first and he wrote in to say so, and that's just fine. It's even better that he changed his mind about me after he seen what I did. But what's the best thing is that he wrote that second time. He could have just said nothing, but he was fair enough to say, 'Hey, wait a minute; old Say did what he said he was gonna do.' I'm gonna give those kids over there a free barbecue, and that boy's gonna be the guest of honor."

McIntosh throws a lot of free barbecues. He throws them for people he likes, to thank them, and for people he doesn't like, to embarrass them. He gives away hundreds of free meals—advertised for the needy and homeless but open to everybody, no questions asked—at Thanksgiving and Christmas. He is fond of asking young

Black children questions about racial pride or good citizenship and rewarding a correct answer with a ten-dollar bill. As a result, he is often broke, and there are several judgments against him in the local court for nonpayment of bills, mainly from food wholesalers. Once, after a newspaper article quoted McIntosh at length about his desire to live like Jesus, a local lawyer representing some creditors wrote a sarcastic letter to Say, urging him to do a little rendering unto Caesar that which was Caesar's. McIntosh thinks people like that just aren't looking at the Big Picture.

"People shaming me for owing money ought to be ashamed themselves that a man can work as hard as me and still not pay his bills," McIntosh says. "I know I owe people money, and they're going to get it." Pause. "They're just not going to get it as soon as they want it, that's all."

It seems almost impossible, but there was a time not too many years ago when Say McIntosh was virtually unknown outside Little Rock's Black community. As a teenager, he had gone to work as a busboy at Franke's, the popular Little Rock cafeteria that was located in downtown Little Rock, on Louisiana Street. For a busboy at Franke's, the money was in the tips earned by carrying diners' trays to their tables, and the more trays you carried the more money you made. McIntosh soon proved to be the all-time, A-number-one, bullgoose busboy. He brought helium-filled balloons to work and passed them out to the children of customers, who would then, of course, ask for "the balloon man" at all future trips to the cafeteria. The busboy gig had started as a part-time thing, but McIntosh was soon making more in tips than most of his friends' parents, so he quit school. He now calls that the worst mistake he ever made, and he spends much of his time urging Black youngsters to continue their educations.

The first that most white people heard about Robert McIntosh was in the middle 1970s, when the *Arkansas Democrat* ran a feature article about him and his annual custom of dressing up as Santa Claus to distribute gifts to needy Black children at Christmastime. He was dubbed "Little Rock's Black Santa," and his first soul-food restaurant, at Wright Avenue and High Street, in the heart of one of the city's roughest Black neighborhoods, soon became locally famous for being the cleanest spot in the blighted area, and for being the home of Say's delicious sweet-potato pie. McIntosh received plaques and awards for his cleanup efforts. City, county, and state officials had their pictures taken with him.

But even back then there were signs that he was not as simple a study as the mavens of the daily press had thought. In 1974, Orval Faubus was having his next-to-last hurrah as a gubernatorial candidate, stumping the state in a pale imitation of the days when he had ridden the tide of racial hatred to an unprecedented six terms in office. To be fair about it, Faubus ran a moderate campaign in 1974 against the ultimate winner, former Congressman and future Governor and Senator David Pryor. He still defended his actions in the white-hot Little Rock school crisis of 1957, of course, but he concentrated on pushing an enlightened program to combat drug abuse. Despite Faubus's new face, however, the people who came to hear him on the stump came for the old reasons, and so it was worth noting that the former governor was heckled unmercifully during a flatbed-trailer speech in North Little Rock by a Black man who danced—danced!—around the trailer as Faubus tried to speak, waving a big blue towel and yelling "No! No! No! No!", reminding the audience—none of whom needed to be reminded—of the Bad Old Days of '57. It was like a photographic negative of that old "Hell, no, I ain't fergettin'!" caricature, and the Black man who did it was, of course, Say McIntosh.

McIntosh's next big media splash came when he fed a rag-tag bunch of Ku Klux Klansmen who had straggled into Little Rock for some sort of regional konklave. The Kluxers had had a hard time hiring a hall and were generally getting the kind of reception they themselves advocated for Blacks, Jews, Catholics, and other non-Aryans, and it was left to McIntosh to remind the liberals what liberalism was about. Even a Kluxer's got rights, he said, and, besides, when a white guy's wearing a sheet, at least a Black guy knows where he stands with him.

It was the kind of left-handed logic that would come to characterize many of McIntosh's subsequent homilies. When I was a child, my father once kept me occupied for days with his plan for a car that wouldn't need an engine. Its back tires would be bigger than its front ones, he said, so it would always be rolling downhill. Even after he let me in on the joke, there seemed something so right about the idea that I hated to give up on it, and I have discovered over time that many of McIntosh's ideas have struck me the same way. When I talked to him during the Little Rock teacher's strike, for instance, he had a simple solution. "The teachers say the district's got the money, the district says it don't. Give the teachers just what they're asking for and, if the money runs out, close the schools, send everyone home, and remind everybody it was the teachers that done it." The implication was that some kind of retribution would fall like rain upon the pedagogues should the unhappy scenario come to pass. It was simplistic, irresponsible, and totally out of the question, but something about it appealed to the long-suffering patron in me, and I had to remind myself that it was a dumb idea.

(And some of the points McIntosh makes are anything but dumb. One can agree or not with his position as one of the most vocal and visible advocates for a commutation of the death sentence received by Barry Lee Fairchild, the Black man convicted of raping and murdering a white nurse, but when the backlash to the commutation effort started building, with letters-to-the-editor writers and call-in radio screechers demanding the death penalty, it was McIntosh who was the first, as far as I know, to remind us all that there had been no similar hue and cry for vengeance after four young white men were convicted of raping and murdering a Black schoolteacher at Dumas.)

Some years ago, McIntosh began printing and distributing hand-lettered flyers in downtown Little Rock, slapping them under a windshield wiper of any car that wasn't moving. One side of the handbill was usually an advertisement for his restaurant, listing specials on such items as the Li'l Robin, a hamburger named for one of his daughters, or the Big Bad Say, the heaviest hamburger in Arkansas; on the other was a short polemic, often profane, occasionally libelous, but almost always entertaining, on some issue of the day. In both style and content, they owed much to the late Joseph Weston, the pathologically idiosyncratic newspaper editor from Cave City who dubbed state Representative John E. Miller of Melbourne "The Lizard of Izard." The flyers have become an integral part of McIntosh's persona, and there are people in Little Rock who go to great pains to collect them, complaining if they miss a single one.

It was while distributing flyers last year that McIntosh got into a fistfight with an off-duty police officer. The officer claimed that McIntosh was blocking traffic by stopping in a street that had been temporarily narrowed by a construction project, and that when he, the officer, pointed this out, McIntosh flew into a rage. McIntosh contends that the officer, who was not in uniform, was the one who was in a rage, that he showed no identification, and that the fisticuffs broke out only when the officer reached inside McIntosh's van in an attempt to grab the ignition keys. The incident had not come to trial as this article was being written, but McIntosh had made it grist for his mill, devoting several flyers to his version of the incident and advertising a "Peckerwood Smasher Burger" for a while at his eating establishment.

In his handbills and his conversation, McIntosh uses the word "peckerwood" a lot when referring to white people. To be fair about it, he also uses the word "nigger" a lot. He says he uses the words to get attention, and to make a point. Actually, he wants to make two points, and not surprisingly—because this is, after all, Robert McIntosh—the points are contradictory. On one hand, he says, he wants people to understand how people can be hurt and shamed by racist labels, either white or black. On the other, he says he'd like to take the sting out of such epithets, make them neutral or even positive, by using them so much that they lose their potency.

"Deep down," he says, "everybody wants to say 'nigger' and 'honky' and 'peckerwood.' I can go ahead and say 'em because everybody knows I got no hate in my heart for any child of God. I may hate what people do, and I may get mad as hell about it and scream and holler, but I don't hate nobody, and everybody knows that."

Don't hate nobody? How about Bill Clinton? He has certainly dealt the governor enough misery. For a while there, it seemed as though Clinton couldn't stick his head outside his office without McIntosh popping up and popping off about it. Betsey Wright, the guv's faithful majordomo, physically intervened on one occasion, and on another, a state trooper hustled the yam-pie king away.

"I'll tell you something. People all the time saying about how I hate Bill Clinton. I'll tell you something that will surprise you. Bill Clinton is a good man. Bill Clinton is doing the best he can. Bill Clinton's a politician, and he's got to get re-elected. He's got to be popular, and what's popular ain't always right. I don't have nothing to lose. I'll just say what's right, but Bill Clinton's got more sense than I got. He knows if he tells the truth all the time, he'll be gone. I used to think that if you do the right thing all the time, everybody will be there to help you. Well, that ain't so. Bill Clinton wants to do right as much as he can, so he's got to say some things and do some things that I'm going to get on his ass about. There's a whole lot of peckerwoods still out there, and they vote, too."

Okay, then, Say McIntosh likes Bill Clinton. Does he like white people?

"I love white people!" he replies with enthusiasm. "They are so funny! They're natural comedians. White people just can't stand to be criticized by a nigger like me, that's all. Back when I was trashing Black people for not having pride in their neighborhoods, boy, the white people couldn't get enough of ol' Say. They was giving me awards and shaking my hand like I was an honorary white man. Then I started talking about what was wrong with white people, and all of them white folks just disappeared. The white business at my restaurant went down to about a nickel. What did they expect? Did they really think I hate my own people and think white folks was perfect?

"Anything bad you can say about a nigger is gonna be right about *some* niggers, but you can turn it right around and it'll be right about some white folks, too.

"Here's one for you: I went down to that soup kitchen at the church downtown, where all the winos go for a free lunch, and I went up to all those white winos, and I said 'You need some money?' and they all said, 'Yeah, man, sure,' but when I said they'd have to work with me over at Central High picking up some trash, there wasn't a one of 'em wanted to work for their money. Now, how many times you heard a story just like that about niggers? Well this was white people.

"Now, I ain't putting the winos down for being broke or going to the soup kitchen. Being poor ain't nothing to be ashamed about. I'd go on welfare; I wouldn't be ashamed. But if I did, I'd go out and pick up trash by the side of the road or something to earn what they gave me."

And probably have a television news crew there to film it. For no matter what you might think of McIntosh's opinions, or his methods, or even his sweet-potato pie, you have to admit that his ability to get media attention is impressive. Part of it comes naturally: Simply because of his public-affairs activities, Say McIntosh is seen at a lot of meetings, ceremonies, and public hearings. But he also has the ability to draw reporter types to events of his own creation. There is no telling how many times newspaper city editors or TV assignment editors have vowed to cut McIntosh off from the news pages or the airwaves, but he always manages to get back on, either with something so plainly public-spirited that it shouldn't be ignored, or so outrageous that it can't be.

"Sure, I use the media; I know what they want. They wouldn't have no newspaper if people like me didn't go and do stuff. That's another funny thing about white people. They say, 'Ol Say is just a dumb nigger, we're tired of listening to him,' and then they turn around and say, 'That Say sure does know how to get on the news,' like God made me smart enough to dominate the media."

White people are so funny.

When a man invents a hamburger to commemorate a fistfight or stands in a radio-station parking lot for an hour just to get a chance to scream at Tommy Robinson in front of a television camera, there is an understandable tendency to dismiss him as a kook or a publicity-seeking clown. To take the easier of the two possibilities first, Say McIntosh certainly has his clownish aspects, but those who know him, even his detractors, acknowledge that he is deeply committed to improving the community. There is no doubt that he likes to see himself on television and in the papers, but the same certainly applies to every politician who ever kissed a baby. The thing that no one should ever forget about McIntosh is that he really cares about all this stuff.

He really cares about clean neighborhoods: "If you don't respect yourself enough to keep yourself and your place clean, ain't nobody else gonna respect you. A doper and a hellraiser don't want nothing to do with anything or anybody that's clean."

He really believes that Black people must be responsible for their own destiny: "It just makes me sad to hear Black folks say, 'The white people did all this to us: the white people brought us over on slave boats; the white people sold us dope; the white people kept us down.' So what? All that means is that we better save ourselves because the white people sure ain't gonna do it for us. Truth is, nobody in this country wants to fool with Black people. You just got to accept the realities; you got to work for yourselves."

Arkansas's Next Bill Clinton?

Arkansas Times
January 1987

IT STARTED SOMETIME during the last legislative session. Nothing big, really—no trumpet fanfares or anything like that, but just quiet talk by the Capitol's third-floor, blind-stand coffee sippers about one of the young senators, Mike Beebe of Searcy, and how he was making a name for himself in the stuffy and hidebound old upper chamber. Beginning with the 1983 session, they said, Beebe had somehow managed to ignore the unwritten rule about freshmen being seen and not heard and had, at the same time, avoided the general opprobrium that normally accompanies such rash behavior. He had, they said, been assertive without being pushy, confident without being cocky, independent without calling down the wrath of the testy old bulls of the Senate. That's not as easy as it sounds; one observer likened it to running at top speed through a cow pasture without stepping in anything.

It's one thing to be Rookie of the Year in the Arkansas Senate; it's quite another to be tagged as a "comer," a figure whose future in electoral politics transcends the confines of the state Senate chamber and extends to the Governor's Mansion and beyond. Mike Beebe, the experts say, is a "comer"; some even call him "the next Bill Clinton." Beebe himself demurs, but it isn't the aw-shucks of a timid man.

"I don't think of myself as the next Bill Clinton," he says. "I think of myself as the first Mike Beebe." When asked whose political style he admires, his first answer is "mine." To be fair about it, Beebe laughs when he makes those statements, but he makes them, and he seems to mean them.

When asked if he's going to run for governor some day, Beebe takes an obligatory swipe at trying to be coy, but finally succumbs to his own natural candor and self-confidence and says probably, one of these days, if he doesn't run for the United States Senate first. The most amazing thing about the fairly amazing statement is that when Mike Beebe says it, it doesn't sound offensive. Bill Clinton can speak ten times as modestly and sound twenty times as conceited.

Mike Beebe

If you press Beebe again about his political role models, and ask him to except present company, he recites a fairly conventional list of national and local politicians, beginning with John F. Kennedy and ending with David Pryor, Dale Bumpers, and Bill Clinton.

"Now, when I say I admire the style of these people, I'm saying that I think they've found a style that works for them and that they do it well. I'm not saying that I've modeled myself after anyone. Except maybe Kennedy. I just admired the guy so much when I was a kid—his wit, his dignity, the energy he brought to the presidency. I guess it's only natural that I might try subconsciously to emulate him a little bit."

He's got the equipment. Good-looking and fit at forty, Beebe need not worry over the fact that the day is probably past when a homely man can be elected to statewide public office in Arkansas. His good looks, however, come as something of a surprise after a careful perusal. His eyes are a little close together, and his chin is weak. It's the kind of countenance that gets you called Ratface in junior high school, but the mature Beebe mug would look just fine on a campaign poster, aided as it is by a slightly roguish Pepsodent smile and a haircut of a kind you don't get in barbershops where the barbers are named Otis and the magazines are named *True* and *Field and Stream*. (The hairdo costs him a little ribbing from his fellow senators but not much; they realize it's just one of those things a young "comer" has to do, like selling the Corvette.)

There's a slight chance that Beebe's handsome visage was a factor in being unopposed in his first political race in 1982, but a fellow has to have something more than looks going for him when he manages to make a second race, also without opposition, two years later. (He and seventeen other senators reached into a hat upon taking office in 1983 and drew out two-year terms, a circumstance brought about by a statewide redistricting that resulted in all thirty-five Senate seats coming up for election at once.) By all accounts, Beebe hit the ground running in January 1983. His Senate colleagues—and, one supposes, his constituents—were impressed by the freshman's grasp of state government and of the arcane rules and customs of the upper chamber. He insinuated himself into the Senate's clubby inner circle with seeming ease, and was soon named to the prestigious Legislative Council, a relatively rare plum for a senator with so little time in grade.

Part of that was luck, Beebe now says. "There were eleven of us freshmen after the '82 election, and out of thirty-five senators, that's a lot of new folks. As a result, a lot of us new guys got positions of responsibility a lot quicker than we normally would have. To a certain degree, we were courted by the established leadership."

On the floor of the Senate, Beebe's votes were those of a moderate Democrat who nevertheless refused to be chained to the policies of the governor. He was a staunch supporter of Clinton's educational standards, but he says he never liked the teacher-testing provision and voted for it only because he was convinced that Clinton would veto the sales-tax increase that was so vital to the standards if the teaching provisions weren't included. He later voted for the unsuccessful bill that would have repealed teacher testing.

Beebe's credentials as a face man and his skills as a state senator are part of the reason that he's talked about as a future candidate for statewide office, but another part—a large part—is his obvious eagerness to make such a race. Legislators are used to competence—there are a lot of competent legislators around—and they're used to ambition. It's when competence and ambition coalesce in one person that the veterans begin to take notice—and they've taken notice of Mike Beebe.

"He wants it, there's no doubt about that," says a veteran state representative who's observed a lot of gubernatorial-fever cases in his day, and has even survived a mild dose of it himself. "But the difference between Mike Beebe and a lot of other guys who want it just as badly is that he's never going to let his ambition cloud his judgment. He'll bide his time, do a good job at whatever he's elected to do, and make as few enemies as possible along the way. He's also going to be tough as a boot when he needs to be."

Beebe's political luck began at birth. Had his mother not been visiting her grandfather when she went into labor, Beebe would have been born in Detroit, where his family lived, and would have been subject to charges of being a carpetbagger. As it happened, though, he was born December 28, 1946, in the Jackson County community of Amagon—and in a log cabin, no less!

His parents were divorced when he was an infant; Beebe says he has no recollection of his father. His mother, Louise Reynolds, remarried more than once, but he has little to say about any of his stepfathers. One of them was an electronics technician who traveled the country for an aircraft company, and as a child Beebe moved around a lot: Festus, Missouri; St. Louis; Houston; Alamogordo, New Mexico; Fort Walton Beach, Florida. "I went to five different schools in the fifth grade," Beebe recalls.

For long periods—and for just about all of Beebe's adolescence—there was no man in the house. About the time he entered the ninth grade, he and his mother moved to Newport, where his mother made a living as a waitress, working at Kelly's and at the Midway Cafe, both locally famous eating spots.

"I would describe our circumstances as modest, and that's probably an understatement, but I would not want to even hint that my mother wasn't a good provider, because she was. I always had everything I needed, and we've always been close." Mrs. Reynolds now lives with her sister in Tuckerman.

Many of Mrs. Reynolds's working hours were spent on the night shift, so young Beebe had an unusual amount of freedom for a high-school lad. Did he abuse it? You bet. Newport was the home of the legendary Silver Moon roadhouse, and was a good place for some decidedly high-spirited running around.

"I was an old-timer at the Silver Moon," he says, "but listen, I wasn't the only one. I've seen thirteen-year-olds raising hell at the Silver Moon."

Despite his modest economic standing, Beebe says he "ran with the 'in' crowd." He describes himself as "sort of the sane guy in the animal house" in those days. "I'd always be the one to say, 'Hey, maybe we shouldn't do that,' and everybody else would call me a wimp, and then I'd be too much of a wimp not to go along. Then I'd be the one who had to try to figure out a way to get us out of whatever mess we got ourselves into."

In school, he says, "I guess I was the kind of kid that teachers don't like too much but can't really do anything about. I never caused them any trouble, but I never really did anything good, either. I did what I had to do to get by in school, which was practically nothing."

He was on the basketball team, but apparently wasn't very good; he dismisses his athletic efforts as not worth recounting. He was the manager of the football team one year, and he sometimes ran for class office and sometimes won, but he says he wasn't what you would call a campus politician. It was just something to do.

After graduating from Newport High School, Beebe enrolled in Arkansas State University, financially backed by a student loan, his own summer jobs, and whatever money his mother could provide. He was used to living close to the vest financially so he wasn't tempted to squander his money like so many college freshmen unleashed with a checkbook for the first time in their lives, but he was also used to pretty much blowing off school, a practice he continued for another two years.

"I pledged a fraternity and did all the social-chairman stuff," he says. "The fraternity gave me a reason to make my grades, but that's about all I did for a while; mostly C's, with a B thrown in here and there."

Finally, in his junior year, the light bulb came on over his head, and Beebe began to go to college in earnest. He was accepted to the University of Arkansas Law School at Fayetteville after graduating from ASU, and he compiled an enviable record there, finishing as editor of the *Law Review*. In August 1972, he went to work for the Searcy law firm of Lightle, Tucker and Hannah, an established White County firm with deeper roots in Democratic

Party politics. Lightle was a state senator and Hannah later a Supreme Court justice.

He was the fourth lawyer in a four-man firm, and Beebe started out just as every new associate does—handling the legal scut work: the divorces, the wills, the abstracts, the occasional unglamorous criminal case. Beebe discovered that he liked trial work, liked thinking on his feet and getting a jury or a judge to come around to his way of thinking, and he gradually evolved into the firm's principal trial lawyer. By 1980, he had earned quite a reputation in legal circles as a trial lawyer, a reputation that was enhanced by one of the biggest judgments ever obtained in a civil suit in Arkansas. On December 21, 1979, Charles Chastain, a Cleburne County chicken farmer, was killed in a fire in one of his chicken houses. The structure had been insulated with a cellular plastic substance manufactured by the Celotex Corporation of Tampa, Florida. Beebe sued Celotex on behalf of Chastain's estate and convinced the jury that Celotex knew that the insulation material gave off noxious fumes when burned, that the firm warned against its use in residences—but not chicken houses—for that very reason. The jury awarded the estate more than four million dollars. It was the largest jury award ever made in Arkansas up to that time, and Beebe was named Arkansas's Trial Lawyer of the Year in 1981.

The big awards from juries may get the big awards for your wall, but home folks, Beebe says, base their opinions on more important things. He recalls a case in which he represented a foxhunter whose dog had been shot by a woman who believed the dog was stealing her chickens. The plaintiffs sought a hundred and fourteen dollars in damages. Beebe for the plaintiffs; Ed Bethune, no lightweight himself, for the defense.

"We won," says Beebe, "and it was all over the front page of the local paper. Ed Lightle got a sixty-thousand-dollar judgment the same day, and he got a squib on an inside page."

And there was the case of Amos Lester, the self-taught vet. Lester had been taking care of White County animals for years, but he had never got around to filling out the forms necessary to grandfather himself into compliance with new regulations on veterinary licensure. When the state cracked down on him, local folks were outraged.

Beebe for the defense: "I walked into that courtroom to start the trial and I swear it was the closest thing I've ever seen to that courtroom scene in *To Kill a Mockingbird*. There were people literally standing on the windowsills. I've never seen a room so crowded." The judge ruled that Lester had "substantially complied" with the state regulations except for some doodly-squat paperwork, and while there are those who might note that Arkansas judges are elected and cite the *Miracle on 34th Street* precedent, Beebe understandably maintains that it was his incisive legal argument that carried the day. It really doesn't matter. The point is: All a big judgment will get for you are money and clients; defending the rights of a veterinarian without portfolio can translate into votes somewhere down the line.

Beebe apparently started thinking about that fairly early on. He had risen quickly in the Lightle law firm and had all the accoutrements of the successful small-town lawyer: a growing reputation, plenty of pocketbook change, and a picture-book family. Beebe married during his senior year in college but was divorced in 1976. He remarried in 1979. He and his wife, Ginger, have a son, and Mrs. Beebe has two children by a former marriage. Beebe wanted more than membership in the White County jet set. He wanted to be on the Board of Trustees of Arkansas State University, and lo and behold, on January 4, 1974, Governor Dale Bumpers appointed Beebe, then only twenty-eight, to the ASU board. Beebe had voted for Bumpers—he was a Democrat in a fiercely Democratic law firm, after all—but he hadn't particularly noised it around, and he was pretty sure that Bumpers didn't know Mike Beebe from Adam's off ox. How, then, did he get the job?

"I lobbied for it," Mike Beebe says. "I politicked real hard for it. I wrote letters. I got my friends to write letters. I made phone calls and got my friends to make phone calls. And, son of a gun, I got it!"

Beebe spent five years on the board, including a term as its president, but when his board term expired in 1979, Bill Clinton didn't reappoint him.

"I was steamed," says Beebe. "The governor and I have joked about it since. He says getting off the board was the best thing that could have happened to me, but at the time I was hot."

The governor may have been absolutely right, for when Beebe no longer had the ASU board to occupy him, he started looking ahead to the redistricting that would occur after the 1980 Census and started thinking about the state Senate. (Four years later, in the fall of 1985, a few legislators who were disgruntled with Clinton for one reason or another circulated rumors that Beebe, by then making big tracks in the Senate, was being urged to run against Clinton in the 1986 gubernatorial primary. Did Clinton look ruefully backward at the non-reappointment that eventually landed Beebe in the Senate? Is that exactly what the legislators wanted him to do? Does an accordion player wear a diamond ring? But we're getting ahead of ourselves.)

Looking at possible redistricting plans after the 1980 Census, Beebe figured that Searcy would be in a district with Independence County, which would pit him against veteran Senator Bill Walmsley of Batesville. That would be a tough race for a newcomer, he figured, but he was ready to make it. As it turned out, the state Board of Apportionment created a long, skinny, north-south Senate district out of Arkansas and Prairie counties and parts of White and Woodruff counties. Frank White, then the governor and a member of the Board of

Apportionment, opposed the configuration, arguing that no candidate from Searcy would ever stand a chance of getting elected. Beebe says he wasn't sure either, but he announced anyway, and prepared to face incumbent W. N. "Bill" Hargrove of Stuttgart in the Democratic primary.

"I traveled all up and down the new district making speeches to any group that would listen to me, and then Bill Hargrove announces that he's not going to run again."

Beebe didn't have any Republican opposition either, and he was likewise unopposed when he ran for his first full term of four years in 1984. Senator Walmsley, by the way, was defeated in 1982, but that's another story.

So that gets us more or less up to the present, a present that finds knowledgeable political observers touting a potential gubernatorial candidate who hasn't ever even run against anybody, for Pete's sake, a potential candidate who may pass up the governor's race entirely to run for the Senate of the entire U.S. of A, and without, mind you, taking that obligatory middle step, the race for the House of Representatives.

No good politician ever says "never" but Beebe seems pretty adamant when he says he has no interest in running for the United States House of Representatives.

"I just don't see myself ever trying for the House," he says. "It's too big a pond. You get lost in there; you can't get anything accomplished. I don't want to be a little bitty dog in a big machine. I want to be where the action is."

This despite the fact that no one has jumped directly from the legislature to the Governor's Mansion or the United States Senate in recent memory. This despite the political axiom that you get statewide media exposure in the House without having to be elected statewide. The last state legislator considered a good bet to make such a jump was Hayes McClerkin of Texarkana nearly two decades ago, in 1970. A young, progressive, and popular speaker of the Arkansas House, McClerkin had years of experience, miles of good press coverage, and a short ton of money with which to make his race. Even then, his supporters knew that statewide recognition would be a problem, so they covered the state with billboards emblazoned with the candidate's name and image. You couldn't drive three miles in Arkansas that summer without gazing into McClerkin's greatly enlarged puss. It was a textbook name-recognition campaign. McClerkin got beat like a government mule.

So how is Mike Beebe any different?

"That thing about having to take that congressional stepping-stone—they're just myths that have become self-perpetuating. They used to say you couldn't go into one of these little rural counties with a lawsuit and win a six-figure judgment. My answer to all those myths is that the right case, presented in the right way, will throw out the old norms and create new ones. That's just as true in politics as it is in the law."

But he hasn't ever campaigned.

"I campaign every day. That's the only way to campaign. Every day I spend in the state Senate I spend it as though I had an opponent breathing down my neck and the election was a week away. And remember, for three months there in '82 I presumed I was running against Bill Hargrove. Until he withdrew late in the game I was in a contested race for all intents and purposes."

But White County doesn't even make up the biggest part of his own Senate district. How does that build a statewide constituency?

"Well, for one thing, it causes someone from the *Arkansas Times* to drive up and put your name in his magazine."

You might as well face it; you're never going to shake him. Whether his legislative peers have done it, or whether he's done it himself, Beebe has put himself in contention in the political hot-stove league, where observers watch the candidates and—even more fun—watch the candidates watch the other candidates. This is the game that takes on two fascinating new dimensions during this off-season. We've got two players who might be going for the national ticket, and the players now have twice as long to either oil up their machines or get completely forgotten by the electorate. (What will Sheffield Nelson do to stay on the six o'clock news for the next four years?)

Mike Beebe is confident he can compete with any of them if he chooses—from Steve Clark, who may have at long last got off the dime only to discover that somebody else has swiped it out from under him, to Tommy Robinson, a legitimate political phenomenon who has forged an improbable coalition of rednecks and Blacks, to Bill Clinton himself, if it comes down to it.

Beebe may be right: People who ask if he's the next Bill Clinton may be asking the wrong question. This is not to suggest in any way that Beebe is a stronger candidate or a better public servant than Clinton (or any other potential opponent), but to suggest that one very great difference between the two men far outweighs the superficial similarities, and that the big difference is self-confidence.

"Sure, ego plays a role in what I do," Beebe says. "If it's properly channeled, I don't see anything wrong with that. Self-esteem is a healthy thing. Every parent tries to instill self-esteem in his or her children; I don't see why that should stop when you're a grownup."

Clinton can probably match or even beat Beebe when it comes to ambition, intelligence, and political savvy, but you get the feeling that the governor would never feel quite secure enough to gripe good-naturedly to a reporter about not being able to drive a foreign car. You feel that every time Clinton finishes a speech, he turns to an aide who already knows what answer to give and asks, "How'd I do?"

Mike Beebe would never need to ask that question. Mike Beebe would know.

[**Editor's Note:** State senator Mike Beebe was elected attorney general in 2002, defeated Asa Hutchinson for governor in 2006, was elected to a second term in 2010, and retired in January 2015 to the Searcy Country Club golf course.]

Mixed Nuts

A more-or-less historical anthology of military misfits, mystical Bible-thumpers, medical mountebanks in pinchback suits, and other out-of-the-ordinary Arkansawyers, a few of them running about half a quart low.

Arkansas Times
February 1986

THERE IS NO PROOF that Arkansas has had more than its share of strange and wonderful characters; it probably only seems that way because, in a state where for many years there was little else in the way of entertainment, we have sought them out and reveled in their idiosyncrasies. More often than not, our eccentrics, oddballs, and outright lunatics have gravitated to politics, maybe because that was where the action was, or maybe because they felt more at home there.

A sampler such as this will naturally be incomplete—one man's meatball is another's Socrates—and it will be further constrained by the bounds of good taste and libel laws. In culling Arkansas Originals for this list, for example, we decided that an account of the state's only recorded necrophiliac didn't fit the tenor of the piece or what we like to think of as the generally uplifting tone of the magazine, and that to go into detail about the Cummins Prison Farm inmate who pleaded guilty to having two wives and later turned out to be a woman might run afoul of case law in the area of invasion of privacy.

Here then is an admittedly expurgated, blatantly subjective, and possibly wrongheaded review of a few of our own originals— men who for good or ill were not your average, run-of-the-mill guys. Plenty more candidates are out there; you probably know who they are.

W. H. Kruse
Gold Miner, Seer of Visions

Henry W. Kruse moved his family from Ohio to Rogers, Arkansas, in 1883. His eldest son, W. H. Kruse, was reared on his family's farm there, but he had a hankering to go into business, so when he became a man, he headed for Minnesota and the world of commerce, settling first at Le Sueur, south of Minneapolis. He proved successful in commerce and banking, but in 1900 he wrote to his parents that he thought he was losing his mind. He was having visions, he said, and was powerless to stop them.

His parents were distraught, but Kruse himself finally solved the problem by deciding to quit fighting the visions and begin doing what they told him. He would sit at his desk with a pencil in hand, write what his vision told him to write, and then follow the instructions he had written. He was to live by his visions for the rest of his life.

Kruse swore by his visions, claiming that he had accurately predicted the great Kansas City floods, the death of Queen Victoria, the San Francisco earthquake, and the assassination of President William McKinley. But his most important vision, or at least the most important as it pertained to the people of Rogers, turned out to be a bust.

On January 27, 1903, fifty Rogers residents received identical telegrams from Kruse: "TEN MILLION DOLLARS FOR ALL

THE PEOPLE OF ROGERS." It turned out that Kruse's vision had told him that a rich vein of gold existed under a wild apple tree on his father's farm. When his relatives informed him that there was no apple tree on the property, Kruse appealed to the vision, which told him his kin just didn't know how to look for apple trees; he should return to Rogers and find the tree himself.

He did, and was successful; the stunted tree was found surrounded by underbrush. The people of Rogers were beginning to get very interested at this point.

Kruse dug up a few ore samples, and assayers indeed found traces of gold, but not enough, they said, to make a mining operation feasible. The vision told Kruse that the assayers were incompetent and described a better test. The assayers refused to accept the testing methods prescribed by the vision, and the wrangling went on for two years. Finally, Kruse said to hell with the assayers, and he started to dig.

The big day was September 15, 1905. A parade began, and the Rogers Cornet Brass Band marched and played "Silver Threads Among the Gold" and "In the Shade of the Old Apple Tree." Thirty stalwart locals, hired as miners, occupied places of honor in the procession as it made its way to the Kruse farm. A wooden tower a hundred feet high was built over the proposed mine shaft, which was to be dug to a depth of one hundred twenty-five feet. Three crude smelters were set up nearby. The town was alive with excitement. "TEN MILLION DOLLARS FOR ALL THE PEOPLE OF ROGERS."

The balloon deflated quickly. Within a couple of months a high wind had blown over the tower, and nobody ever bothered to repair it. Although the shaft never reached a depth of more than a few feet, the miners managed to scrape up a carload of ore by November 1905, but it never got smelted, and, reports say, the ore was finally dumped into a river.

Every once in a while, Kruse's vision would tell him to resume digging, but no pay dirt was ever found. The visions took up other matters, such as predicting that a Minneapolis man would be raised from the dead and that God Himself would appear in the air over Rogers to deliver a speech. Kruse died on December 12, 1925, still believing in the visions that had ruled his life.

Joseph Harry Weston
Editor

He was a quiet, almost courtly, man in person, but you had to read his newspaper only once to know that Joe Weston, the editor of the *Sharp Citizen*, was crazy as a loon. The *Citizen* and Joseph Weston burst on the Arkansas scene in 1972, and there were times when we wondered if the state could survive them both. His little paper at first took out after public officials around Weston's hometown of Cave City, but soon branched out into neighboring counties (he branded state Representative John E. Miller in nearby Melbourne [Izard County] "the Lizard of Izard") and eventually the whole state. Lots of folks were amused at first, maybe even a little admiring—there is always some admiration for the little guy who takes on the establishment—but it soon became apparent that a lot of stuff in Editor Weston's paper had no basis in fact.

Joe Weston's problem—well, *part* of his problem—was that he simply believed almost anything anybody said to him, and was more than happy to put it in the paper, no matter if it came from a disgruntled jobseeker, a jealous housewife, or a space cadet as loony as Joe himself.

He once explained himself this way to a bunch of "establishment" reporters: "You gentlemen take at face value what the government hands out to you, what the police tell you, what the sheriff tells you. I take at face value what my sources tell me. You cover the establishment; I cover the anti-establishment."

120

Not surprisingly, it wasn't long before Joe Weston got sued. He got more than sued; he got charged with criminal libel, a felony that could have landed him in the pokey. Joe seized the opportunity for martyrdom and went into hiding; the next issue of the *Citizen* blazed this second-coming headline: "EDITED IN EXILE!"

Actually, Weston wasn't in exile; he was holed up in the Hotel Posey in Sheridan, but it made a great headline, done up as it was in Weston's familiar hand-drawn block letters.

Joe Weston ran three times for governor. In 1972, he was a write-in candidate in the Republican primary. Two years later, he got a fourth of the votes in the primary against Ken Coon, the Republican Party leader. In 1976, he bullied his way onto the Republican ballot, running on a platform of war with Panama. Republican stalwarts got a plumber named Leon Griffith to run for governor to prevent Weston from becoming the party's standard-bearer, but he had scared them to death. Griffith beat him by 3,300 votes.

Joe Weston

Weston wasn't totally consumed with politics. He once proposed a statewide monorail system, and designed the thing himself. He displayed the system at a press conference at the Capitol. It consisted of a state roadmap crisscrossed with parallel horizontal and vertical lines. One spoilsport noted that Joe's routes bypassed such cities as Little Rock, Fort Smith, Pine Bluff, El Dorado, and Jonesboro in favor of such places as Cooterneck, Blue Ball, Fouke, and Monkey Run. Weston shrugged. Those big towns had had their time in the sun, he said; it was time for other places to go big time. Actually, he added, he hadn't paid much attention to where the monorail line went when he laid it out. He was after symmetry; he liked things to be neat.

Joe Weston's personal life was as weird as his newspaper. Reared a Mormon, he divorced his first wife when she failed to bear him a son, and married her daughter, his stepdaughter. All three lived together in harmony for the rest of Weston's days, and his second wife indeed delivered herself of a son, whom Joe named Benjamin Freepress Weston.

If Joseph Weston—"Editor Weston," as he referred to himself—served any purpose at all in Arkansas, it was as a test of just how strongly its citizens were committed to the First Amendment. Ted Boswell of Bryant, a respected lawyer and political figure, represented Weston against the charge of criminal libel, and defended his client by arguing that people like Weston—people who push against the side of the envelope of free speech and free press—are a test of whether the free press will survive. He was successful in having the state's criminal-libel law, the only one in the nation, declared unconstitutional by the Arkansas Supreme Court, and that is probably Joe Weston's legacy.

Weston was a diabetic, and he was always too spaced-out to take care of himself. He spent the last months of his life in a Missouri veteran's hospital, and died November 15, 1983. Until his last few days, when he slipped into a coma, Weston was still writing long letters to "establishment" reporters, telling them of his plans. He was just finishing up a campaign plan that would elect Bill Clinton president, he wrote, and the young Arkansas governor was anxious to get the show on the road.

John A. Battenfield
Millennialist, Town Builder

It was in 1912 that Reverend John A. Battenfield cracked the secrets of the Biblical books of Daniel and Revelation. He wasn't the first to take up the chore, and he wasn't the first to claim success, but his efforts led him to found the Searcy County town of Gilbert on the Buffalo River.

The prophecies of Daniel, and those contained in Revelation, have proved tough nuts to crack, but biblical scholars have never hesitated to take a shot at it. "Numeric" interpreters have abounded, and their efforts—counting the number of words in certain key passages; counting the number of letters in certain key words—have produced some of the most amazing instances of theological convolution in the history of the planet. Battenfield, an Illinois minister in the Christian Church, used numeric techniques based on the number seven, and determined that the Millennium would begin in 1973. The destruction of Roman Catholicism—necessary for the Last Days to commence—would come in 1923, at the close of a World War between Catholics and Protestants.

Along with his brother Ben, Battenfield began spreading his theology through a newspaper called *Kingdom Harbinger* and by

John Battenfield

means of his own fiery sermons. The brothers decided that communities of the faithful must be established in isolated settings so as to avoid the destruction from the coming conflict and give the world a coterie of right-thinking believers once the dust had settled. Communities were formed in several states, but the most successful was at Gilbert. Perhaps that was because the Battenfield brothers made their homes there, or maybe it was the idyllic location on the beautiful Buffalo River, but, whatever the reason, the Gilbert community, launched in 1920, soon had more than two hundred residents, and it was relatively free of the doctrinal backsliding that plagued a few other settlements, such as the one in West Virginia where recalcitrant members still insisted on observing the pagan holiday of Christmas.

All went well for a while. Battenfield's interpretations of prophecy seemed to be right on the button. The Zionist movement had begun in 1897 in Switzerland, obviously presaging the return of the Jews to their native land as predicted in the Book of Daniel. The Irish uprising in 1919 seemed to be the start of the Great War between Protestants and Catholics. Somewhere along the way, however, Battenfield began to amend his original teachings, and his flock became confused. Gilbert colonists believed that the Book of Romans decreed that all Jews would be converted to Christianity in the days before the millennium, and Battenfield had taken a large part of that task upon himself. It is safe to wonder now just who got converted, because Battenfield, while holding to his basic tenets, also came to advocate observing the laws set forth in the Torah and to denounce the Christian concept of the Trinity.

Although 1923 came and went without the predicted World War, the colonists at Gilbert remained steadfast. God simply needed a little more time, Ben Battenfield wrote. What did unhinge the colonists at Gilbert was John Battenfield's unsuccessful attempt in 1925 to raise one of their number from the dead.

Battenfield announced on St. Valentine's Day of that year that he would resurrect a Gilbert colonist who had died the day before. The clergyman had made an earlier attempt to heal the man's illness and had blamed his failure on the fact that there were those in the community who lacked faith. When the first resurrection attempt also failed, Battenfield revealed that God wanted the body to be entombed for three days, whereupon the minister's efforts would be rewarded. It was done, and after three days excited townspeople gathered at the cemetery for the big event.

But Battenfield never arrived. He was taken to the home of his brother, in a state of collapse, and it was later announced that he had suffered a nervous breakdown. Soon thereafter he departed for Washington, D. C., never to return.

The little community on the Buffalo did not disband, but it dwindled, and John Battenfield's teachings gradually came to be regarded as moral guideposts rather than as predictions of the future. Battenfield's little church and the community of Gilbert still exist, occasionally being mentioned on the television news as one of the coldest spots in Arkansas. None of the original colonists is still alive.

William Hope "Coin" Harvey
Prophet of Apocalypse

William Hope Harvey enjoyed in his lifetime a popularity and favorable repute that are today almost impossible to figure out. A hugely successful land speculator, he was a free-silver advocate and a friend and political ally of William Jennings Bryan. When the country indicated its preference for the gold standard by repudiating Bryan's presidential candidacy in 1896, Harvey decided that economic collapse was at hand and started to prepare for it. He retired from his business enterprises, moved to Rogers, and made his living for a time as a pamphleteer.

His business instincts got the better of him, however, and in 1901 he opened the Frances Hotel and eventually two others at the nearby community of Monte Ne. The Frances was a wonder for its time, located near a lagoon over which paying guests were transported in a Venetian gondola after their arrival at the railroad station. (The extension of the rail line to Monte Ne had been a key factor in the enterprise, and its completion was observed with proper gravity: Bryan, the Great Communicator himself, appeared and unloaded a speech.)

Despite the initial success of his enterprises, Harvey remained convinced that the gold standard was about to wreck the world economy, and perhaps he thought his theories had been confirmed when bookings for the resort began to dwindle in the early 'Twenties. At any rate, he retired again from the world of commerce and announced that since the end of civilization as we knew it was at hand, someone should preserve the explanations for its fall as a cautionary tale for future societies. That someone was to be W. H. "Coin" Harvey.

Harvey envisioned a gigundo obelisk, one hundred thirty feet tall so as to still be visible to future archaeologists as they dug into the rubble and sediment from earthquakes and volcanic eruptions and found the remains of a bygone society. At the top of the obelisk would be a plate of "the most enduring metal known," and on the plate would be the inscription: "When this again be read, go below and find a record of the details of the death of a former civilization."

In the base of the concrete structure would be stored Harvey's theories on the demise of western civilization, as well as its history.

Coin Harvey

All of these documents would be printed on the finest paper, milled to last thousands of years. Also available would be a guide to unlocking the secrets of the English language, Harvey reasoning that the King's English would be as dead as the dodo by the time civilization rose again from the ashes of gold worship. (One of the things that Harvey didn't think of—and that's odd because he seemed to have thought of everything else— was how the diggers of the future were going to decipher and obey the inscription at the top of the obelisk if the key to the language lay sealed at its base.)

The cost of the monolith was estimated at seventy-five thousand dollars. Harvey poured about ten thousand dollars of his own money into the project, but was able to raise only about another thousand in contributions. With the money he had, he was able to excavate the base of the structure and construct in it a concrete auditorium and anterooms that were to contain his valuable information.

126

Harvey undoubtedly saw the stock market crash of 1929 as proof of his economic philosophy, and apparently believed that the American people would respond to the Great Depression by repudiating gold at last. They would need a leader, and he was ready. He formed the Liberty Party—its motto was "Prosperity in Ninety Days!"—and scheduled a national nominating convention for 1932, at Monte Ne.

Harvey had predicted that tens of thousands of Americans would attend the maiden convention of the new political party, but only a few hundred showed up. Harvey was duly nominated for president by the handful of Liberty Party delegates and was smothered in the presidential election. He was eighty-two by then, tired of being a voice in the wilderness and generally disgusted with the multitudes who chose not to listen. He retired a third time, this time for good, and died in his sleep on February 11, 1936. The hotels fell into disuse; the concrete amphitheater he built at the base of what was to be his pyramid became a scenic portion of Camp Joyzelle for girls and a popular spot for University of Arkansas students, who would journey from Fayetteville to drink beer there in the daytime and smooch at night.

Coin Harvey's kingdom and the amphitheater that was to tell the story of our demise to a future civilization was covered as he figured, not by earthquakes and volcanic eruptions but by the waters of Beaver Lake, built by the U.S. Army Corps of Engineers in the 1960s.

David A. Cox
Gubernatorial Candidate

Arkansas's history is replete with dark-horse political candidates, but Dave Cox of Weiner represents the best of them. He was not the perennial crackpot who runs unsuccessfully every time the ticket opens, occasionally for an office higher than the one he lost the time before, and for which

Monroe A. Schwarzlose, the somnolent turkey farmer who made four races against Bill Clinton, later became the archetype. Nor was Cox the professional stalking horse, financed by an established candidate to help muddy the electoral waters and splinter the opposition support.

Dave Cox ran for governor once, in 1962, and he ran because he could not stomach the racial politics of Orval Faubus. He got buried, but he made a few friends, and he made his point.

When Dave Cox filed for governor, nobody knew who he was, and nobody could find out. He didn't have a telephone at his farm near Weiner in Poinsett County, and he didn't get to Little Rock much. The papers called him "the mystery candidate." When he did crash the papers, though, he crashed them with a bang. A Little Rock lawyer and racial rabblerouser named Amis Guthridge had announced his infamous "Reverse Freedom Rides," whereby civil-rights freedom rides from Mississippi and Alabama would be countered by giving destitute Black families in Little Rock one-way tickets to Hyannis Port, Massachusetts, the home of the Kennedy clan. Guthridge had been publicly chortling over his brainchild, but Cox was outraged. He bearded Guthridge in his office on West Markham Street, shook his finger at him, and called him "inhuman."

Later, in the language of a farmer with an eighth-grade education, which was what he was, Cox expounded on his candidacy. Orval Faubus was inflaming the people with his politics, Cox said, and he had to be stopped. There would come a day when his five children or his grandchildren would read the histories and ask him what he had done to fight Orval Faubus and it wouldn't be enough to say that he had voted against the demagogue.

With that, Cox plunked down cash money for a brand-new red Chevrolet Impala for a campaign car and hit the road, vowing to halt the Faubus juggernaut and have a high old time doing it.

128

He may not have achieved the first objective, but there was no doubt that he accomplished the second. He scheduled his campaign opener, a fish fry in downtown Weiner, and then announced to the sparse but hungry assemblage that Faubus had scared off the fry cooks, so there would be no food that day. He had lugged two dozen bottles of good whiskey and tubs of iced beer to

David Cox

a grain dryer where the fry and speechifying were to occur, and a newspaper reporter had to help him carry the booze across the railroad tracks back to his truck. The fish went in the freezer. They hit the grease a few weeks later, but observers noted that Dave Cox wasn't as dumb as he looked: He had drawn two fish-fry crowds with one mess of fish.

Cox was nothing if not candid. The six Democratic candidates appearing before the Arkansas Press Association at its annual convention were asked by a guest high-school graduate what advice they had for graduating seniors. Each of the other hopefuls droned about the Land of Opportunity and grand opportunities that lay ahead of the kids, and then it was Cox's turn. He hitched up his pants, strode to the microphone and said, "I'd tell 'em she's a low-wage state. Git out and git out fast!" Then he sat down.

Cox loved campaigning. He loved speaking from the stump and he loved shaking hands, but more than anything else he seemed to love the big horn-shaped loudspeakers he had fixed atop his new red Impala. He loved to mosey through neighborhoods in the late evening playing Sousa marches or Guy Lombardo hits to drum up a crowd or just to prepare people within earshot for a few sentences of invective against Faubus and the racists. Campaigning in a Springdale residential neighborhood late at night he was stopped by the local police, jailed, and charged with public intoxication. He tried to offer his glass eye—a shotgun accident on the farm had cost him an eye, fingers and part of an ear—as collateral when he couldn't post bond the next morning and then said he was taking his campaign out of the Arkansas mountains and into nearby Missouri for a few days. He later retracted that statement and said he would never again set foot on ground that was higher than Crowley's Ridge near his home in the flatlands. He was arrested the next week at the county seat there for packing a pistol in the doorway of the Harrisburg bank.

When a member of the press was around, he was prone to claim that he would lead the ticket in the Democratic preferential primary and might win without a runoff. It was simple logic, he said: He was the only farmer candidate in a state of farmers, and he would get all the Black votes because he was the only candidate to promise Blacks a fair shake.

At the biggest political clambake of the season, the Mount Nebo Chicken Fry, he told the assembled crowd that he hoped to live to see the day when a Black man would be president of the United States.

As the race drew to a close, however, a reporter asked him how many votes, candidly, did he expect to get. He gazed at his hands for a while and answered very quietly, "about two thousand." Faubus's campaign manager had just cited the governor's poll, which Cox said indicated that the powers would let him have one percent of the votes. He figured that would be two thousand. He was off about five hundred votes.

He had made his point for his descendants. He took the speakers off the Chevrolet's roof, ripped the taped "Cox for Governor" sign from the door, and drove back to Weiner to get his rice crop ready for harvest.

Major Homer Berry
"Moisture Control Consultant"

Homer Franklin Berry was born in Mayflower, and he settled in North Little Rock after spending twenty-one years in the Air Force. The major had always been fascinated by the weather, and in January 1964 he made a novel offer to city officials in Little Rock and North Little Rock: He would fill the undernourished Lake Winona reservoir with rain for seventeen hundred dollars and would keep it filled for a yearly retainer. He was not a rainmaker, Berry told the city fathers, because "rainmaker is synonymous with dunce." He could, however, make it rain when he wanted to. "I am a moisture-control consultant," he said.

The city fathers said no thanks, but a local radio station, in need of a little publicity, possibly, remembered the incident, and in August 1964 it offered Berry five hundred dollars if he could produce an inch of rain over Little Rock. Berry was equal to the challenge. He went on the radio and television to warn people to postpone their picnics and then went to work, burning chemical-soaked hunks of charcoal in a fifty-five-gallon oil drum lined with firebrick and set in the bed of a pickup truck.

Major Homer Berry

On August 23, it rained a smidgen, but Berry said it wasn't his rain; his rain would be a frog-choker. On the next day, it rained an inch and a half, and Berry collected his five hundred dollars.

This was how Homer Berry's career as a rainmaker launched. He produced—or, at any rate, collected for—a gullywasher at Joiner, and even produced a white Christmas, defying the predictions of the Weather Bureau. The state Fair and Livestock Show hired him to make sure it didn't rain on opening day; Berry collected.

No meteorologist ever called Berry a fraud. Indeed, they conceded that the silver iodide he used to prime the heavenly pumps was the same stuff that was dropped from airplanes in more widely recognized methods of rainmaking. They were skeptical, however, about his delivery system. Berry didn't care.

"I am an artist," he said. "I paint a picture in the sky. I care nothing for the little people or their opinions."

On another occasion, the major was a little more realistic about his standing in the community. "Fifty percent of the people think I'm a fraud, and the other fifty percent aren't sure."

Whatever else his critics said about Major Berry, nobody ever accused him of being a slacker. He would travel the dusty back roads for days on end, pausing only to mix more chemicals. Once, in the twilight of his career, he failed to produce the agreed-upon amount of rain for parched farmers in Stonewall County, Texas, and his expense checks stopped, but he kept at it anyway, for nothing.

The major complained in later years that producing rain was a young man's game—all those sacks of chemicals to lift, all that breathing of fumes, all that driving along dusty roads, and he finally extinguished his barrel for good in 1972 and moved to Chandler, Arizona. He died September 18, 1975, in a Phoenix hospital and was buried two days later in a national cemetery at Fort Huachuca. It did not rain on the service.

Albert Pike
Genius, Egoist, Mystic

Albert Pike was a man of many parts—so many, in fact, that his memory shouldn't be diminished by the realization that a few were distinctly odd. He was a man of extreme intellectual and physical appetites; a man of action whose inaction in battle earned him a Jubilation T. Cornpone reputation as a general; a gregarious raconteur who spent his reclusive last years immersed in impenetrable mysticism.

Pike was born in 1809 in Boston, but as a young man he settled in the Arkansaw Territory, read the law, and soon rose to power in political circles. In the 1840s he headed up a cavalry company that, by all accounts, acquitted itself well in the war with Mexico; after returning to Arkansas, he interrupted his career again to fight, this time in a duel during which three shots were fired by each participant and neither was hit.

Albert Pike

Originally a Whig, Pike later was linked with the Know-Nothings, a shadowy bunch with antipapist leanings. Possibly because of his involvement with Freemasonry, Pike was accused of having written several virulent anti-Catholic tracts, but the charge was never proved.

Things started coming apart for Albert Pike with the outbreak of the Civil War. He had argued against secession, but when Arkansas left the Union he cast his lot with the Confederacy and was commissioned a brigadier. He proved himself an able military governor, but failed his only major test as a field officer in the Battle of Elkhorn Tavern, near Pea Ridge.

After overrunning a Yankee gun emplacement, Pike's army of Indian troops began to celebrate wildly, losing all semblance of discipline. An Indian trooper shot a wounded federal soldier to death, and at least one Union corpse was scalped during the short-lived celebration. When federal artillery counterattacked, Pike's troops fled in disarray.

Bitter about a resulting controversy over his performance in the battle—he had been unable to figure out what to do with those soldiers who didn't run away—Pike refused to obey marching orders and resigned from the Confederate army.

Meanwhile, Union propagandists and journalists were inflating the scalping incidents into mass atrocities and portraying Pike as a merciless, uncivilized butcher. When Pike's presence was discovered in New York after the war, the public outcry forced him to flee to Canada.

After the war, Pike lived for a time as a recluse, then exploded with a body of writing that probably has never been equaled for sheer volume and incomprehensibility. His monumental work on the symbols of Freemasonry, *Morals and Dogma*, although it seems prolix today, was hailed as a major philosophical work. "Who knows but that Albert Pike was a reincarnation of Plato, walking these Nineteenth-century streets of ours," wrote a contemporary admirer.

Later scholars were less enthusiastic. One Pike biographer estimated that the number of persons who had actually read every word of *Morals and Dogma* could have convened in a coat closet and that those among them who actually understood the tome could be counted on the fingers of a catcher's mitt.

Pike kept churning it out. Ensconced in quarters provided by his order in Washington, D.C., he delved into the mysteries of the East—he mastered Sanskrit while in his seventies—and produced such tributes to the bookbinder's art as *Translations of the Rig-Veda, the Maruts* (four volumes, 2,641 pages), *Irano-Aryan Theosophy and Doctrine As Contained in the Zend-Avesta* (2,344 pages), and *Lectures on the Arya* (1,499 pages). He also found time to fall in love with a nineteen-year-old girl and write a tome of grandiloquent essays in praise of her virtues. She married someone else, and Pike was plunged into a deep depression for months.

The years of turmoil and overindulgence—he weighed more than three hundred pounds before his health cracked—finally took their toll, and Pike died on February 28, 1891. His last words, written on a scrap of paper because he could not speak, were "Shalom, Shalom, Shalom." One of Arkansas's most contentious figures, one of its most tortured, had found peace.

"Dr." Norman Baker
"Dr." John Brinkley
Mountebanks

The careers of these two enterprising mountebanks are startlingly parallel; each man started out as a petty grifter, each more or less stumbled upon the medical dodge; and each made an inordinate amount of money. Neither man won his initial fame in Arkansas, but each found an appealing haven in the Wonder State when things got too hot in other climes. Each man denounced the other as a charlatan and a thief, and each man was correct in that assessment.

Norman Baker started his adult life innocently enough as a manufacturer of steam calliopes, and then drifted into vaudeville as a mentalist. He also operated a correspondence school, offering to teach oil painting in ten easy lessons, and put out a magazine, *T.N.T.* (The Naked Truth), a sort of forerunner of *The National Enquirer*. He finally got into the medical game by selling a horse-bunion paste to humans as a cure for cancer.

For his part, John R. Brinkley was bumming around in Carolina when he happened upon a fellow who introduced him to the joys of hot checks. As a boy, though, Brinkley had had a yen to be a doctor, so the two set up a storefront medical clinic specializing in prostate massage. The other chap later went on to more honest grifting. Brinkley stayed in medicine, except for a brief fling at bootlegging. (He later laughed off a bootlegging conviction as a boyish indiscretion.)

Baker's scam was cancer. Brinkley's was sex. Although Baker claimed at one time or another to be able to cure just about anything, most of his notoriety and money came from his "miraculous" cancer cure. Brinkley, on the other hand, claimed to transplant the gonads of goats into the scrota of his aged male patients, thereby, he claimed, restoring their sexual vigor. "Why be a capon?" the good doctor asked in his radio commercials.

Brinkley came to fame in the flatlands of Kansas, in the sleepy town of Milford. It was there that he performed his first "goat gland" operation on an old duffer who, according to Brinkley propaganda, soon thereafter sired a son, who was appropriately named Billy.

(That goat, incidentally was an Arkansawyer. Early experiments using any old goats had left the human subjects smelling rather rank, Brinkley said, but the Tannenberg goats raised in Arkansas caused no such indelicate problems.)

Dr. Brinkley may have been short on medical training, but he was a genius at merchandising. He started a radio station—a fifty-thousand-watter—and flooded the nation with preachments and testimonials from satisfied customers. People started coming to Milford in droves. Brinkley ran for governor as a write-in candidate and damned near won.

When his past began to catch up with him, he split for the border, literally. He set up another radio station, XERA, at Villa Acuna, just across the Mexican border from Del Rio, Texas, and continued to do business from there. It was calculated that he grossed twelve million dollars at Del Rio.

Meanwhile, Baker was advancing his career in an almost identical way. A snappy dresser given to wearing white suits and purple shirts over a bulletproof vest, Baker set up shop in Iowa. When things got hot there, he followed Brinkley to Texas, where he set up his own station and clinic. He had less success than

136

Brinkley, though, and ended up serving a jail term for fraud in the Lone Star State.

Brinkley also suffered adversity in Texas. He had sued the *Journal of the American Medical Association* for calling him a quack. The medical journal said his goat-gland operation was no more than a vasectomy and his Formula 1020 for restoring male virility was colored water. The courts held for the magazine. Brinkley had at last been officially branded a fraud, so in 1938, while keeping his radio station, he closed his palatial estate at Del Rio, with his herd of Galapagos turtles and a piano that had belonged to Norma Shearer, and moved his clinic to Twelfth and Schiller streets in Little Rock. The city fathers there were reluctant to grant zoning variances, so he finally moved to a beautiful former nightclub and Shriners' retreat about fifteen miles outside the city off the Arch Street Pike, which later became the Carmelite Monastery for nuns.

When Baker finished his jail term in Texas, he settled in Eureka Springs. His "cancer clinic" occupied what is now the Crescent Hotel at the top of the mountain town. Then he attempted to horn in on Brinkley's trade by hiring a fellow to perform goat-gland operations. Brinkley denounced Baker as a crook. "You're another," Baker responded.

Medical officials finally cracked down on the pair, and a Federal Communications Commission agreement with Mexico put an end to their stations, which had beamed powerful signals northward for years. Brinkley declared bankruptcy in 1941 and a federal grand jury soon indicted him, his wife, and several former employees for using the U.S. mail for Brinkley's fraudulent schemes.

Arkansawyers tried to forget both gentlemen, but for a few years the expression remained: "Faster than a goat at Dr. Brinkley's clinic."

Arkansas Times
May 1990

DULL WHITE MEN'S
Historyʝ Month

M AY IS ARKANSAS DULL WHITE MEN'S HISTORY MONTH, A FACT that has gone generally unheralded in the public prints, partly because dull white men are traditionally—and justifiably—modest about their accomplishments, but mostly because Arkansas Dull White Men's History Month did not exist until it was created in the editorial offices of this very magazine.

It was a rainy day in March, and a *Times* editorial staff member, himself a dull white man, was reading a newspaper.

"Good grief," he said—"Good grief" being a typical dull white man's expletive—"we just got through Black History Month, and now it's Women's History Month! When are *we* going to get *our* history month?"

It was clear what he meant by "we"; there were only three people in the *Times* editorial office at that moment, and all were dull white men. The *Times* has on its staff a person who is neither dull nor male, and even one white male who is not dull, but they were out of the office, as they often are. Thus, dull white men were in command of a quorum at a hastily called editorial conference, during which it was unanimously decided that May would be Dull White Men's History Month in the pages of the *Arkansas Times*.

For good or ill, this nation has been shaped in large measure by dull white men, faceless men who managed to slip into the river of history without making a ripple. We cite, for example, Patrick Yawn, who, in the turbulent days leading to the American Revolution, stirred the Continental Congress with the immortal words: "Give me liberty or give me death, but whatever you give me, try not to make a lot of noise about it, okay? I'm trying to sleep back here."

Or the dull white male supply clerk, his name forgotten in the annals of the Second World War, who said: "Patton, shmatton! If the son of a bitch wants gasoline for his precious tanks he can file a requisition in triplicate just like everybody else."

Likewise, the accomplishments of Arkansas's dull white men have been eclipsed by the deeds of their more colorful counterparts—men who horsewhipped editors, closed the public schools, or chained prisoners to fences. Because we have had more than our share of colorful characters, our dullards have been shoved even farther back in our historical pantheon. It is our hope that Arkansas Dull White Men's History Month will help restore dull white men to their proper place in our collective consciousness—that the dull white men of the past will come alive to bore us anew, and the dull white men of today will be recognized for their contribution to the state's never-ending fight against insomnia.

by MIKE TRIMBLE, D.W.M

Walter Hussman Jr, newspaper publisher—Called "Boo," reportedly because he resembles a ghost eating a cracker.

Marshall Schuster, cheap furniture man—Another day, another once-in-a-lifetime sale.

Tom McRae candidate—We didn't know they stacked dull that high.

Dr. Morriss Henry, doctor, lawyer, legislator—And boring at all of them.

Ray Thornton, candidate—He's probably smarter than David Pryor, and wittier, and he's only a little whiter, but he's dull and Pryor's not. Go figure.

HERE BUT

FORGOTTEN:

ARKANSAS'S

TOP TEN

DULL MEN

Frank Broyles, athletic director—Used to be kind of interesting many years ago, but became dull by dint of hard work, dedication, and "tending to his knitting." Assured himself a place on this list by inventing the pooch kick.

Dr. Hampton Roy, eye man, candidate—He's running for lieutenant governor. We rest our case.

Sam Walton, rich guy—Not only is he dull, he's a carrier; check out his top executives.

Jack Stephens, rich guy—His brother got all the interesting genes.

Ernest Dumas, editor, columnist—Excellence can be dull, too.

139

GATHINGS: *Reports of his demise were a trifle premature*

HATFIELD: *An animated bore*

LUNDY: *Dull in living color*

ADKINS: *With a name like Homer, he's got to be dull*

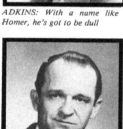

PURCELL: *The ideal—a Dull White Man for all seasons*

GONE BUT FORGOTTEN:
DULL WHITE MEN OF THE PAST

Governor Joe Purcell—Capable, honest, hard-working, idealistic, and probably the dullest white man ever to make his mark on Arkansas history. The *Arkansas Gazette* once reported that "people have been known to go to sleep while shaking hands with Joe Purcell," and nobody challenged the statement; not his wife, not his campaign manager, not Purcell himself, not anybody. Joe Purcell was so dull that most readers are probably thinking at this moment that "Governor Joe Purcell" is a typographical error. Well, it isn't. For a few boring weeks, Purcell was actually the chief executive officer of the state. His program consisted mainly of getting his portrait painted. He had begun his political career as a dull attorney general, and then honed his dullness to perfection as lieutenant governor.
(Note: any person who has served as lieutenant governor of Arkansas automatically qualifies as a dull white man, including Footsie Britt, Nathan Gordon, and whatever-his-name-is, that guy who has the job now.)

Governor Homer Adkins—He looked just like Estes Kefauver, but duller. His fate was sealed as soon as his parents named him Homer.

United States Representative E. C. (Took) Gathings—An east Arkansas congressman for many years, Gathings was so dull that the *Gazette* once referred to him as "the late Took Gathings" in an editorial while he was still alive. Gathings informed the paper of its error, and a rather abashed apology appeared on the editorial page. About a year later, the paper did the same thing again, and had to apologize again when Gathings protested. Gathings is dead now. Or at least we're pretty sure he's dead.

Ken Hatfield—Technically still alive, but with people like Hatfield, out-of-sight is more than out-of-mind; it is out-of-existence. Hatfield's contribution to the History of dull white men in Arkansas was that he managed to be dull while never acting dull. Most of the time, Hatfield was wildly enthusiastic about one thing or another; other times, he was deeply and unconsolably sad, usually at the perfidy of fickle fans or sportswriters. And it didn't make any difference in which mode Hatfield was operating: the boy was slug-dull in either case.

Walker Lundy—Though still alive biologically, former *Gazette* editor Lundy is dead as a hammer journalistically. His is an intriguing case, for Lundy was a dull man who seemed to believe with all his heart that he was interesting. He took a newspaper that was dull-looking but interesting and made it into one that was interesting-looking but dull. A singular accomplishment.

SOON-TO-BE-
FORGOTTEN:
CIPHERS OF
THE FUTURE

J. Keith Moyer—Some are born dull, some achieve dullness, and some have dullness thrust upon them. He's got pretty interesting hair, but our bet is that the *Gazette*'s new editor is a corporate tapdancer, and that means dull—cunning, but dull.

Scott Trotter—Showed early potential as a dull white man when he bored people even while making headlines a few years ago as a gadfly of the utilities. Has since become a lawyer, and, we're told, doesn't feel nearly as antagonistic toward big business as he used to.

OUR HONORARY DULL
WHITE MAN

Sidney Moncrief—A GMC dealer who supports Sheffield Nelson for governor. Is that dull? Is that white?

Preaching in the Paper

When John Workman takes to the pulpit in the columns of the Arkansas Gazette, *some of his readers respond with hosannas, but others wonder what in God's name is going on.*

Arkansas Times
May 1985

I'm a Methodist, a Methodist;
'Tis my belief.
I'm a Methodist till I die.
Till old grim death comes a-knockin' at the door,
I'm a Methodist till I die.

—Methodist Pie

THE REVEREND John S. Workman's very first column as the religion editor of the *Arkansas Gazette* was about the energy crisis.

"And he was wrong about that, too," snorts a constant and disgruntled reader, who then goes on to say that it really wasn't so much *what* Workman had to say about the energy crisis that gave him the willies as that he said it at all, the critic thereby establishing himself as a man who, while he may occasionally agree with what the Reverend Mister Workman says, does not necessarily defend his right to say it.

"He's the *religion* editor, for God's sake," the critic continues, unintentionally turning a pretty nifty phrase. "Why doesn't he talk about *religion*? Why does he have to talk about the *energy* crisis? It just seems to me that the religion editor should mention the Deity every once in a while."

Workman, on the other hand, maintains that he is talking about religion when he talks about secular matters. In Workman's view, a Deity who marks the sparrow's fall would hardly be expected to ignore the energy crisis. As he wrote in that first column:

"When people in gas lines lose their tempers and assault their neighbors, those happenings are much more than energy crisis matters alone; they are problems of human relationships that involve such traditionally religious concerns as greed, covetousness, and what it means to be a neighbor."

John Workman

Or, as he put it in a recent interview in his cluttered cubicle at the *Gazette*: "There is no such thing as a topic that has no religious dimension. Once you accept the fact that God exists, you have to accept His abiding concern over everything that affects the human condition."

In his weekly column of opinion on the *Gazette*'s Saturday church page, Workman manifests that belief by bashing away at such topics as gun control, American foreign policy, capital punishment, nuclear proliferation, and—yes—the energy crisis. His mildly stated but fiercely uncompromising opinions have made his column one of the most hotly debated features in the paper. There are those who consider him an eloquent voice for justice and compassion, and a like number who consider him a dangerous leftist radical. Whichever he is, he is certainly more than a religion editor. He is the *Gazette*'s preacher, using his bully pulpit to add a spiritual dimension to that paper's traditional—late twentieth-century—espousal of orthodox political liberalism.

Readers could certainly be forgiven for assuming that the addition of Workman to the *Gazette*'s chorus of liberal voices was part of a calculated plan, but it wasn't. As a matter of fact, there is considerable evidence that the paper got more than it bargained for when it put the mild-mannered preacher on its payroll. That's not to say that the *Gazette* is unhappy with its religion editor, because it isn't. It's just that it didn't turn out to be quite what they expected.

For years, newspapers pretty much ignored news of religion, and the *Gazette* was no exception. Many papers, the *Gazette* included, had a "Saturday church page," but it was merely a compilation of local church handouts about special activities and guest speakers.

At the *Gazette*, as at most other papers, the title of "religion editor" was held by a staff member who juggled the job with his or her left hand while performing other editorial duties with the other. For years, the *Gazette*'s church page was edited by a staff member who also was the paper's radio and television editor. As far as is known, the only requirement for a religion editor was that he or she be able to make page layouts and write one-column headlines. One was never required to know anything about religion. To even inquire about a potential religion editor's religious leanings or expertise was unheard of, and probably considered impolite. (The use of the term "potential religion editor" should not be construed to mean that there were people actually vying for the job. It was simply another assignment, and, for many irreverent reporters, an odious one. *Gazette* general-assignment reporters had been known to hide under their desks when it became known in the newsroom that the regular radio-TV-religion editor was about to go on vacation.)

The *Gazette*'s cross-town competitor, the *Arkansas Democrat*, had a religion editor—the Reverend Erwin L. McDonald, a highly respected Southern Baptist minister—and he wrote a column, too, but rarely if ever ventured into what religionists of the day rather scornfully called "the Social Gospel." The *Democrat* also had in its employ for years a lady whose job it was to write a weekly Sunday School lesson for the Saturday church page. Her name was Lela Maude Funston, and the wonderful title "Democrat Lesson Writer" appeared under her byline.

John Workman became the *Gazette*'s full-time religion editor in June 1978, and it wasn't long before the Word hit the fan. It had been understood by everyone concerned with Workman's employment that he would write a weekly column of opinion and personal observation, but it's probably safe to say that none of the paper's face cards ever envisioned that their religion editor would one day scold Mother Teresa in the columns of the staid old *Gazette*.

The revered Nobel Peace Prize winner from Calcutta, in Little Rock to visit a Catholic home for unwed pregnant women, had characterized abortion as "murder." Workman thought the use of that term was harsh and inappropriate, and said so—albeit gently— in his column. A flurry of angry letters to the editor ensued. "Congratulations, Workman," a fellow *Gazette* staffer greeted him one morning during the midst of the firestorm, "you're the only reporter in the history of this newspaper ever to dump on a saint."

Carrick H. Patterson, the *Gazette*'s editor, stoutly denies ever having choked on his Wheaties upon scanning a Workman column on a Saturday morning, but he acknowledges that Workman has charted his own path at the paper.

"I'll accept that we got more than we bargained for, only in the sense that John carved out his own role for himself at the paper with no direction from us as to what he would say or not say in his column. He did it himself; he established his own voice, and our hats are off to him."

Patterson takes pains to point out that Workman is more than an opinion columnist at the *Gazette*. As religion editor, Workman also handles all those mundane chores that his predecessors did: the editing and compiling of the weekly church page. Patterson also points to Workman's other writing efforts: his reporting and interpretive pieces on religious issues in the news.

"We had always been good at reporting the political side of issues," Patterson said, "but, quite frankly, the *Gazette*—and most other newspapers in the country—had neglected the fact that most of our readers were churchgoing people who were interested in news of religion and in the moral aspects of social and political issues as well. In John, we found someone who was not only a deeply religious man and learned in religion, but who also was a qualified journalist."

Indeed, Workman's controversial columns have tended to overshadow his work as a reporter, which has been considerable. He has interviewed such disparate figures as maverick theologian Hans Kung and Moral Majority leader Jerry Falwell, and has produced long and thoughtful pieces examining such developments in religion as the rise of the charismatic movement and the anti-Catholic campaign of the Arkansas cult leader Tony Alamo. But it is as a liberal commentator that Workman has drawn the majority of both his praise and his criticism.

His belief that "there is no such thing as a topic that has no religious dimension" springs not only from his own personal background and religious faith, but also from political and social changes that had their beginnings more than thirty years ago, when Workman was a young Methodist minister. In later years, these developments would have an effect on such issues as poverty and foreign policy, but the first and most explosive issue was race.

In the 'Fifties, the backbone of the fledgling civil-rights movement in the South was the Black church. Black churches provided a meeting place, a sense of community, and a sense of purpose, and Black clergymen provided much of the young movement's leadership. As newspaper accounts and television news coverage of the struggle pricked the conscience of the nation, white churchgoers joined the movement; clerical collars and nuns' habits became familiar sights in footage of civil-rights marches.

At first, most of these clergymen were from the North, but Southern churchmen of conscience were beginning to take their stands, too—if not actually taking to the streets, then taking to the pulpits to urge calm compliance with the law concerning public school desegregation.

The issue of race shaped the political thinking of many young Southerners. Before the civil-rights movement began, most of them, if they had thought about politics much at all, would have declared themselves conservatives, as their fathers and grandfathers had. But the sight of Bull Connor's police dogs in Birmingham caused many young Southerners—and many Southern clergymen—to embrace the civil rights movement and the entire spectrum of liberal political thought. They came to see liberalism as the philosophy of racial equality and Christian love for one's fellow man. Conservatism, on the other hand, was seen as the defender of segregation and of bigotry. Liberals didn't bomb Black churches; conservatives did. From a historical perspective, it may have been a bum rap, but there was no way the conservatives could avoid it. To young idealists, it was a matter of simple logic: I am against racism; therefore I am a liberal.

That perception—if you're a racial liberal, you're a liberal all the way—has left us with some interesting but skewed historical images. The late Governor Winthrop Rockefeller, for example, was a racial liberal by any standard, and on other issues he was firmly ensconced in the liberal wing of the Republican Party, but he was *still* a Republican, a fact that a lot of people—righties and lefties alike—tend to overlook today.

Many young Methodist seminarians in the 'Fifties who were moved to activism by the civil-rights movement doubtless found it easier than their counterparts in other denominations to accept liberal political thought. The Methodist Church certainly couldn't be confused with the Unitarians, but its theology was more liberal than that of, say, the Southern Baptists. Liberal in theology, liberal in politics; it wasn't that great a leap. Also, Methodist ministers may have found it easier to voice their convictions about civil rights from their pulpits than did their Baptist counterparts. Methodist preachers are assigned to churches by their conferences; Baptist congregations are pretty nearly autonomous, and pastors serve at their pleasure.

John Workman was a young Methodist minister when the civil rights tide was sweeping the South, and he joined it.

Current events, however, were not the only things that shaped Workman's thinking. He comes from a family "with a deep liberal tradition, not so much in the sense of political issues as in the sense of moral issues."

Workman's father, the late Reverend James W. Workman, was a fourth-generation Methodist minister who studied at Yale and served as the last president of the old Henderson-Brown College in Arkadelphia (now Henderson State University).

"Dad was not your typical Bible Belt minister. He was considered very liberal by Southern standards, at least for that time, and, in matters of religion, he was a very ecumenical thinker. He even played golf."

Workman was born in Fayetteville and spent his early years there, but the church later sent his father north, and Workman graduated from high school in Winnetka, Illinois, the home of the legendary Big Noise.

Despite the long tradition of Methodist preachers in the family, Workman says there was never any pressure on him to enter the ministry. (He has two brothers; one is a social worker and the other is a lawyer.) As a matter of fact, Workman says, he was "just sort of sitting around after high school graduation in Illinois wondering what I was going to do with myself" when his Uncle Sam made the immediate decision for him.

"When I learned that I was about to be drafted, I went to the local board office," Workman recalls. "Back then, the Navy was drafting, too, and I was interested in sailing, so I thought I'd prefer the Navy, if they gave me a choice. Sure enough, they asked me which I preferred, and I said the Navy. Next thing I knew, I was in the Army."

Workman spent the next two years in Japan and Korea, monitoring Chinese radio transmissions.

"It wasn't really all that exotic," he says. "Not really cloak-and-dagger stuff at all. It wasn't as though we had access to super-secret materials. We just listened to these telegraph key transmissions and passed them on to the intelligence people for decoding. We didn't have any idea what they said."

After being discharged in 1948, Workman entered Hendrix College on the GI Bill, and it was there that he decided he would enter the ministry.

"It was a gradual decision; there wasn't a bolt of lightning or anything like that. I think my decision centered on my own perception of what really mattered, what really made a difference."

After graduating from Hendrix in 1950, Workman entered the Perkins School of Theology at Southern Methodist University in Dallas, where he earned his theology degree in 1953. It was as a theology student in Dallas that Workman received his first preaching assignment, to a five-church circuit based at Acton, Texas.

"I remember my first visit to one of the towns on the circuit, Falls Creek. I paid a courtesy call on the Baptist preacher there and learned that one of the pillars of the Baptist church had died. The minister asked me to help with the service, so I did."

Workman was continuing the ecumenical tradition of his father: his first funeral was for a Baptist whom he had never laid eyes on.

Workman and his wife, Liz, herself the daughter of a Methodist minister, returned to Arkansas in 1955 and for the next nearly twenty years he preached in churches at Newark, Oil Trough, Cabot, Berryville, Sylvan Hills, and Little Rock. As the civil rights movement gained momentum, however, and as more ministers began speaking out, not only on civil rights but also on a number of other social issues, he began to wonder if his true calling was in the pulpit.

"I loved preaching, and I loved my parishioners, but I came to realize that a lot of the people in my congregation were a lot more conservative than I was. I had to examine whether I was serving them in the way they wanted and deserved to be served and whether I was compromising my own principles in doing so."

In 1973, he was offered the editorship of the *Arkansas Methodist*, the statewide weekly church newspaper, and he took it. He was the principal writer for the paper and also took most of the pictures.

"I suppose it was a lot like working for my little weekly," Workman says. "We had a small staff and an even smaller budget, and everybody ended up doing a little bit of everything. A lot of us worked eighteen hours a day just to get the paper out."

In the six years that Workman edited the *Arkansas Methodist*, the political pendulum was swinging to the right, and many fundamentalist denominations that had decried the entrance of the church into "secular matters" in the 'Sixties were now making pronouncements from their own pulpits about political and social issues. All of a sudden, liberals who had applauded William Sloan Coffin and Milwaukee's fiery Father James Groppi were taking umbrage at Jerry Falwell and James Robison for doing pretty much the same thing. The liberals weren't ready for that. Fundamentalist preachers were supposed to confine themselves to holding baptisms on riverbanks and condemning dancing and card playing. As long as such preachers had confined their political activities to endorsing the Sunday blue laws, everything was fine, but now they had stopped preaching and gone to meddling. They were talking about busing and civil rights and foreign policy, and what was worse, oh Lord, they were urging their congregations to register to vote. The first reaction of the liberals was to assert that the right had no right to do what the left had been doing for years. It was not the liberals' finest hour.

Workman stepped into this free-swinging atmosphere in 1979 as the *Gazette*'s new religion editor. While he didn't intend to compromise his own strongly held views—and there probably isn't anyone, right or left, who would contend that he has—he was determined to bring a little more reason into the debate. Whether he's done that is itself debatable, but a careful re-reading of his columns confirms that there probably is no other person in Arkansas writing on controversial subjects who takes such pains to avoid shrillness. (He did once come very close to accusing the president of the United States of blasphemy, but everybody deserves one fall from grace.)

Like most any journalist who writes from a liberal perspective, Workman often gets accused of reflexive reactions to events of the day. It goes with the territory: when writers hew unerringly to the liberal line, they're "knee-jerk liberals." (Don't conservative knees ever jerk?)

Workman denies that he shoots from the hip, and his columns for the most part back him up, but he has, on a few occasions, been amazingly fast on the draw. He began questioning the Grenada invasion before the soldiers' boots were dry, and the controversial "60 Minutes" segment that accused the National Council of Churches of subsidizing terrorist groups drew a speedy Workman condemnation. It should be noted, however, that those who accused Workman of shooting from the hip on those two occasions were not people who had thoughtfully withheld judgment on either event; they were people who had voiced their wholehearted support for both, and they hadn't wasted any time, either.

Actually, Workman is less doctrinaire than some of his critics might suspect. The Mother Teresa column notwithstanding, his views on abortion are tentative, almost anguished, and have drawn criticism from both pro-choice and pro-life groups. On a few other issues, he is downright conservative. He shares the *Gazette*'s straitlaced opposition to gambling to the extent of writing against the latest bingo bill, as much as it must have strained his natural ecumenical tendencies. Although the *Gazette* might be called a tippler's newspaper, endorsing as it does on its editorial page most proposed liberalization of the state's Byzantine liquor laws, Workman—a teetotaler himself—has written strongly about what he sees as the dangers posed by "the liquor interests." After some municipalities declared themselves "nuclear-free zones" to protest nuclear proliferation, Workman wrote a column declaring his cubicle at the *Gazette* a "tobacco-free zone." As far as his fellow workers at the paper can tell, Workman's only vice is an addiction to M&Ms, the plain kind in the brown sack. In deference to the Methodist temperance tradition, Workman says, he's been trying to cut down.

Workman is also careful not to limit himself to controversial or weighty subjects. At the *Arkansas Methodist*, he wrote two regular columns. One, "From the Bottom of My Heart," dealt with serious subjects, and the other, "Off the Top of My Head," was reserved for lighter observations. At the *Gazette*, Workman still juggles the sublime and the ridiculous in the context of his column. He has taken a text on the glories and tribulations of being bald-headed, fumed over the mechanical vicissitudes of his ancient Volkswagen beetle, and rhapsodized over long, solitary excursions aboard his faithful bicycle, Old Jim.

And the man *will* write about spring.

Rare is the editorialist or columnist who can resist an occasional, seasonal urge to write about spring, but Workman is positively nutty about it. He writes about spring not only in the spring, but in the fall and winter as well.

"My wife has begged me not to write so much about spring," Workman says, "but I can't help it. I just flat like spring."

Workman also leavens his more serious columns with humor occasionally. Much of it is self-deprecating, a refreshing change from your average sober-sided pundit. He has begun a column by waxing indignant over a radio commentator's assertion that the United States would never again have a bald-headed president and has gone on from there to make some serious observations about how America's leaders are perceived by their constituents and about how they are packaged and sold by advertising men.

In another column, he outlined a political controversy with immense moral and religious ramifications and then wrote: "Only a fool would attempt to answer that question. What follows is an attempt to answer that question."

Workman's greatest fear about his work—other than that some puckish copy editor may someday insert a dirty limerick into his column—is that readers may be so turned off by his conclusions that they ignore the reasons he gives for coming to those conclusions. It's a symptom of the times, he says; everybody has their minds made up and nobody—right or left—seems to want to listen to what the other side has to say.

"A piece of writing deserves to be read with the same care with which it was written," Workman says, "and I'm afraid there is a shortage of careful reading, among both liberals and conservatives."

Workman himself is very careful in his writing; he has to be. It is a relatively simple thing for an editorialist or a political columnist to condemn his opponents as fools or brigands, but when a man is writing from a religious perspective, when he is criticizing views that are bound so closely to religious beliefs, he is talking not only about judgment, but Judgment; he is commenting on the salvation of his adversaries' immortal souls.

That's one reason why a dialogue between the religious right and the religious left is so difficult. Although they both use the same Rule Book, they interpret the rules so differently that it's hard to find any common ground.

Workman, for his part, often criticizes the positions of the religious right, but he is careful never to question the movement's motives, or the status of the adherents as "good Christians." He does not question these things because accepting the beliefs of others is part of his own deeply held religious faith.

Many fundamentalists, on the other hand, do question the standing of their opponents in the eyes of God, which gives rise to countercharges that the fundamentalists are lacking in the basic Christian virtues of tolerance and compassion.

It is not that easy, though; the religious right's literal interpretation of the Scripture demands that they question their opponents in that way in order to be true to their faith: there they stand; they can do no other.

Workman understands this, he says, and in fact he has become "a little impatient" with the widely held attitude among mainline churches that the fundamentalists have nothing relevant to say.

"Having come from a liberal background, I'm still a little critical of the mainline clergy because they have not taken the trouble to become aware of what is going on in the evangelical movement," Workman says. "Some liberals tend to dismiss fundamentalist beliefs as primitive, when in fact there is a vast body of serious scholarship in that area. The point is that nobody has a monopoly on virtue; nobody has all the right answers. I'm not really sure where I come down on all of these issues. I'm a little

154

concerned about people—liberals and conservatives—who are so sure they are right."

Because of that, Workman says, he writes his controversial column not so much to try to convert people as to stimulate discussion, another example of the clear differences between soft-sell, mainline Methodism and the hard-shell proselytizing of the fundamentalists. What he is doing, in essence, is climbing into the ring with one hand tied behind him against opponents whose interpretation of the Marquis of Queensberry rules allows them to drop horseshoes in their gloves.

None of which seems to bother Workman, an unflaggingly cheerful man who looks all of his fifty-seven years but who at the same time somehow manages to resemble a mischievous bald-headed little boy. He will continue to write about arms control and capital punishment and Latin America—and spring—and will consider each angry letter to the editor a victory instead of a rebuke.

"If my columns stimulate discussion then I'm satisfied," he says. "That's generally all a preacher can realistically hope to do—submit his beliefs to his congregation in the hope of stimulating them to serious thoughts.

"It's been said that if Saint Paul came back to earth today, he'd be a journalist. I don't know about that, but I do know that some of the best preaching down through the ages has been done by writers."

Facing the Facts of Life

Arkansas Times
January 1989

[**Editor's Note:** Four years after this article appeared, President Clinton appointed Dr. Elders surgeon general of the United States but then, in December 1994, asked her to resign in the midst of a controversy over her frank remarks about sex education at a national forum. He would later say he regretted doing it.]

BILL CLINTON once said of Dr. Joycelyn Elders that the thing that made her different from all his other appointees was that when he told her what he wanted her to do, she took him seriously. Only the governor knows for sure to what extent he was joking.

As director of the state Health Department, Elders has set for herself no less a task than cutting Arkansas's teen-pregnancy rate in half before the end of the decade. She has persistently and publicly advocated sex education in the public schools beginning in kindergarten; classes in which parents learn how to talk and listen to their children; and school-based health clinics that would, among other things, dispense birth-control information and devices. Her proposals, especially the first and the last, have been condemned by many conservative Arkansawyers, who say such an approach is morally nearsighted and will only exacerbate the problem. Elders has met those criticisms head-on, often in heated face-to-face confrontations, without either retreating into concili-

156

atory bureaucratic crabwalking or losing her temper and braining somebody with an umbrella.

Health Department directors have made headlines before, become the object of controversy before, but usually it has been over politics: a disgruntled governor here, an insulted legislator there. The stew that Elders has stirred up isn't about appropriations or bureaucratic turf; it's about public health. She's stayed on the good side of the governor, and has even managed to win over a legislator or two.

After Elders presented the Health Department budget to the Legislative Council in November, Representative Tom Collier of Newport, about as reactionary an appleknocker as there is in the General Assembly, appeared to praise her proposals with faint damnation: "When it first came out, you were going to put the condoms out there and everything, and, of course, man, I went through the ceiling on that. But I'm listening to you lately. I'm leaving an open ear and I think maybe you're getting ready to do a pretty good job." That's not exactly an unqualified endorsement, but even accounting for Collier's typically impenetrable phraseology, it does seem to be an endorsement of sorts, and that's how Elders chooses to interpret it.

"I think the council was very responsive," she said recently. "I think they're finally aware of the severity of the problem we have in this state with teen pregnancy, and they're willing to entertain ideas now that they might not have just a few years ago. There wasn't any hostile questioning. One gentleman just asked me to explain what it was I wanted, and I talked about the education programs, including parenting education, human-sexuality classes beginning at the kindergarten level, classes for boys about male responsibility, and, for schools that choose to ask for them, in-school health clinics that would provide a variety of screening and diagnostic services and, again, if the local school district asked for it, birth-control counseling. Everybody seemed very open-minded about it. I felt it was a real plus."

Not every encounter has turned out so well. Not long after Elders began speaking out in favor of the school-based health clinics, which was not too long after she was appointed director of

Dr. Joycelyn Elders

the Health Department in October 1987, she invited twenty-three people to her office to discuss the proposals. Those twenty-three had written to her opposing the concept of school-based clinics, she recalls, and she thought it would be a good idea to talk to them about their objections. When the delegation arrived, it comprised almost a hundred persons. Some were carrying signs expressing opposition to Elders's proposals. One of them read, "Sex Education is Pornography." Someone had called the papers and the television stations. Reporters, photographers, and TV crews were there to record the whole thing.

"We had to move the meeting into the auditorium. I was totally unprepared."

Prepared or not, Elders climbed into a ring crammed with a passel of vociferous opponents—a kind of verbal *rassle royal*—and proceeded to match them blow for blow. The abiding image of Elders since that encounter, an image created by newspaper and television accounts of the set-to, is that of a controlled but tenacious advocate.

Elders had been in the public eye before being named to head the Health Department, but the public's perception of her was much different from what it is now. As chief of pediatrics in the College of Medicine at the University of Arkansas for Medical Sciences, Elders had a Sunday-feature-story image: an attractive and articulate Black woman in a world that for years had

158

traditionally been reserved for white males. She was a respected physician and teacher, a success in business (she was a founding director of a central Arkansas bank), the wife of a man who was something of a celebrity in his own right (Oliver Elders, the successful basketball coach at Little Rock's Hall High School), the mother of two boys. She was a society editor's delight.

Then came the confrontation in the Health Department auditorium, and Elders was no longer a journalistic warm fuzzy; she was out of the features section and into the hard-news pages.

She laughs when asked about the transformation. "Anybody who thinks I'm just now developing a tough side should have a little talk with my husband, or my boys, or my brothers and sisters. That's the problem with media coverage; it only looks at one side of you, and the people who see it think that's all there is to you; they think they know you from what they see on television or in the paper."

Elders was born Joycelyn Jones on August 13, 1933, in the farming community of Schaal in south Howard County. She was the first of eight children—four boys and four girls. Her father made a living by farming on shares—cotton, some corn, and a few cucumbers. Elders remembers her childhood home as neat and clean but spartan—there was no electricity or gas, and water was fetched from a well. As the family grew, the children were expected to help with the farm work.

"My mother really valued an education, and my father felt the same way, but he had to look at it from another way, too. He needed all the help he could get just to keep us fed, and it hurt losing a farm hand, even a little kid. Both of my grandmothers were very influential; they helped me scrape together the pennies I needed to go to school."

Elders began school in a stereotypical one-room schoolhouse at Schaal; later she transferred to a consolidated school at Tollette, about four miles to the east. Black students were bused to the school from all over Howard County, and from Fulton and Saratoga in Hempstead County. The segregated school was staffed by poorly paid Black teachers and equipped with castoff books and materials from the area's white schools, but, to Joycelyn Jones, it was all very impressive.

"Coming from my little one-room school, everything at Tollette looked pretty wonderful. I had never set foot in a white school, so I had no way of knowing how much better they were."

Elders learned later that many rural schools adjusted their class schedules to accommodate farm kids; the school at Tollette did not.

"They didn't let school out for planting or picking; the kids had to just work their chores in as best they could. Most of us missed a lot of school because we had to work. Then you'd get behind, and that's when a lot of kids would drop out. I would guess we had a dropout rate of between thirty and sixty percent. There were only ten people in my graduating class." All the Jones children stayed in school, but it wasn't easy. "We'd milk cows and feed the hogs in the mornings, and then go to school. When we got back, we'd work in the fields.

"When there was a lot of work to be done, we wouldn't go to school at all. We missed a lot of school."

Elders' absences disturbed her science teacher, who considered her a promising student, and he asked her why she didn't attend more regularly. Elders was ashamed to say that she had to farm, so she tried to assume an air of nonchalance, telling her teacher that she simply didn't care for school.

"I'm pretty sure he knew the real reason, because he helped me make up the work I missed."

Elders apparently made up for her absences in fairly good order, for when the end of her senior year came she was the valedictorian of her class, and she received a scholarship to Philander Smith College in Little Rock. All that summer, she picked peaches for

160

money with which to buy school clothes, and her brothers and sisters donated some of their cotton-picking money for her bus fare. In the fall, she and her grandmother boarded the bus for Little Rock and college. She was fifteen years old.

Elders' scholarship provided her with tuition, but it also gave her something equally as essential for the continuance of her education: a job. Hers was as a cleaning woman in a Philander Smith dormitory.

"I swept, mopped, and waxed the halls and cleaned the bathrooms," Elders recalls. "It was so much easier than picking cotton that I thought I had it made. Besides, there wasn't any stigma to working when I went to school. Everybody I knew was working, too."

Elders had excelled at science in high school, so she majored in chemistry and biology at Philander Smith. Her ambition was to be a laboratory technician, because, she says, "I thought that was the top of the world for a girl like me."

In her freshman year, however, she heard a speech at the college by Edith Irby Jones, who at the time was a student at the University of Arkansas College of Medicine in Little Rock and would become the first Black woman to graduate from that institution.

"I was completely and totally inspired," Elders says. "I didn't know at the time how I was going to swing it, but somehow I was going to get into medical school." How she swung it was to work for a while as a lab technician upon graduation, and then to enlist in the Army to train and work as a physical therapist. By the time she left the service as a second lieutenant, she had been accepted to the medical school at Little Rock. She started medical school in September 1955, attending under the G. I. Bill.

When Elders completed medical school, the University of Minnesota offered her an internship in pediatrics, and she took it. Before heading north, however, she took care of one other little item of business: She got married.

As a medical student, Joycelyn Jones had given preseason physical examinations to local high-school athletes. While checking the athletes, she also had the opportunity to check out one of their coaches, a young man named Oliver Elders. He coached basketball. He apparently did some checking out himself, and the two were married just before Joycelyn Elders reported for her internship in Minnesota. Oliver Elders stayed behind in Little Rock.

"That made me a super intern," she says. "I didn't have anything else to do up there but work."

Elders returned to Little Rock to a residency in pediatrics at University Hospital, and later was named chief pediatric resident, supervising nine white male doctors.

This was in the 'Sixties, remember, when Black physicians were rare in Arkansas, and Black female physicians were rarer still. Elders says she never encountered any resentment or bigotry from the men she supervised.

"Thinking back on it, I guess that's pretty remarkable, considering the time and the place, and the fact that there are a lot of big egos in a hospital. Maybe the Med Center was just a little ahead of its time, or maybe everybody was just too busy for that sort of foolishness; I worked seven days a week for that entire year. Later on, as things began to open up for women and minorities, I was there in the right place at the right time, with the right bag of tricks."

After her residency, Elders returned to the classroom again, this time earning a master's degree in biochemistry as part of a National Institutes of Health program to train academic physicians. That was followed by an NIH Career Development Grant and an appointment to the faculty at the College of Medicine. That's when Joycelyn Elders broke into the Sunday feature pages of the newspapers, which is where she might still be today if she hadn't got steamed at Bill Clinton.

"It was during the governor's first administration," Elders says, "and there was a lot of controversy in the Health Department. I wrote the governor a long, very critical letter about his Health Department policies. I think I remember him sending me a nice polite response, but there wasn't anything much said about it at the time.

"Then, in 1987, I got this call from the governor, and he said he wanted me to do something for him. I asked what, and he said to head up the Health Department. Well, I reminded him about my letter and said that when I made those recommendations, I wasn't the person I had in mind to implement them. He said he realized that, but that he thought I could handle the job. I thought about it for a couple of weeks, and then I said yes.

"My first day on the job, there probably wasn't a greener beginner in the world. About all I knew about the Health Department was that they gave baby shots. But there were great top-level management. They took me in and taught me what I needed to know in a hurry."

Elders quickly learned that there was more to the Health Department than baby shots. She spent her first year on the job wrestling with such problems as the state's infant-mortality rate, asbestos in public buildings, safe drinking water, home health care, and acquired immune deficiency syndrome. The more she looked at the state's health problems, the more convinced she became of what the Health Department's first priority should be: school-based general health clinics and a reduction in the teen-pregnancy rate.

"Any way that you looked at it as a physician or as a government administrator, we're wasting our resources. We're spending millions on the consequences of teen pregnancy without effectively attacking the cause of it. We're pouring money down the drain and continuing a problem that will double in the next ten years. To people who say that we can't afford to fight it, I point out that Arkansas spent $192 million in 1986–87 on teenage families. I say we can't afford to continue like we are doing. We can pay now to attack the problem at its roots or we can keep on fighting the problem of cleaning up the mess and paying forever.

"And I'm not just talking about health expenditures. The state's prison budget is nearly two and a half times the Health Department budget, and if we don't stop this flood of teen pregnancies, we're going to have to build bigger and better prisons, because kids born into circumstances like that are more than likely headed for trouble with the law down the road."

To reverse the trend of teen pregnancies—and she says the rate can be cut in half by 1990—Elders proposes first of all a comprehensive sex-education program in the public schools, beginning with kindergarten.

"I'm not saying I know how to teach sexuality to kids in kindergarten, but there are people who do, and we've got to get them to work on it. We've got to teach these young people from the very beginning to respect their bodies, respect their sexuality, and not let someone else take advantage of them. In the tenth grade, the hormones are already raging and there have been ten years of watching easy sex on TV and movies. In poor homes where teen pregnancy is now a two- or three-generation tradition, tenth grade is just too late to instill that self-respect you need to be able to say 'no' to sex."

Elders also proposes classes for parents on how to communicate with their children on such subjects as sex, drugs, and alcohol.

"You can say all day long that the place to teach kids about sex is in the home," Elders says, "but how many parents do it? Of the ones who do it, how many are just one-shot, awkward little speeches about the birds and the bees?

"You know what I realized one day when I was giving a speech advocating classes in sexuality awareness? I was making the same point I'm making now, and I asked everybody who had neglected to teach their own kids about sex to raise their hands. All of a sudden I realized I needed to raise my hand, too; I had never talked to my sons about sex. I went home and asked Oliver what he had told the boys, and he said, 'Hey, you're the doctor, I thought you handled it.' So here we are, a physician and a teacher, with two grown sons who found out about sex God knows where. I'm one of those people I'm talking about."

The third proposal and the most controversial one is for the school-based health clinics. Opponents have been outraged that clinics could offer birth-control information and contraceptive devices. What good are parental entreaties for abstinence, they say, when schools provide birth control?

Elders has attempted to defuse those objections with a bevy of options. First, clinics would be placed only where local districts asked for them. Second, they wouldn't provide contraceptives or birth-control counseling unless the local district approved it. Third, any parents who didn't want their child going to the clinic could simply withhold permission.

Still, some people object, and Elders can't figure it out.

"You've got selective veto power all down the line," she says. "A school won't even have a clinic unless the local district requests it. The clinic won't unless the district requests it. And kids won't go unless they have their parents' permission. That should take care of anyone's objections. I can see what people are saying when they say you should just teach abstinence. I absolutely support abstinence. Every school health nurse in these clinics supports and counsels abstinence. Everybody you meet on the street supports abstinence. But what do you do with the teenagers who choose to be sexually active? Does that mean we have no responsibility to try to keep that teenager from getting pregnant?"

Elders reckons that 80 per cent of the parents of teenage children in the public schools would approve of the clinic proposals. "The biggest protesters are those with no kids in school," she says. Other opponents, she says, simply have no idea of the size of the problem.

"Number one, I think most of the organized opposition comes from the bigger areas, where there are more health facilities, both private and public. People in the poorer, rural areas know how bad this problem is. And I think a lot of the opposition comes from happily married, middle-class people who mean well, but who don't have an accurate view of the problem. I'm not talking about a middle-class teenager who gets 'in trouble'; I'm talking about a thirteen-year-old girl whose mother may be only twenty-seven, and who may be a prostitute, or who may bring men home, have sex with them, and encourage her daughter to join in. I have seen these situations; I am not exaggerating."

Elders is normally very controlled in her public statements or in interviews, but when she talks about the poverty she's seen since becoming director of the Health Department, there is an emotional edge to her voice. She has seen poverty all her life, she says. She experienced it herself as a child. But there is something different about this poverty. It is meaner, she says, seemingly without any hope of any kind, without any moral rudder within the family unit. It saps the spirit, leaving only fear and bitterness.

Her opponents say that is exactly what one must expect as a result of a welfare state that destroys any initiative. Elders disagrees vehemently.

"That's the same thing as saying we've done too much for our poor," she says. "I think we've done nothing, or else we've given the poor just enough to survive, not to live. We've started a miserable cycle of slavery. Our society as a whole has progressed, but to the poor that only makes it seem like they're even poorer. They see all of the glamour and the good life on television, but they don't see any hope of things getting better for themselves. When I was little, we knew we were poor, but we never thought things were hopeless. We always believed there was a way out of poverty. Many of the poor I see today don't have that hope.

"When I talk about sex education in public schools and parenting classes, and school-based health clinics, and making it a law that any case of pregnancy in a girl fourteen or under be investigated for the possibility of child abuse, I'm not talking about throwing money away. That's what we're doing now. I'm talking about a plan that will get results, and it's ethically right, medically right, and economically right."

And then there was one.

If they haven't already, proponents might want to take a look at how the state's first school-based clinic came into being, about two years ago at Lincoln, in Washington County. The sequence of events at Lincoln was, on a much smaller scale, almost identical to that now being played out on the state level, at least so far.

During the school year of 1985–86, there were ten pregnancies in the twelfth grade of Lincoln High School. That amounted to about 30 percent of the girls in the senior class, and it got the undivided attention of the Lincoln School Board. The board formed a communitywide committee to propose a plan of action, and the committee recommended that the district avail itself of the Washington County office of the state Health Department and augment its own school-health-nurse program with a Health Department clinic at the high school. In addition to backing up the school nurse on established health programs, the Health Department clinic—it originally would be scheduled for a half day every other month—would provide birth-control information and, through the county health office, access to contraceptives. There was strong local opposition. Lloyd Jones, the Lincoln superintendent of schools, recalls that "basically, the objections were about the clinic being on school property, and that students who went could have access to birth-control materials without the consent of their parents."

The school board didn't dismiss the objections out of hand, Jones says.

"The opponents had a point, and the board understood how they felt."

In the end, however, the board decided that the situation warranted the establishment of the clinic. "The school district is not dispensing contraceptives," Jones says. "They are available through the county health office, just as they have always been. Essentially, we moved an existing program to the high school, and that ended up being the main controversy.

"We're also attacking the problem through education," Jones says. "We don't have specific sex-education classes, but it is included where it's appropriate in the curriculum. We're even talking to elementary students in terms of self-awareness, self-esteem, and being able to say no in the face of peer pressure."

Jones is careful when speaking about the clinic. There is still a lot of opposition to it.

"We have tried to keep everyone, the opponents included, honestly informed as to what we're doing and how the program's going," Jones says. "We've invited people who opposed the clinic to serve on committees to help oversee the program."

The clinic now operates once a month for about two hours, and while Jones isn't ready to say the teen-pregnancy problem in Lincoln is licked, he does say the program "has done some good."

In 1985–86, there were ten pregnancies in the Lincoln senior class. In 1986–87, the first year of the clinic's operation, there was one.

The Sundance Kid Grows Up

Architect James Lambeth, the 'Seventies wunderkind of solar design, didn't disappear in the era of Reagan and oil gluts. He stuck to his principles, stayed busy, and got rich.

Arkansas Times
October 1989

JAMES LAMBETH of Fayetteville does not appear to be a man who would have much truck with the sun. He is fair-skinned and redhaired, a burn-and-peeler if there ever was one. Despite that, or because of it, or for reasons having nothing at all to do with it (it doesn't pay to lean too heavily on these flimsy journalistic frameworks), Lambeth has a long-standing relationship with the sun: studying it, drawing pictures of it, writing little illustrated stories about it, listening to what it tells him, and learning from it. Lambeth is an architect, and you might say that the sun has been a silent partner in his firm. During that portion of the 'Seventies when every day was Earth Day, Lambeth was known worldwide as an exponent and innovative practitioner of passive solar design. His buildings were featured in national and international journals. He was invited to lecture, consult, and design all over the globe.

Lambeth had first drawn the attention of the architecture establishment with an iconoclastic house he designed and built for himself in Fayetteville in the late 'Sixties. The house was shielded on the north side by the south face of Fayetteville's Mount Sequoyah; it surged outward and upward to face the southern sun with three stories of wood, brick, and glass—*lots* of glass. It was something of a back-to-the-land, flower-power palace that was just right for its time (the 'Sixties) and place (Fayetteville, also known as Marin County East, or Little Sur), with the tradition-shattering look and feel of the 'Sixties and the emphasis on the simple and natural that soon would come to the fore in the environment-conscious 'Seventies. And, more or less to his surprise, Lambeth says now, the house was incredibly energy efficient, as well as being cheap to build.

"It's kind of funny how everything came together," Lambeth said to a recent visitor at his Fayetteville studio. "I was still in my twenties, teaching architecture at the university, full of that 'Sixties adventurousness and rebellion and looking for an aesthetic that made sense to me. Everyone seemed to be teaching fashion architecture—folded concrete plates were real big about then—and it seemed silly to me that something as permanent as a building would be subject to fads and fashions. So I designed this place strictly on what I liked and what made sense to me. I built it in 1967 for about $27,000 (it would cost much more now, he notes) and pretty soon it was getting written up in all the journals. It was also very energy efficient, although that hadn't been my first concern. I guess it probably wasn't even considered a 'solar house' for another five years or so, until the energy crisis came and utilities hit the roof."

More houses followed, all of them arresting and innovative, some of them whimsical (Lambeth designed one house for friends of his who were expecting a baby, and in honor of the new arrival he made the driveway a huge face of Mickey Mouse), and all of them energy efficient. A few of them, in their quest for the winter sun, resembled high-fidelity loudspeakers that had been ripped from their cabinets: low and narrow at the north end, which was

170

often bermed into a hillside; high, wide, and handsome on the south side, where glass panels rose to meet the winter sun and eaves shot outward to minimize the harsher summer rays.

Others looked like tilted cubes.

Lambeth designed a solar chicken house that used fifty-five-gallon drums—painted matte black and filled with water—to catch, store, and radiate heat. He designed a mountain cabin for a couple of ground hippies and then couldn't find out if it ever got built. About a year later, he heard of a cabin in Newton County that sounded like his, and he found it by flying over the area in an airplane. His original clients had never got around to constructing the cabin, but they had passed the plans on to a couple that had.

All of Lambeth's projects worked, and a lot of them got a lot of attention, which meant that he got a lot of attention, too. He wrote a book, *Solar Designing*, that was named one of the best books of 1977 by the American Institute of Architects. It's interesting to look at the book twelve years later, for although it was published privately and inexpensively, it was stylishly done, and reflected the period about as well as Lambeth's houses themselves. *Solar Designing* opened with diagram after diagram of solar angles at different latitudes and different times of the year, and there were more diagrams of how light behaves when bounced off a mirror. Lambeth's style—he included stylistic figures along with the arcs and angles—was a cross between geometry and modern art. The text, too, was different, a composite of technical expository writing, poetry, and mystical guru-babble.

Lambeth won the Prix de Rome in 1979 and traveled the world spreading the word about paying attention to what the sun was telling us. He consulted on ambitious building projects in Germany, Japan, and—before the fall of the Shah—Iran.

Then, all of a sudden, we were in the 'Eighties, and we were all Republicans whether we liked it or not. The voice of the yuppie was heard in the land, and it was saying, "What energy crisis? What climate crisis?" Detroit started cranking up the horsepower in its cars again, and we cranked up our air conditioners at home. It seems like a long time since we last saw an article in the papers about passive solar houses, and a Little Rock architect engaged in cocktail-party small talk a few months ago wondered what had ever become of James Lambeth.

About every three years or so, some TV network news department will get hard up for a feature spot and drag a crew out to a ballroom or a society dance or a college prom, there to ask some barnacle-encrusted orchestra leader: "Are the Big Bands back?" whereupon the dinner-jacketed maestro avers that he's "never been away." James Lambeth gives a similar response to an interviewer's "Quo vadis?" with its tacit implication that he's not been heard from much lately, and he makes a better case than does the average bandleader.

"After the Prix de Rome thing, I came back to Fayetteville and started lecturing all over the place, teaching again, and tending to my architecture practice. Then my brother and I went into the real-estate development business and were very successful. Motels, apartment buildings, things like that. My brother tended to the development end of things and I handled the design chores. Then my brother died in 1985, and I had to assume a much larger role in the business. That meant cutting the teaching, and it meant less residential designing. I'll still do two or three residences a year, though, so I haven't fallen off the face of the earth. I'd say I'm doing pretty well."

Just how well, of course, is a private matter between a man and his CPA, and we still haven't become quite Geraldofied enough to ask, "Hey, you rich, or what?" Perhaps it will suffice to relay Lambeth's report that he is adding a seven-car garage to his house on Mount Sequoyah, a garage where will dwell a Mercedes, a

Ferrari, and a Corvette, the last a perfectly restored 'Fifties classic, the kind with the tea-strainer headlights.

Which is not to say that Lambeth is no longer dancing with what brung him. He's waltzed with the sun since the 'Sixties and he figures there's still a turn or two in the old girl yet. Just because a building has a commercial application, he says, doesn't mean you turn off your brain—or your soul—when you design it.

"Some of the most daring things we've done," he said, "are things we've built ourselves, in our real-estate developments."

A couple of examples of that can be found in Springfield, Missouri, where both a motel and an apartment building developed by Lambeth's firm catch the eyes of passersby with huge concave mirrors that reflect the sun's rays into solar collectors that heat a swimming pool below. Lambeth said he became fascinated with lenses while designing a ski lodge in Aspen, Colorado; here, he used a concave panel of mirrors over the front door to focus the sun onto the driveway and melt the snow.

"Some of the locals were afraid that the mirrors would focus the sun's rays on other buildings and burn the town down," he recalled. "But my mirrors are friendly. They warm, but they don't set anything on fire."

Lambeth likes the big mirrors over the swimming pools not only because they heat the water but also because they also produce a kaleidoscopic reflection of the water and the bathers below that he finds pleasing. The combining of the aesthetic and the utilitarian, he says, is what architecture is all about.

Not everyone agrees. Lambeth said that a British architectural journal named the pool mirrors one of the seven worst utilizations of solar technology, presumably on grounds of triviality, which gets us into the politics of architecture, an area in which Lambeth seems firmly ensconced on the right, at least when it comes to designing buildings. When discussing the fortunes of solar design, which seemed to soar, explode into brilliance and then fade, like a Fourth of July skyrocket, he laid at least part of the blame for the fizzle on the federal government.

"Back in the 'Seventies," he said, "the oil embargo hit and energy costs soared, and all of a sudden the government got very interested in energy conservation. It dumped incredible amounts of money into the system, but it all went into hardware—stuff like flat-plate solar collectors, which were a waste of time."

Lambeth has never thought too highly of flat-plate collectors, which are an example of "active" solar design as opposed to "passive" solar design. Flat-plate collectors—you've seen them; they're those large, black glass plates set at an angle to catch the sun's rays—store the heat of the sun and then use an energy-consuming means (fans, usually) to distribute the heat. Although he has used flat-plate collectors himself, most notably in his pool-heating systems, Lambeth considers it a mistake to use them as a major design tool. Even back in the 'Seventies, when flat plates were the rage, Lambeth expressed his opinion of them in his book when he portrayed a flat-plate collector being carried by a dodo.

"Now all this hardware used energy in order to save energy, which always seemed to me to be the wrong way to go about it," Lambeth continued. "Flat-rate collectors last only about twenty years anyway. Plus they were very expensive. The only way they could be cost-effective was if you were heating water with electricity, and then only if the government paid for it with direct subsidies or tax credits, or something like that. Everything was fine as long as the subsidies continued, but when the Republicans got in, the subsidies stopped, and nobody could afford this stuff anymore." Meanwhile, Lambeth said, he and other architects were working on passive solar designs, designs that captured, stored, and radiated the sun's energy in the winter without using energy to do it, and turned away energy in the summer heat. They were con-

174

sidered innovators, he said, but so much of what they did was very old. He talked about visiting ancient Indian cliffhouses in Arizona and how their south-facing mud walls caught the winter sun and stored the heat, releasing it slowly during the night, and about how the overhanging cliffs shielded the pueblos from the harsher summer sunlight and made the walls cool to the touch even in the hottest months.

"So much that we needed to know was already there," he said. "It had been around for five hundred years or more, but we forgot about it in the 'Forties and 'Fifties when we were obsessed with high-end technology. A lot of what we were doing was no more than avoiding stupid things like putting a bunch of windows on the east and west sides of your house. There were times in the 'Seventies when I was a little embarrassed at all the attention I got. People would pay my way to Germany or somewhere for a lecture, and what I was saying essentially was that the sun comes up in the east and goes down in the west. It's really fairly simple once you've mastered that low-end knowledge and realized that just because it's low-end doesn't mean it's unimportant. There are just basic things you do: The south side is where you reach up and catch the sun; the east and west sides are where you bundle up; and the north side is where you do your architectural tricks. It's a matter of looking at the earth and the sun and doing what they tell you to do. Buildings should look different in different parts of town. You should be able to tell which direction you're walking by looking at the buildings."

At the same time that Lambeth deposed on the apparent decline of solar architecture, he also took pains to say that the decline was more apparent than real—that, like Big Bands and James Lambeth, solar design had never really gone away.

"Think for a minute," he said. "You're always hearing the words 'energy efficient' in commercials for everything from house trailers to furnaces. A lot of times, it doesn't mean what it's supposed to

175

mean, but it does show that people are conscious of the need to conserve energy. And a lot of solar design concepts are pretty much standard equipment now; they've entered the mainstream without much notice. Nowadays, even real-estate people know the difference between a north-sloping lot and a south-sloping lot, and why that's important. Some things are cheaper, too. When I first started designing houses, double-pane glass was almost unheard of, and it was awfully expensive; now, relatively speaking, it's not. A lot of ideas and equipment have got to the point that they're cost-effective now. Insulation isn't appreciably more expensive now than it used to be, and it's a lot more efficient. They've developed 'selective' surfaces for glass that reflect heat away from the house in the summer. The developments in the future are going to be more in the high-tech photovoltaic cells and things like that, but when that happens, I'll just call the experts and tell them what I want. My job will still be just to make the design right to begin with."

Lambeth says the houses he designs now are more mature than those that caused such a stir in the late 'Sixties and 'Seventies. An example is one he designed for Drs. Tom and Sharon Leslie of Harrison. The house at first glance does not appear to be designed by the same man who created Lambeth's Fayetteville home. The Fayetteville house is fanciful, deceptive in its many reflections and delicate in appearance; it seems as though it might fly right off the hillside if it got the notion. The Leslie house, on the other hand, seems to be hugging the ground, not struggling to be free of it. It is a substantial-looking structure, its front a facade of masonry highlighted by an entryway that could be the entrance to an ancient Mayan or Egyptian temple. Windows are on the front of this house, but you don't look "into" it as you do with Lambeth's residence. Where Lambeth's home in Fayetteville seems consciously to break every architectural tradition, never looking in any direction but straight ahead, this house looks to the past, unashamedly. Art Deco is in the stairwells and railings, a feeling of Twenties Hollywood opulence in the pool area around back. But Lambeth's basic stuff is all there. The east and west sides of the Leslie house are buttoned up against the morning and evening sun. While the south side doesn't exactly soar, plenty of glass catches the winter sun, including a large wall of Twenties Moderne glass bricks. And the north side is still for architectural tricks. Two monolithic chimneys stand guard at the front—the north side—of the house, and stairstep down to meet the massive entryway. Square windows sit recessed in the angles formed by the stairstepping. Above the doorway is a square stone inset that is translucent; at night it transmits an amber glow from inside the lighted entry hall of the house.

Something else remains from James Lambeth's earlier days. The front doors of the Leslie house, sunk back into the entry so as to be almost unnoticed from the outside, are etched with an intricate pattern of wide arcs and lines. Only after studying them for a while one realizes that the patterns appear in Lambeth's 1977 book. They are the tracks of the sun, as they angle in to mark the seasons, or dance along a mirror's edge.

The Phantasmal World
of H. E. Harvey

Arkansas Gazette
April 1979

H. E. HARVEY is sitting on the side of his bed, feet under a makeshift table, committing two-fingered assault and battery on a defenseless portable typewriter. He reads aloud as he pounds the machine at a rapid hunt-and-peck pace.

"Your issue of the thirty-first is examined," he types aloud, punctuating his verbal transcriptions with a snort. He leans on certain words as he reads; on the typing paper, those words appear in capital letters. "It is easy to think that the EDITOR relished trotting forth Bruce Bennett for ANOTHER LASHING, if for no other reason than to prove that the ED has a long MEMORY, like a camel and an elephant are reputed to have. And a HORSE."

The horse reference pleases him; he whoops as he reads it, almost as if the word's sudden appearance on the page surprises him. He continues.

"Well, now, if the said EDITOR wishes to establish that he has a 'long memory,' he should have listed FDR and LBJ and others along with RMN when he lists RMN's BIG pension, which is $241,000 a year. But NO. He forgets his DEMOCRATS who paraded up and down the Potomac."

Having established the connection between a former Arkansas attorney general and the spending policies of national governments, Harvey surges along, pausing only to look quickly through books and magazines for figures as he chronicles American payments to such countries as Great Britain ("Dismantled by one WIN CHURCHILL"), France, the Soviet Union, and China ("LOST under the DEMOCRATS, regained by RMN"), and as he finally lays the blame for all that free-spending perfidy:

"QUESTION: Where were our beloved second-class journalists while the Democrats were ladling out the millions in foreign aid? REPLY: They were polishing their VERBS, or so they pretend. Actually, they were existing as cur dogs and SCOUNDRELS SCOUNDRELS SCOUNDRELS SCOUNDRELS SCOUNDRELS SCOUNDRELS ..."

H. E. Harvey is writing another letter to the editor of the *Arkansas Gazette*.

Of all the readers who contribute to the *Gazette*'s "From the People" column, none is as prolific as H. E. Harvey of Route 1, Clarksville. It is a rare week that does not see four or five H. E. Harvey missives dumped on the editor's desk; often there are more. Each letter is typed on Harvey's plain white personalized stationery; they are from one and a half to two pages, double-spaced. The letters often include handwritten marginal notes. Sometimes, the notes direct attention to a thought he wishes to emphasize ("This is the MAIN POINT!"); more often, they are ribald greetings to the editor ("Just a little BULLS***"), or an informational tidbit for the editor's eyes only ("BIG SNOW HERE: 4 or 5 inches ...") Each letter is signed in Harvey's steady, Spencerian hand.

Harvey writes more letters than could ever be published in the newspaper. Because of space limitations, only about 20 percent of the letters written by readers appear in the "From the People" column, and a *Gazette* editor estimates that only about 10 to 15 percent of Harvey's output ever sees the light of print. At that, no name appears more frequently in the letters column than his.

The editor who handles the letters column was asked how he chose which of Harvey's letters to print. He looked intently at his fingernails for a while, twisted his mustache, and then began to pluck listlessly at his clothing.

"Well, uh ... I generally look for one that's coherent—no, that's not the word ... uh, one that makes a point, that is, a single point, in the course of the letter. I think that's what I'm trying to say. Does it make any difference?"

Probably not. The letters editor said that since Harvey's letters arrived nearly every day, sometimes two a day, he felt more and more guilty every day that he didn't pluck one and stick it in the paper since the fellow spent so much time composing them. H. E. Harvey never runs out of new ways to make his points, but, like most things, the more his letters change, the more they stay the same. The Democrats are the party of war and waste, the Republicans the party of peace and prudence. Former President Richard M. Nixon is destined to be remembered as a giant in American history, a martyr driven from office by the lying jackals of the Press.

Ah, the Press. It is for that institution that Harvey reserves his most scornful and high-spirited invective. The Editors (or "The Eds," as Harvey often calls them) are, according to his mood, classified as power-mad and purposeful Rasputins intent on destroying the republic or as oafs who are unqualified to wield the power they possess, rather like a willful and rather stupid child who has just been given custody of a loaded Gatling gun.

"Why," he asks in a typical letter, "does the common reporter fail to measure up and at least TRY to perform a useful role amongst his hard-pressed brethren? Well, it is easy to believe that

180

a majority of them yearn for a nomadic lifestyle, as they instinctively dislike a fixed location where folks would note that their 'reportings' are great figments of their hallucinatory imaginations."

While Nixon, party politics, and the press most often occupy Harvey's thoughts, he occasionally takes a swipe at other institutions, such as the American Medical Association and the memory of Winston Churchill, and, on occasion, he will abandon current events entirely and relate a bucolic remembrance of his childhood. It is in reading these infrequent essays that one comes to a startling conclusion: H. E. Harvey can write. To wit:

"Old Uncle Will Dobbs was, come to think of it, just another hillbilly, but he was considered an impressive man in these parts, especially by the younger folks. He was not, however, a saint, nor did he pose as one, and bad things were said about him."

There are people who make their living at the writing trade who would gladly claim authorship of a paragraph like that.

Given Harvey's prolificity and outspokenness, it seems a little strange that he does not participate in one of journalism's finest old traditions, the long-distance debate in the letters column. You have seen it countless times: One correspondent writes to take an unassailable position on an issue, and another quickly writes to assail it. The decision can go on for weeks, providing humor, excitement, and sometimes even a little information. Occasionally, someone will throw a gauntlet at Harvey's feet, but he lets it lie. Only once has he come close. It was after a letter of his appeared praising several Republican heroes, including Nixon, Herbert Hoover, and U. S. Grant. An incredulous reader wrote in to wonder why Harvey didn't include Warren G. Harding in his pantheon to make the rogue's gallery complete. Within a week, another letter from Harvey was published. It did not mention the challenge at all, but it began: "Warren Gamaliel Harding was born on a farm near Blooming Grove, Ohio…" It was a long letter.

It is also well to note that Harvey's letters do not exactly lend themselves to reasoned replies. It is difficult to transcribe a sputter. One contributor to the letters column probably summed up the feelings of a lot of readers when he asked, "Is there really an H. E. Harvey?"

There is, indeed, though there are occasional doubts as a visitor drives deeper and deeper into Johnson County, along a county road that gets narrower and muddier as the miles wear on. You can get stuck on Stone Hill Road this time of year, and you can get lost any time of year. The time is well spent, however, in anticipating what the visitor's host will be like. A retired Army major, perhaps, or a retired country lawyer, not the kind who went to law school, but the kind who read law as an apprentice or got his degree by mail many years ago. One thing for sure, he will be an old man, in his seventies at least, probably a little stooped with age. Being forewarned of the interview, he will be wearing a coat and tie, and there will be a tiny metal American flag on the lapel. His wife, if he has one, will collect state plates, and he will call her "Mother."

Hopelessly lost now as the road becomes little more than two muddy ruts through the woods, the visitor stops one last time to ask directions. The house, set back from the road and protected by a gate made from two bedsprings, is in the middle of about an acre of closely cleared land. The outside walls are covered with patterned tarpaper, the kind that is sometimes called "Sears and roe-brick." The house is set about two feet off the ground on stacks of bricks; sections of tree trunk are the steps to the front and side entrances. The roof is sheet tin. As the lost visitor gets from his car, a robust man of middle age comes around the corner of the house. He is dressed in a faded blue shirt, striped denim overalls, boots, and a battered western hat. He examines the muddy car, then the visitor, and he extends a beefy hand.

"You Trimble? I'm Harvey. What kinda mileage you get in that thing?"

H. E. Harvey is fifty-six years old, a stocky, handsome man with a neatly trimmed mustache and a military haircut. He was born in the house he lives in now, a house built by Elmo Harvey, his father. Harvey has raised eight children there; the three youngest still live with him. They all sleep in the larger of the house's two rooms. Each room is heated by its own wood stove. There is electricity and a telephone, but no plumbing. The smaller room is furnished with an old platform rocker, a battered office swivel chair on casters, a castoff school-desk chair, and a small television set on a table. One corner of the smaller room is filled with one-gallon plastic milk cartons filled with drinking water. There are a couple of "Star Trek" posters on the bare wood walls, and a shelf full of snapshots. The table by Harvey's bed supports his typewriter, several books and magazines, and a dime-store world globe. Clothes are hung on nails. There is a broom in the corner; the house is spanking clean.

"Want to take a look around the place? My daddy built this house with his own hands in 1922. I was born here; we moved a couple of miles off in 1927. I came back to the place when I got married. Paid it off in 1953, added that other room myself when we started havin' a lot of kids.

"This here's my gear, hanging on the wall here. Why don't you get a picture of me and my gear. That's just an old cheap western saddle, but that English saddle, that's a good one. An English saddle, once you get used to it, it's a pleasure to ride in."

A friendly black dog rounds the corner of the house and commences to sniff tires and feet. Harvey bends down to scratch the animal's ears.

"His name? Now that you mentioned it, I don't reckon he's got one. We've got a cat, too, and a pony that's out there in the woods. The pony's what keeps this grass so short."

Harvey's "farm" is eighty acres, but he doesn't grow anything on it—"just grass and a few trees." He gets by on a veteran's pension; he served in the Army Air Corps in World War II "working on propellers."

Out away from the house is an artesian well, and still farther away is an open-sided shed that houses a couple of years' worth of firewood and an old buckboard wagon. Nearby is a weathered privy, a two-holer. Back of the house is a root cellar with a hand-poured concrete roof. "My father dug it in 1927. You can see the date scratched there on the roof."

Inside the house again, Harvey talks about his letter writing.

"The first letter I ever had published was in *The Progressive Farmer*. They didn't print it all, just a couple of lines. Then, in 1966, I had a couple of boys in the Army, and I wrote hundreds of letters to the Pentagon, asking about my boys. That's about when I started writing to the papers, too. I started out writing to quite a few, but I just sort of narrowed it down to the *Gazette*.

"When I first started, I couldn't hardly write a sentence. I went to a little old school out here; the teacher had got through about the sixth grade. I made it through the ninth grade myself before I quit. That's one of the things I wanted to learn when I started writing letters, to write out a thought, to make myself clear."

As Harvey talks, the visitor feels uneasy. This plain-spoken man in overalls bears little resemblance to the H. E. Harvey who comes storming off the editorial page in the mornings, metaphors cocked and ready. It is only when he moves to his typewriter to pose for a photograph that the man of letters appears.

Harvey sits down and inserts a sheet of stationery in the machine. "I'll just fire off a little shot here to show you how I do it."

As he begins to type and read aloud, it is as though a switch has been thrown somewhere within H. E. Harvey.

"The MDs, AMA monopolists, drug and munitions tycoons, auto chieftains, rail barons, and others, including the insurance

184

lords, have not been, and are not likely to be, condemned by the lowly JOURNALISTS. And worse, FAR worse, if they were—that is, if the journalists got up on their hind legs and fired both barrels—the lowly and bedraggled lower classes would remain mute, unconcerned, and unimpressed."

Harvey stops typing and looks up, and the switch is turned off.

"That's it. Nothin' to it. I just start out and go till I run out of gas. No, I don't ever go back and rewrite one. I tried that some, and I ended up writing every letter about eight times and then throwing it away."

What Harvey does is collect all his thoughts before he even sits down to write.

"The paper comes in the mail about noon. I go to get it and read it over. Then I think about what I read. Sometimes I won't get started writing till late the next day. By then, I know what I want to say. Sometimes I'll just do one letter, sometimes more."

Harvey's typewriter table is littered with magazines, esoteric publications from both right and left—*National Review, Mother Jones, Human Events, Inquiry.*

"I'll tell you something about those magazines," he says. "If you write off and ask for a complimentary copy, sometimes they forget and leave you on the list for a whole year. *New Times* went broke."

Harvey is self-deprecating about his reading, the magazines as well as the numerous books that lie about the house.

"Aw, I'm not smart enough to read all that," he says. "I just sort of skim through 'em when I get the time."

A look through the books, however, reveals that each one is heavily underlined, with notes in the margins. Most of the books are contemporary histories or memoirs, *History of the Second World War* by B. H. Liddell Hart, *The German Army: 1933–1945* by Matthew Cooper, Eisenhower's *Crusade in Europe*, and, of course, Nixon's memoir, *RN*.

There is other evidence of Harvey's literary bent. He keeps carbon copies of his letters to the editor, those that were printed and the more numerous ones that weren't—all stacked flat and then rolled into a wad about the diameter of a basketball and fastened with an old belt. He displays the collection for another photograph, holding it as an angler would a prize catch.

There is also a scrapbook containing a chronological collection of all of Harvey's letters that have been printed on the editorial page of the *Gazette*. There are other items in the scrapbook, too: birth certificates, an obituary of a baby who died at birth, a news account of the violent death of country music star "Stringbean" Akeman.

Harvey's books and magazines provide statistics to back his arguments, and an occasional quotation, but his basic ideas are his own. The idea of a poor man—and Harvey is undeniably poor—stoutly defending orthodox Republicanism might seem odd to some, but not to Harvey. It is not rich people that a poor man hates, he explains; a poor man looks with admiration upon a man who has made a lot of money. It is a waste of that money that makes a poor man's blood boil, he said. That is why he no longer has any truck with the Democrats.

That and war. America has gone to war under Democrats and has made peace under Republicans, and nothing can change the importance of that to Harvey. Two of his sons served in Vietnam; one was seriously wounded.

"A man with two boys in a war is in a terrible position," he says. "That Vietnam was terrible. There was no reason for it except that a Democrat president got us into it. But when you got two boys over there, you can't turn your back on them. That's why I kind of had to go along with Lyndon Johnson. I didn't like it, but it didn't seem like I had a choice. It tears a man apart, something like that."

The Vietnam War ended, of course, while Richard Nixon was in office. That, ventures the visitor, is the main reason behind Harvey's loyalty to RMN.

"Nixon, Nixon, Nixon," Harvey muses quietly. "You know, it's a good thing the press ran him out of there. I think he was about half nuts there at the last. Have you read *The Final Days?*"

The visitor's uneasy feeling returns, only this time it is a full-blown panic. He is sure of it now: He is interviewing the wrong man. The real H. E. Harvey is still sitting in his coat and tie somewhere in the wilds of Johnson County, waiting for the visitor to arrive.

Harvey sees the uncomprehending look in his visitor's eyes, and he knows why it's there.

"I bet you never expected to hear that from me, did you?"

Then he explains the real reason behind his letters, and his explanation goes a lot deeper than Republicans and Democrats. It is about a poor man's need to speak his piece, an unlettered man's late and sudden discovery of the intoxicating world of words and thought, the joys of verbal combat.

"I'm an ignorant man. I started learning late, and the more I've learned, the more I've found out I didn't know. I read those editorials in the *Gazette*, all of 'em written by educated men, and my first thought is, 'This guy's right, there's no doubt about it. He's made his point.' But I make myself search for a loophole, see. I go over it again and again till I find a weakness. There's no use writing if you agree with a guy. Then I go at it with everything I got. That's the fun part.

"There are too many people won't say what's on their minds. They're afraid to speak up for what they believe in. A poor man especially, he'll be afraid of getting stepped on some more. But what I say is a poor man's got nothing to lose. A poor man's got to speak his mind. It doesn't really matter all that much what he says."

Carrick Patterson, executive editor of the *Gazette*, said much the same thing the other day when he was asked about Harvey's rather special status at the paper. The framers of the Constitution, Patterson said, didn't have *The New York Times* in mind when they drafted the First Amendment; they were thinking, although they didn't know it at the time, about H. E. Harvey.

"The First Amendment was drafted to protect the pamphleteer," he said, "the little guy with a printing press and an idea. H. E. Harvey is the direct descendant of that little guy. It's part of our responsibility to provide him with his printing press. It's a responsibility we can't afford to take lightly."

The late Jerry Neil didn't take it lightly. Until his death late last year, part of Neil's job as a *Gazette* associate editor was to assemble the letters column. He never met Harvey, but he cherished his contributions and printed as many as he could. More, some thought, than was necessary.

In H. E. Harvey's scrapbook is a letter from Jerry Neil, a gentle note of condolence written in 1977, when Harvey's wife died and his letters stopped coming to the paper for awhile. Pasted beside the letter in the scrapbook is Neil's obituary, clipped from the Thanksgiving Day edition of the *Gazette*.

Was he aware, the visitor asks, that Jerry Neil was the author of many of the editorials that Harvey attacked so virulently in his letters?

"I never was sure, but I kind of figured he was. I hoped he was, anyway. He was a good 'un. They all are, if you ask me. All that stuff I write about 'em, that's just part of the fun. Living way out here like this, I don't have a lot of friends. I feel like those boys at the paper are my real friends."

The interview over, the visitor leaves, but Harvey has to lead him to the main road in his vintage Volkswagen, partly to show the way and partly to push him out of the mud when he gets stuck. By the time the man gets back to his office, the mail has come, bearing another letter from H. E. Harvey to his friends at the *Gazette*:

"Re: your effort of last Thursday. Wrong! Stupidly, idiotically WRONG, WRONG, WRONG, WRONG! ..."

The Reigning King
of That Odd Fish

Arkansas Gazette
April 1979

DEVALLS BLUFF—The catfish is an odd duck. There
are about two thousand species of catfish, although only about
twenty-five normally reside in the waters of North America. Adult
catfish can range in size from an inch to ten feet and can weigh out
anywhere from an ounce or two to more than six hundred pounds.

Catfish don't have scales, but some have horny plates,
something like those found on certain species of rhinoceros. Catfish
have spines that can stick you, and some can expel venom through
those spines, venom that has been known to kill human beings.

Some catfish live in the mud on the bottom of rivers; some
gnaw holes in the sides of larger fish and live there, surviving on
their hosts' blood, like a tick.

Catfish can hear better than most other fish, because their air
bladders are connected to their inner ears by a series of small
bones. They are a sort of underwater bass fiddle.

Some male catfish carry the female's fertilized eggs in their
mouths.

There is a catfish that can walk on land for relatively long dis-
tances, and one is called the upside-down catfish because it likes
to flop over and swim on its back for no apparent reason. There is

an electric catfish that can give a person a pretty good shock. It lives in Africa.

Catfish will eat anything. That's right, anything. For that reason, most reference books class catfish as trash fish, and generally not fit to eat, which shows two things: It shows that most reference books are written in the North, and it shows that people in the North don't know what they're talking about, at least when it comes to eating catfish.

Northern people are funny about food. There is a documented case in a Little Rock household of a transplanted New Yorker who declined a serving of fried okra on the ground that he was a vegetarian. The man seemed to be under the impression that each segment was a tiny crustacean scraped from the bottom of an Arkansas River towboat. It should be noted in fairness, however, that the chances of the man's partaking of that Southern delicacy could not have been helped by the sight of his host spitting in the grease to make sure it was hot enough.

Southerners know about catfish, just as they know about barbecue, and they love it. This devotion has its drawbacks. It results in Southern people's placing the eating of catfish and barbecue in the same category as sex—that is, the worst there is is wonderful—and it allows scores of less-than-excellent catfish to be served under the premise that mediocre catfish is better than no catfish at all.

There is nothing shameful in that; when you need a catfish fix, you need it right away, and even frozen Brazilian fish is not proscribed, though it is nothing to be especially proud of, either. There comes a time, however, when the soul demands something more, something approaching perfection, and for hundreds of Arkansas catfish lovers, that means piling in the car and driving to DeValls Bluff on Highway 70, turning west between the old Moore hotel and a place that makes concrete steps, crossing a treacherous-looking wooden bridge and an equally treacherous-looking low-water bridge and stopping finally at what appears at first glance to be a minor train derailment but is actually Murry's Cafe.

In this rabbit warren of a restaurant, Olden Murry cooks up catfish and other wonderful foods. He has been at the same location since 1967, although it seems longer, and there probably is no restaurant in Arkansas that has a more loyal or illustrious clientele.

Paul Bash, the *chef de cuisine* at Restaurant Jacques and Suzanne, is not a man most people would lump together with Olden Murry, despite the fact that the two men are in the same business. At Jacques and Suzanne, the *cuisine* is about as *haute* as you can get in Arkansas: continental dishes served in an atmosphere of muted lighting, fine china, and lots of forks. At Murry's, it's heavy restaurant crockery on folding tables, and watch out for the gas space heaters. The two men have met, however, and they share a professional respect that transcends economic and cultural lines. Bash says that he and Olden Murry have more in common that most people might think: They both run "an honest kitchen," where the energies of the staff are devoted to turn out food of the highest quality.

"That's the mark of a fine restaurant," Bash said. "It makes no difference if you serve nothing but hamburgers, as long as you are devoted to making the best hamburgers it is possible to make."

(For his part, Olden Murry has eaten once at Restaurant Jacques and Suzanne. It is, he says, "a nice little operation.")

United States Senators Dale L. Bumpers and David Pryor are devotees of Murry's, as are a large percentage of the state's other well-known political figures. Before ill health forced him to stop, prominent Little Rock contractor Jack Pickens used to bring busloads of friends to Murry's a couple of times a week.

Bumpers says he would rather eat at Murry's any day than at *Sans Souci* in Washington. In fact, he says, Murry's is one of the three best restaurants he's ever eaten in. (The other two: Jacques and Suzanne and Fisher's Barbecue, both in Little Rock.)

Bumpers is a compassionate man who realizes that a lot of his colleagues in the Senate have never had the chance to taste Murry's catfish, and he is trying to figure out a way to remedy that situation. Suitcases full of Fisher's ribs have been successfully transported from Little Rock to the Senate Office Building by trusted Bumpers aides, but it is not yet known how well fried catfish travels across state lines. The senator has just about decided that the only thing to do is put Murry himself on a plane with an appropriate mess of iced-down catfish and let him do his stuff right there in Washington. Bumpers thinks such an undertaking might even have a positive effect on the quality of federal legislation coming out of the Senate.

"It certainly couldn't hurt," he said.

People who are not famous are just as devoted to Murry's. For instance: A telephone call to Senator Bumpers's Washington office to elicit a comment about Murry's was answered by a polite but briskly efficient receptionist with no trace of regional accent. Before learning the nature of the caller's business, she informed him that the senator was very busy, and that it might be several days before the call could be returned. Then the caller said he wanted to talk about Murry's.

"Oh, my God! It didn't burn down, did it?" the receptionist cried, this time in a voice that was pure Arkansas in origin. "I'll have the senator get right back to you."

It took a while to allay her fears.

For another instance: A party of nine Little Rock people was eating at Murry's the other night, and one fellow had a camera with him. The first thing his wife did after finding her place at the table was to demand that her husband take her picture alongside Olden Murry. As it happens, this woman works for the governor of the state, a man people line up to be photographed with, but she's never expressed an interest in being photographed with him, or with anyone else for that matter—not even her own husband. Just Olden Murry. She is now trying to get back to DeValls Bluff so Murry can autograph the picture.

The object of all this devotion is a 54-year-old father of seven who learned his trade at now-storied eating places at DeValls Bluff and perfected it during more than twenty years as a riverboat cook, plying the Mississippi for the Army Engineers.

Now he works seven days a week at his business and has taken one four-day vacation since he opened the place in 1967.

Murry's quit serving lunch a couple of years ago and now opens at 4 p.m. each day except Sunday, when the family gives itself a rest and opens at 5 p.m.

Murry is busy early in the evenings, and questions result in polite but brief replies as he runs the big electric deep-fat fryers in his kitchen. Later on, when things slow down a bit, it is Murry's custom to wander around the restaurant to chat with his customers, the new ones as well as the regulars, and after a little unwinding, he gets expansive.

"I was born here in DeValls Bluff in 1922. I never lived anywhere else. I finished high school over at Biscoe. When I came on, that was about as high as a Black man could go. I started cooking for a living when I was eighteen. I cooked at Moore's Hotel, and the Journey's End and Rex's Grill. All those were famous all over the state.

"I was working at Moore's in 1940 when a man from the Corps of Engineers came in and wanted me to go to work cooking on a snag boat for twenty dollars a week. I hired on, and I was on the boats until 1947, except for the time I was in the service, and I was cooking then, too.

"I cooked on snag boats and towboats, and on the pleasure boat, too. That was the boat the Corps had for big shots like congressmen and senators. Whenever they got a trip on the big-shot boat, they'd pull cooks off the other boats to cook, and I always got picked.

"You worked two weeks on the river, and then you got one day off. After your day off, you had to check to see which boat you had been assigned to and catch up with it no matter where it was. Sometimes we'd ride the train, but, most of the time, we'd drive our cars to Greenville or wherever we had to meet the boat.

"I got to New Orleans a lot. Now there's a town! That's where I found out I like crablegs. I saw people cracking open those claws and sucking that meat out and I didn't think I'd ever do that, but I tried it once, and man, oh man!

"They drafted me off the boat in '43, and I went to the war, cooking all the way. I saw some awful bad food cooked when I was in the war. Horsemeat and everything else.

"I got back with the Corps in '47, back on the river. I loved it at the time, but I wouldn't give you a nickel for it now."

In 1962, Murry broke his arm in an accident on the boat, and the injury didn't heal properly. It still bothers him at times.

"I left the Corps after my accident and cooked around town. Back at Journey's End and Rex's, that's where I learned to cook catfish. I also did a lot of catering for private hunting clubs and parties and things like that. It was pretty good work."

In 1967, Murry decided he wanted to open his own place. A Forrest City woman owned a diner, actually an old trolley that had seen transit duty at Pine Bluff, and she let Murry have it. He moved it to its present location and opened up shop.

"We started out serving plate lunches and barbecue. We didn't really push the fish all that much at first, but the word just sort of got around about it. I can't ever remember doing much advertising at all. People just told other people, and the customers started coming in."

Murry had fixed up his diner by adding a cinderblock foyer, but it soon became apparent that further expansion would be needed. That's when he bought his first house trailer and bolted it onto the trolley car. There have been two more additions since then, and the result is a fire marshal's nightmare that can seat 350 people, if they can ever find their way to their seats.

On Friday and Saturday nights, Murry needs all the seating he can get.

"We stay busy from opening till closing on Fridays and Saturdays. There's not much time to do anything but stay at the cookers. We probably sell more catfish than any other one thing, but you might be surprised to know how much other stuff we sell: froglegs, barbecue, quail, crappie. And steaks. We sell a whole lot of steaks."

Indeed, while Murry's reputation has been built on catfish, he is just as proud—maybe prouder—of his other culinary efforts. He says there is no secret to cooking catfish ("You roll it in the meal and you put it in the grease"), but questions about the preparation of some of his other items bring only enigmatic smiles from Olden Murry, and polite refusals to discuss the matter.

There is, for example, Murry's barbecue. It takes a brave man to sell barbecue in DeValls Bluff, which is the home of Craig's, one of the best barbecue houses in the state, and thus one of the best in the world, but Murry does it, and his ribs rate right up there with Craig's. Murry, understandably, thinks his is the better product, although "I sure wouldn't say anything bad about old Craig." It would be foolish indeed for an outsider to declare a preference. The safest thing to do is simply to declare Murry's the world's best barbecue served at a place famous for catfish, and to note that there is a Little Rock man, a serious eater of both catfish and barbecue, who has almost come to dread an impending trip to Murry's and the attendant decision it involves.

Usually, he solves the problem by ordering both and suffering the consequences later.

And there are the froglegs, covered with a batter that Murry says is the secret to their other meritorious attributes.

"You see, I can't get enough froglegs around here on a regular basis, so I have to get 'em frozen. If it weren't for the batter, they'd be dry and tough. The batter's the secret."

And it will remain a secret. Other restaurateurs have begged and offered bribes for the recipe, he said, but to no avail.

One recent customer, a man on a gluten-free diet, told Murry that he had passed up the froglegs because he was afraid the batter might contain flour. There was an unspoken question in the statement, and Murry gazed at the man a long time before answering, gauging the fine line between courtesy and a serious breach of security. Finally deciding that the man's motive was pure, Murry gave his reply, a reply calculated to answer the specific question and nothing more: "You did the right thing."

(It is interesting to note that Olden Murry himself does not like froglegs. He does not even deign to call the dish by its popular name, referring to it accurately, if not appealingly, as "frog," as in "I do not eat no frog.")

When Murry says there is no secret to cooking catfish, he is probably being honest; indeed, there seems to be no magic in the way he dredges the fish in meal and throws it into the big electric cooker in his kitchen. That is not to say, however, that there is not a lot to know about cooking catfish, and Murry knows it all.

The first thing to know, of course, is to get the best possible fish, and being located as he is hard by the White River, Murry is in a position to do just that.

"The river fish is the best. A river fish has to suffer to get his food. A pond-raised catfish, they just feed him while he sits there. The White River fish are the best of all 'cause the water's so clean.

I go over to Clarendon every day and buy two hundred to three hundred pounds of catfish from Mr. Bob George. I'm one of his biggest customers, and we've got a good relationship.

"The size of the fish I buy depends on the kind of catfish. Most of 'em I get are between two and three pounds. That's the best size for your blue or white catfish. I never buy blue or white over seven pounds. A yellow cat bigger than seven pounds is okay, 'cause he won't eat anything that's not moving."

Although Murry doesn't like it, he's forced during some winter months to buy pond-raised catfish.

"It's not White River fish," he said, "but it's not a bad fish."

Murry has never served frozen catfish.

"I would tell you that I will never serve frozen fish, but there's one thing that would make me do it. I would serve frozen fish before I would serve that Brazilian fish. I would tell my customers I was out of the catfish business."

Knowledge is essential, too, once the fish enters the kitchen.

"A lot of people will cook catfish at 350 degrees, but that's not hot enough. It's got to be 375. And that's not all of that. If I'm cooking up a bunch of dinners at once, I know that the cold fish is going to lower the temperature of the grease, so I get it up to 400. I can tell if it's hot enough the second the fish hits the grease, just by the sound.

"A lot of fast-food places, they'll cook fish with a timer, take it out when the buzzer sounds no matter what. Every batch is different. What I do is, I go by the time a little bit, but mainly I go by looking at the fish and listening to the grease.

"Another thing, a lot of places, they'll take a knife or a cleaver and just whack up the fish, and you'll get different-sized pieces. What that means is that some of your pieces are going to be cooked too much and some aren't going to be cooked enough. I've got a band saw over there, and I cut every piece the same thickness."

198

Murry attends his kitchen with the help of a staff that consists, with one exception, of members of his own family. Five of his seven children work at the restaurant.

"If it hadn't been a family thing," he said, "I don't think we ever would have stayed on this long. Back when the kids were little, we had outside help, and we was helping them, not helping ourselves. Like it is now, everybody knows what to jump on when things get busy. There's no bosses in the kitchen. We're all bosses."

Several of Murry's grown children have families of their own that depend on the restaurant for a living, so despite his heavy volume of business, Murry is not a rich man, and he still can't see his way clear to ponder retirement, take a vacation, or even cut down on his seven-day work week.

"As long as I'm here, things are running okay, so I'm going to be around as long as I can. There's nothing else for me to do anyway. I'm a cook, so I'll just keep cooking."

Murry has no hobbies, and the only thing he does strictly for pleasure is drink bourbon. ("I don't drink much, but I sure enjoy what I drink.") He confines his pleasures to the simpler things, such as his bourbon and sitting down occasionally to his favorite meal.

"If you ask me," he said one evening as he relaxed with a drink after a day of cutting and dredging and listening to the hissing of the grease, "there is nothing much better in the world than a big old plate of roast beef."

3.

BEST FRIENDS

How to Bury a Dog

Arkansas Gazette
1975

THE MAN and his family returned home on a Sunday afternoon, after a daylong trip out of town, to discover the dog dead, just outside the pen where they had put him early that morning. The animal had accomplished one more successful escape and then had breathed his last. He lay on his side—legs extended, eyes open—looking surprised.

Although technically a family pet, the dog was the spiritual property of the man. Their relationship had begun several years before the man's marriage; he often referred to the dog as his dowry.

Sometimes, though, there was an edge in the man's voice when he made the joke, for he and his dog had had a stormy time. The dog was bad, there was no doubt of it. Not mean, just bad, like some children are bad without really wanting to be or knowing why they are. The dog was a four-legged Huntz Hall, with a dash of low cunning thrown in.

The man was reflecting on these things as he carried his dog into the pen and laid him on the ground, and went to the garage for the shovel. Yes, he would bury the dog in his hated pen. An ironic choice, but practical, too, dictated by the geography of the property.

It occurred briefly to the man that it might be illegal for him to bury a seventy-five-pound Irish setter in his yard in a metropolitan area, but he quickly pushed it from his mind. There was a higher law, one learned in childhood, in a much smaller town, and *that* law said that when your dog died, you buried him in your back yard, where he had chased sticks and buried bones.

Not that yours ever had much affection for this place, the man thought as he turned the first earth inside the pen. Indeed, soon after the family had moved into the place, the dog had made a dedicated and successful life work of escaping from his custom-built, six-foot-high, $650 wood-and-chain-link Xanadu. Within a matter of weeks, the perimeter of the pen was dotted with stacks of bricks, stones, and firewood, each a monument to another successful tunneling effort. Crossties didn't help.

Once free, the dog set about what he deemed to be his official duties: Tipping over every ~~garage~~ garbage can and bringing home every cat-food dish in the neighborhood. The new neighbors, so friendly

at first, grew surly and uncommunicative. The dogcatcher was called. He was unsuccessful but he left notes.

Bad as that was, the man mused as he struggled with the shovel, it was probably better than the early days, when he had been a bachelor, and he and the dog had shared an apartment. A dog like that in an apartment! He shuddered at the memory of things devoured: Rugs, pillows, even a mattress. Eyeglasses. A watch.

(Don't forget the Valium. The vet had said just observe him, so the man had stayed up all night watching the dog as it alternately staggered into walls and sat in the middle of the living room, baying at a light bulb.)

For some reason, the memory of the Christmas tree was vivid as the man dug in the heat. He and the dog had paid a holiday call on his best friend. The little house was lovely—Early American—and the tree was decorated in the old-fashioned way. An errand had to be run, and the man and his friend left the dog at the house. Upon their return, they found the tree on its side, every inch of the painstakingly strung garlands of popcorn and cranberries had vanished. The dog sat, looking regal, in a wingback chair, indicted by a burp and five inches of thread hanging from the side of his mouth.

I'm not being fair, thought the man. I should think of positive things, he thought as he dug.

Once, several years before he had walked over to visit his niece, then a little girl of about three, and had taken the dog. The three friends had gone for a walk and had encountered a woman, known to the man and his niece, but not to the dog. The dog silently interposed himself between the little girl and the stranger, and refused to yield the position. If the woman moved to the side, so did the dog. If the woman came closer, the dog backed up, forcing the little girl to back up, too. If the woman circled, the dog circled, never making a sound or looking anything but friendly. He kept the watch until the woman moved on.

Another time, a dangerously crazy acquaintance made a drunken, nocturnal visit to the apartment, and the dog refused to stay in the same room with him.

That was it. Not a long list, the man concluded, and the second incident was probably a fluke. Generally speaking, the dog was an abysmal judge of character. Benign strangers—mailmen, cookie-vending Girl Scouts—were subjected to truly fearsome barrages of barking and growling; bill collectors and process servers got their hands licked.

He had never, ever, got ahead of the dog, the man thought, and his face reddened as he realized that he wasn't going to get ahead now, either. The ground where he was digging was nothing more than a rock pile disguised by a thin veneer of earth, and the man's limbs protested as he clanged around with his shovel. Finally, as he hove against a stone as big as his head, the shovel handle snapped in two, and the man, moving in a slow-motion fashion not unlike that displayed by the Incredible Hulk on television, tipped headfirst into the hole.

The man was in no shape to call on friends, and Sunday is a bad day to try to buy a shovel. It was almost an hour before the man obtained a new tool and set about to finish his task. When the hole looked about right, the man lay down the shovel and knelt by the still form of the dog.

It was not until he was leaning with his burden over the grave that he realized the magnitude of his defeat. The battle that had begun seven years before had not ended when the dog coughed his last earlier that day; it had not ended with the rocky ground or the broken shovel, and it was not ended now: The dog was stiff as a plank, and would not fit into the hole. The man rolled over on his back and screamed at the sky:

"RED, YOU SON OF A BITCH!"

Then he pulled the dog onto his lap, cradled its head in his arms, and wept.

The relief that came with the catharsis was palpable, but it wasn't complete. Even as he clung to the dog and sobbed, some part of him hung back, unable to accept the balm of grief, unable to do anything, really, but note without comment that the dog had managed once again to make him look like a fool. The proper scene, of course, is for the faithful dead animal to be curled in its master's lap, eyes closed, as though asleep. The reality, however, was a man embracing a comically rigid form, its legs jutting skyward like lightning rods. That tiny part of the man's mind reckoned that, from a distance, it probably looked as though he was weeping over an upturned end table.

It took about fifteen minutes for the man to calm himself and start enlarging the hole. When it was done, he lowered the dog into it, and furiously shoveled the loose dirt back into the cavity, being careful not to look into the grave again.

The job done, he put up the shovel and walked around to his front yard, where he was confronted by a neighbor, a nice man, but one determined at this point to get an unpleasant problem resolved.

"Mr. * * *," his neighbor said, "are you going to be able to keep your dog in its pen?"

"I think so," the man said, and then went into his house.

A Moral Dilemma
(Canine Division)

Arkansas Gazette
December 1973

I HOPE you don't mind my imposing on you like this, but I've got a problem, and maybe you could help me with it.

The problem consists of Pearl, a female dog of unknown lineage who has made a couple of minor appearances in this space since she was saved as a pup from an uncertain future at the pound.

Pearl is loud, impolite, untidy, disobedient, pushy, and a thoroughgoing coward; that is to say, she has acquired all the character traits of her master, and we get along fine.

As with most dogs, she is smart enough to outwit me whenever she really wants to and dumb enough to think I am pretty hot stuff. We have not had a serious difference of opinion since the day she ate my mattress.

Pearl has survived puppyhood without contracting any of the more serious dog diseases, and her innate cowardice has protected her from potentially dangerous encounters with cats or other dogs. The only real threat to her physical wellbeing came the other day when she absent-mindedly backed into my bathroom heater. Luckily, I was seated nearby, and was able to beat out the flames with a rolled-up newspaper, a gesture that went unappreciated by

Pearl, since my quick action prevented anything worse than a singed tuft on the end of the offended appendage.

The problem is that Pearl is fast approaching the age when I must make that age-old decision—to spay or not to spay—and I'm just not sure I'm up to facing the moral implications of the whole thing.

I've searched among my friends for an answer to the problem, and, so far, the overwhelming weight of opinion firmly favors the use of the surgeon's knife. The pragmatists point out the inconveniences of harboring an unaltered female dog, and the animal lovers are all but unanimous in their contention that having the operation is the "humane" thing to do. "They are so much happier after being spayed" is a line I've heard time after time in the past few weeks.

Unfortunately, I have yet to hear it from a female dog, and I hope you'll forgive me if I consider that the only unimpeachable source. Even if the statements of my friends are true, they are disturbingly similar to the statements used a few years ago to describe patients who had undergone prefrontal lobotomies to curb their criminal or otherwise antisocial tendencies.

I would feel a whole lot better about the whole thing if there were some way to drag Pearl into the decision-making process, but she is much too busy eating my shoes and dragging yesterday's underwear around the house to be bothered. It is not quite fair, this abrogation of all moral responsibility on her part, but I suppose it is one of the fringe benefits of being a dog.

Now, Pearl has never expressed a desire for children and, for my part, I feel that I'm just too young to be a grandfather. On the other hand, I haven't been able to figure out just who gave me the right to mess around in another living creature's procreative equipment.

So here's what I'd like you to do. If any of you know a female dog who can express an opinion on this subject, I'd appreciate it if you would help me get in touch with her. If I don't get an expert opinion soon there's not a doubt in my mind that the pragmatists will win out, and good old Pearl will go under the knife for no better reason than that I will be sick and tired of kicking the swains from my front door every morning. If that ends up as the reason, I'd never be able to look her in the eye as I beat out the flames in her tail.

The Public Responds

Arkansas Gazette
December 1973

WELL, PEARL and I certainly want to thank everyone for the way they responded to my plea for advice the other day. I haven't received so much mail since I killed off the wrong lady in an obituary down at Texarkana some years ago. (The lady, incidentally, was very nice about the whole thing and ordered several copies of the newspaper to send to her friends. As for the family of the deceased party, well, that's another story.)

Back to me and Pearl. As you may recall, Pearl is a young female dog who shares my living quarters and who is racing through adolescence at breakneck speed, leaving a trail of chewed-up shoes and overturned ashtrays in her wake. The time is fast approaching when she will—if nature is allowed to take its course—involuntarily become equipped to obey the Biblical admonition to be fruitful and multiply, thereby raising the specter of scores of miniature Pearls, all of them shredding paperback books, throwing up on the sofa, and joining me in the shower.

My general inclination was to employ the skilled hands of the surgeon to forestall any such possibility, but the moral implications of messing around with the plumbing of another living creature without its permission were too much to bear, so I publicly advertised for advice, preferably from a female dog.

The response was overwhelming, although I am sorry to say that I still have yet to hear from a certified bitch. (A few letters were written in the first-person canine, but I recognized them as clever frauds. First of all, dogs can't type, and, second, although they were very nice, they just weren't logical enough to have been written by a dog.)

As it stands now, the advocates of the knife are about even with the proponents of letting nature take its course. This takes into account my personal interpretation of the letters. There was, for example, an anti-spaying letter that joyously—and graphically—described the process of aiding a dog give birth to a litter. Despite the writer's enthusiasm, that letter went in the pro-spaying stack.

It was, however, offset by a letter on lavender stationery that extolled the virtues of the operation, saying it had made a world of difference in the behavior of the sender's French poodle. "She used to be so skinny, and nervous," the letter said, "but now she is fat and healthy and is content to lie around all day." Into the "anti" stack.

The mail also yielded a picture of a beautiful Labrador retriever named Queenie with a handsome brood of pups, probably the most eloquent argument against the surgery. The letter that accompanied it, however, reported that after having two fine litters, Queenie had gone under the knife and was now happy as a bug on ice. The letter went into the "pro" file and the picture was put over with the antis.

As heartening as the response was, I can't say that it has brought me any closer to solving the original problem. All the arguments were logical; each side made valid points to show that it was indeed the more humane. As a result of all this fine advice, I am as confused as ever, and Pearl continues to grow in stature, if not in wisdom.

I have, however, reached a couple of conclusions involving my actions after the ultimate choice is made. If it turns out to be a trip to the vet, no one is going to hear anything about it. If, however, the antis hold sway, I am saving their return addresses, and they will be hearing from me as soon as the gestation period is over. I hope there will be enough pups to go around.

4.

TURNING HOME AGAIN

Johnny Cash Comes Home

Arkansas Gazette
February 1968

DYESS—Johnny Cash had promised last week that he would give as many concerts as it took to make his homecoming celebration here Sunday afternoon a success.

It took two, and Cash, a Dyess High School graduate who hit the top in the country-and-western music field, worked as hard for the five hundred people who waited for the second performance as he did for the more than two thousand who jammed the Dyess High School gymnasium for the first.

The people came from West Memphis, Blytheville, Jonesboro, Marie, Tomato, Bassett, Delpro, and Cottonwood Corner. Some even came from Little Rock.

Each concert was two hours long and featured, in addition to Cash, Mother Maybelle and the Original Carter Family, Carl Perkins, the Statler Brothers Quartet, and a group called the Country Junction Band, the moving force of a regional television show sponsored by the Pride of Dixie Table Syrup Company of Bono.

When it became apparent that it would take two shows to get the afternoon's job done, the starting time was moved up a half hour and the Country Junction boys came on stage.

They warmed up the crowd for about fifteen minutes, relying mostly on country and western standards borrowed from the more established stars. The leader of the band is a fellow named Gene

Williams, and he doesn't do anything but come out of the wings after each number and introduce the next. He is a Dyess boy, though, and his band was well received.

Then Perkins, whose 1956 smash hit "Blue Suede Shoes" predated the Elvis Presley version by about two years and still stands him in good stead, came on and the crowd really began to warm up. Like Cash, Perkins is a big, tough-looking country boy, and when he finished his last chorus of "Blue Suede Shoes," the audience forgot for a moment that Cash was the man they came to see.

The Statlers were next, and they interspersed their songs with what has become known as "country comedy," namely outlandish faces, broad puns, and jokes about toilets.

Then came the Original Carter Family—Maybelle and her daughters June, Anita, and Helen. June, who has begun to sing duets with Cash lately, now is the featured attraction of the act, but Mother Maybelle clearly was the class member of the family Sunday afternoon. When she strummed her autoharp and sang "Keep on the Sunny Side of Life," the Carter Family theme song when they sang with Woody Guthrie in the 'Twenties and 'Thirties, it was the high point of the show up to that time.

But it was Johnny Cash that the entire Tomato, Ark., Future Farmers of America chapter hitchhiked to Dyess to see, and it was Cash who drew the greatest response with his jerky motions, his downright scary voice, and those steely dark eyes that bored big bullet holes in the back of school custodian E. O. Woodie's brand-new gym.

Mr. and Mrs. Roy Cash, Johnny's parents, moved to Dyess from Kingsland in south Arkansas, and Johnny graduated from Dyess High School in 1950. He began recording for the Sun Record Company of Nashville, the same outfit that started Elvis Presley, and he gained a degree of fame in country and western circles with his record, "Ballad of a Teen-aged Queen," the story of a small-town girl who becomes a star, but chucks it all to return home and marry the boy who worked at the candy store.

Then came "I Walk the Line," which was a number-one record in both the popular and country fields, and Cash has been singing to both audiences ever since.

The little town of Dyess, about 170 miles northeast of Little Rock on state Highway 297, hasn't fared quite as well as its most famous son. Established in 1934 by the Roosevelt administration as a colony for destitute farmers, Dyess once boasted about 1,700 inhabitants. That number has dwindled to about 400.

There are about four streets, all of them gravel, including the "main drag," state Highway 297. The town's business district consists of three filling stations, two cafés, a movie house, and the Blue Eagle Malt Shop.

The stately three-story house that once served as the government administration building for the colony now is dilapidated and has been cut up into apartments. The old community hall was bought a few years back by the Church of Christ. Everything in town is closed on Sunday.

(A visitor seeking a restroom was told by the proprietor of a filling station that the place was closed but that "you sure are welcome to use my house over yonder.")

The little town incorporated a few years ago, however, and things are looking up. The new water system has been working for about seven months now. There is an impressive new school to replace the one that burned in 1963. State Highway 297 is going to be paved. And Johnny Cash finally gave a homecoming concert.

There's always been entertainment at Dyess in the form of local talent, but other than a recent visit by Lester Flatt and Earl Scruggs, there hasn't been much in the way of big-name entertainment. One resident recalled that he went to see a whale on a flatcar back during the Depression, but he couldn't remember whether it was at Blytheville or Memphis.

Cash is plenty big-time enough. He's one of the top names in the recording industry because his appeal is almost universal. Nearly every acne-plagued rural teenager in America likes to imagine himself like Cash—handsome, Mean as Hell (the name, incidentally, of one of his albums), but still a good old boy.

Nothing, it seems, can tarnish his image. Even when he was convicted of a narcotics violation in 1965, it was for possession of "pep pills," in the best truck-driver tradition.

Almost every song Cash has ever recorded has become a hit, and by singing a medley at the end of his show he managed to get most of them in Sunday afternoon. He sang about disaster ("How High's the Water, Mama?"), farming ("Pickin' Time"), hard times ("Busted"), and love ("Ring of Fire").

He sang fast songs and slow songs, happy songs and sad songs, and when he finally sang "Were You There When They Crucified My Lord" to end the first show, the crowd was clapping itself silly.

Before he left the makeshift stage on the floor of the gym, Cash invited all the old home folks to come by and see him before they left. A lot of them did, and he talked to every one.

The doors at the front of the gym were closed, holding back those who were waiting for the second show, so everyone had to file out two doors at the rear.

A lot of them went right back up to the front and got in line again.

A Houseful of Children

Arkansas Gazette
December 1973

At Christmastime, no member of a household is any more mature than the youngest member of the household.

THE QUOTATION above is known as Kringle's Law, and what follows is a deposition attesting to its validity.

The pivotal—though not the principal—character in the drama is a one-and-a-half-year-old female person we shall call The Charmer. Others in the cast include The Charmer's Parents, two sets of Grandparents, and a Joe McDoakes-type character known as the Brother-in-Law, he being the brother of The Charmer's mother and thereby uncle to The Charmer herself.

As the curtain rises, it is Christmas Eve, and the Brother-in-Law, having begun his shopping that morning, when the selection was at its best and the clerks at their friendliest, is seriously considering converting to Judaism as he trudges over to the home of the Parents, where the rest of the cast is assembled.

The Charmer is sacked out for the night, and it is time for the evening's big chore: The assembly of the safety-inspected, non-allergenic, nontraumatizing, educational indoor slide, which comes boxed with endorsements from 437 prominent pediatricians but no instruction sheet.

The Brother-in-Law is thinking that this assembly session won't be as bad as last year's, for The Charmer's father, who doesn't know a molly-bolt from a milkshake, is temporarily immobilized due to a tennis injury, and will be unable to contribute his normal share of balling things up.

Poor, naïve Brother-in-Law. Although the father's actual physical participation consists only of leaning over in his Recline-O Chair, giving a bolt a few twists and telling dumb Brother-in-Law that he got the wrong size screwdriver, the unceasing stream of advice and criticism proves to be more of a hindrance than last year's collection of ten stubby thumbs.

The Grandfathers, for their part, more than make up for the Father's inability to foul up the works by picking up each piece to examine it for safety hazards, just as the Brother-in-Law is about to bolt it into place.

The two Grandmothers are thinking this is all pretty charming and they unlimber the old Polaroid to capture forever the image of all the menfolk at work. The resulting photograph shows Father and both Grandfathers poring over the project, looking competent and efficient. At the lower left of the picture is a nice shot of Brother-in-Law's fanny, the rest of him being occupied behind the superstructure of the slide, attaching Brace D-4 to Slot D-4-A.

It is at this point that Kringle's Law begins to apply. Brother-in-Law sees the instant photo and demands that it be reshot. Here he is doing all the work, he whines, and he's damned if he is going to be represented by his rear end in the family album.

The picture is retaken, and he shows up fine. I have seen the picture, and the look in the Brother-in-Law's eyes. You have seen it, too, in those old movies about Czarist Russia when the mad monk, Rasputin, happens to be portrayed by an unusually gifted actor.

The slide is finally assembled, and the casualty list is relatively low. The only blood spilled is that of one of the Grandfathers, who responds to a command of "Watch your fingers!" by sticking his fingers into Slot Z-42-Y. He wears his Band-Aid with pride. He has shed blood for The Charmer.

It is later now, the middle of the night. The Brother-in-Law is home in his bed when the telephone rings. He runs into the door facing and trips over the dog as he gropes his way to the phone. It is a fire at the Parents' house, he thinks to himself. That's the only thing it could be at this hour of the night. He is filled with shame at his next thought: They better have saved the slide.

It is the Father on the line.

"Get up and get yourself over here, Brother. Santa Claus has been here!"

There is a pause. It is a long pause. Then the Brother-in-Law responds: "What time is it?"

It is 6 a.m., says the Father, and it's getting later by the minute.

The Brother-in-Law starts fumbling into his clothes, and throws all the Christmas presents—still unwrapped—into a shopping bag. He is interrupted by another telephone call. This one is from one of the Grandfathers and the message is that the Brother-in-Law is holding up the whole works.

He stumbles over with his shopping bag of unwrapped gifts, and is greeted by the family group: The Parents and the Grandparents. The Charmer is not in evidence.

"Where's the kid?" asks the Brother-in-Law.

The father responds as though a very dumb question has been asked. "It's 6:30, and she never gets up this early."

There is more, but this is a family newspaper, so the proponents of Kringle's Law rest their case.

The Ghosts of Yesteryear

Arkansas Gazette
November 1973

BAUXITE—I'm not sure why, but I prefer to come here now at night, when there's no chance of meeting anyone and I can park the car and walk down the pockmarked streets where the houses used to be.

Daytime visits are disconcerting for some reason. The bank is still here, and so is the post office, and people go in and out during the day. The school is still here serving several rural communities in the county, and twice a day there is a hollering of school kids and the procession of buses as they carry the students to their homes in the country. The presence of the people makes me uneasy.

It's irrational, of course, this discomfiture, rather like resenting the news that a loved one, long comatose and considered dead for all practical purposes, has moved an eyelid or lifted a little finger. Nothing to make you think the patient might recover, just an ironic reminder that there used to be a whole life there, not just involuntary ties sustained by TV tubes and miracle drugs.

The kids who attend school at Bauxite might resent being equated with plastic tubing, and I don't guess I'd blame them if they did. They're used to thinking of Bauxite as a school, not a place to live, and there would be something wrong with them if they thought any differently. But I lived there, and so did a lot of other folks over the years until Alcoa, which owned the town and everything in it, reluctantly decided to get out of the town business and closed it down in 1969.

So, that's why it's better to visit at night, when realities don't intrude as you amble down the winding streets, calling up the pleasant ghosts that hide until the sun goes down.

Like the company store, where you could buy a Coke and a Nickleloaf and stand all afternoon admiring the red and chrome Cushman Eagle motor scooter on display in front. Nobody ever bought that scooter, because every other kid in town would have been deprived of a whole summer of delicious dreaming.

Or the picture show, where Rudy Faulkner would take your dime admission at the first of the week, when the feature changed, but would let you in free until it changed again. There wasn't anyplace else in town to go, you see, and Rudy couldn't bring himself to charge twice for the same movie.

Or the big oak tree smack in the middle of School Street, left there because a former works manager liked it and couldn't bear to have it cut. Earl Lindsay, who ran the filling station, once wrote a poem about that tree, and nobody made a move to cut it down—even though its original benefactor was long dead—until the town itself was gone for good.

Or the mines themselves, once named for the foremen's wives—Bertha, Maude, Prudence—but later designated by drab numbers, an omen that the company was at last outgrowing its paternal attitude toward the insular little community it had created. They were open-pit mines—great gaping, ugly scars in the earth—and nowadays, even Alcoa realizes just how ugly they are and is rushing ahead with "reclamation" projects with environmentalist groups snapping at its heels. For some reason, though, those immense holes used to be considered a town resource, our reason for being there. We'd proudly take visiting relatives to view the holes.

"Just like the Grand Canyon," we'd say. "Look at those colors."

The artificial life in the town during the daytime scares all these things away, but they're there at night, and you can sit on the hood of your car and smoke and call them up one by one. Then you can walk to the yard on Maple Street and try to remember where you buried the last of an interminable string of pirate's treasures, and then go across the street to see if you can still jump the creek flat-footed.

5.

TALES FROM THE ROAD

The Match Is Passed

Arkansas Gazette
May 1973

THE FIRST official act of the new Arkansas Traveler was to clean the coffee pot.

It happened Monday, as I moved seven years worth of old eyeglasses, pencil stubs, and scraps of paper with telephone numbers, but no names, on them from my old desk in the friendly womb of the newsroom to the third-floor office I now share with the *Arkansas Gazette*'s intrepid investigative team of Jones and Patterson, who are forever busy analyzing public records, taking sworn statements, and tossing cards into a hat.

I am, incidentally, going to miss the newsroom. It has been much like Wilbur the Pig's manure pile in *Charlotte's Web*: warm, friendly, and full of just about everything one needs to ease his mind from a world beset by Watergate, inflation, and Wilbur Mills's fourth and fifth lumbar vertebrae. I am going to let the folks down there keep my ashtray.

My box of junk had barely hit the floor in what is called the Muck Room when Jones took immediate charge of the situation, informing me that, as Junior Man, I now was in charge of cleaning the crud out of the percolator. He and Patterson then repaired to the Little Rock Club for lunch, possibly operating on the theory that if you're going to search for corruption in high places you might as well get out there amongst 'em.

So, I am sitting all alone in a red velveteen office chair that looks as though it once belonged to a bookkeeper in a brothel, listening to the Dip-It belch and froth against the innards of the coffee pot, and starting to wonder just what the hell I am doing here.

Since the title of this enterprise connotes some mobility, I spent last weekend racing around North Arkansas in search of salty old characters who had memorized the Bible or built a two-story Holiness Tabernacle out of old Spam cans. What I ended up with was one hangover and a notice on my apartment door that the electric company had shut off the power in my absence because of an unpaid bill of $68.82.

The trip also resulted in my first literary effort in this new position, an expense voucher that has been described by the boss as "quite creative."

The danger here, sitting alone with only the gurgle of the coffee pot to keep me company, is to become, by stages, maudlin, morose, and downright panicky about the departure of the man who previously owned this spot in the paper and who, in the minds of most of the people who read him, will continue to own it in spirit if not in fact.

What Lancaster did during his tenure here was possibly the most important development in daily journalism since the invention of the informed source. The journeys of that Arkansas Traveler often originated inside the Traveler's own shaggy head, and he took us with him, pointing out along the way the things that make us laugh, or cry, or boil with rage.

They can call some appleknocker off the federal courthouse beat to follow Lancaster, but there's no way in the world they are ever going to replace him.

Or, as my mother so encouragingly put it: "My God, son, you're going to look like an idiot!"

But he is gone, and there's nothing we can do about it. At this very moment, he's unpacking dishes in Media, Pennsylvania, and wondering why he forgot to bring light bulbs and toilet paper. All we can do now is wish him well.

As for what's going to appear here in future weeks, there's not much I can tell you except that some of it will be the truth and some of it will be lies.

We're just going to have to wait and see how it works out.

The Goods on
the Good Brothers

Arkansas Gazette
June 1973

I HAVE NO IDEA how many people have sat in the classroom and listened to William J. Good explain the vagaries of the inverted pyramid lead in journalism classes at the University of Arkansas's Fayetteville campus, nor can I estimate the number who may have heard his brother, Reverend C. W. Good, in little Methodist churches around the state. There must be enough of them, however, to allow me to slide by the rule for columnists that states they shalt not write about their friends.

This is generally a pretty good rule, owing to the fact that one man's *bon vivant* is invariably another man's dullard, but I don't know of anyone with any sense who has failed to admire either man once they've met him or who has failed to maintain a lively interest in their activities.

That amounts to a pretty sizable audience right there, and, if the rest of you aren't interested, you may turn now to the crossword puzzle.

Clint Good was the pastor of the Bauxite Methodist Church in the years I was in that disgusting phase of being openly snotty about organized religion and was being booted to Sunday services by my parents on the grounds that "it can't hurt and it might help."

The years haven't done much for my piety—I still can't shake the feeling that the big churches will be the first things thrown into the cosmic trashmasher when Whoever's in Charge has had enough of the killing, double-dealing, and just plain stupidity here below—but Mr. Good made me reassess my adolescent conviction that men of the cloth were invariably charlatans, fools, guilt-ridden neurotics, or dangerous zealots.

Mr. Good sometimes seemed a little puzzled by the Lord, and I respected that, because the Lord kind of puzzled me, too, and still does. He never claimed to know what was on the Lord's mind, and I've been amazed ever since at the number of preachers who do.

"Faith is believing what you know isn't so," he said once, so he never worried too much about whether the Lord actually parted the Red Sea for the Israelites. "I expect that He could have if he had wanted to," Mr. Good said, although he added that it seemed to him that He probably would have preferred something a little less flashy.

Mr. Good relied heavily on Pogo Possum for a few of his sermons, and that was during the time that Pogo and Edward R. Murrow were waging their lonely war against old Joe McCarthy. He also had a few quiet but emphatic things to say about the brotherhood of man in the days when nine Black children were being spat upon twenty miles away as they tried to go to school at Little Rock.

The people at Bauxite in those days weren't any more enlightened than the residents of any other Southern town, and I've wondered since how he managed to escape the wrath of the local yahoos. I still haven't figured it out, but I do remember that about the only disparaging remarks I ever overheard came from a couple of horsey old women who longed for a pastor who was "good with the youth."

What too many parents have in mind when they speak of a preacher who is "good with the youth" is a fool who doesn't mind being even more immature than his charges.

I don't know if that grumbling had anything to do with it, but Mr. Good eventually transferred, and my interest in attending church dropped to an abysmal level that I have managed to maintain over the years. His replacement, as I recall, was a greasy Bible-thumper who wore alligator shoes and a Conway Twitty haircut, and who may or may not have played the accordion.

I heard recently that both Goods were retired, so I traveled to North Arkansas last week to pay my respects. I found Clint Good at Goshen, and also discovered that for him retirement means working for free.

The Goshen United Methodist Church is a nice little brick building set back from the road in a lush meadow, and the church cemetery is nearby. The small parsonage is just in front of the cemetery, and that is where Mr. Good is spending what he calls retirement.

"I had retired and didn't have a house," he said, "and the folks here had a parsonage but no money to pay a pastor, so we worked out a deal."

Bill Good's retirement, on the other hand, seems bona fide. He said he hadn't been back to the university's snazzy new Communications Building since he carted away his belongings last May. He has adopted a foundling dog named Lady and still indulges his passion for fishing. He says he's going to do some free-lancing when he can find a place to work and set up a darkroom.

I hope he does. Things will retain their order a lot better for me as long as Clint Good is preaching and Bill Good is tapping out those good inverted-pyramid leads.

Bats Get a Public Defender

Arkansas Gazette
July 1973

SPEAKING OF BAT GUANO, today's report comes from what is undoubtedly the state headquarters for the stuff.

I've never been what you might call a rabid bat fan, but when I heard reports that the bats had disappeared from the newly opened portions of Blanchard Springs Caverns, I figured I'd better drive up and have a look. After all, every columnist worth his salt has a cause to champion. Since most of the socially acceptable ones are taken, I'm not too proud to settle for bats. Bats have gotten a pretty raw deal in the press over the years, despite the fact that when you get right down to it they're just mice with wings. If you concentrate on that image real hard for a while, it's possible to work up some outrage at the prospects of their being driven from a cave they had been knocking around in for millions of years, give or take an eon.

Okay, it's not exactly your iceberg-lettuce boycott, but it's about as good as I'm going to do.

The only problem is that I needn't have worried. The bats, according to cavern manager Lynn Young, have merely exhibited their good sense by deciding not to have anything to do with the parts of the cave where man has set foot. No one really knows yet how big the caverns are, and Young figures there's room enough down there for man and bat to coexist. Matter of fact, he said, a few bats are returning occasionally to the giant Cathedral Room, although not in numbers that would alarm the visitors.

For the most part, the only evidence of the critters seen by the visitors who tour the cavern's Coral and Cathedral Rooms are the impressive piles of guano that dot the cavern floor. Lots of folks get the idea that the Forest Service piled the stuff up as part of the general cave-keeping procedure, but that's not the case. The piles have been left just as the fastidious bats created them through years of digestion.

Since Young doesn't have to lose any sleep over the welfare of the bats in his cave, he's free to worry about what he calls The Green Monster, which is actually a bright green plant growth that forms on the rock formations wherever artificial light is introduced. So far, he's been able to effectively combat The Monster with periodic steam cleaning.

Young also has time now to reflect on the wave of visitors that descended on the cavern just after its opening in July, some thirty thousand of which never got to see the cave, resulting in a couple of angry letters to the editor and lots of station wagons full of unhappy children.

"We just didn't know what to expect," he said, "and the response was overwhelming." He hopes that the cavern's second tour route will be completed by the summer of 1975, thus tripling the daily capacity to more than two thousand visitors. Cavern business was slow on the Friday that I visited, and Young said that this would be a good time to take the tour—before this month's rush of foliage-seekers starts the congestion again.

I first saw the caverns in 1967, when I and three other newspaper types were subjected to a guided tour of the then-uncompleted facility by Alvis Owen, a friendly Forest Ranger with the uncanny ability to walk up a perpendicular grade with a flashlight in one hand and his lunch in the other. Two of us in the group were

Mike Trimble was among a group of future luminaries pictured here during a tour of Blanchard Springs Caverns before they were opened to the public in 1973. From left: Dick Allen, then a Gazette copy boy, later managing editor of the European edition of the New York Herald Tribune; Trimble, then a reporter for the Gazette; Richard Portis, then a Gazette copy editor and later a physician and, of course, brother of Charles; and Charles Portis, who was at the time working on the novel The Dog of the South.

certified fatties, and we were finally reduced to uttering lines worthy of a British war movie. ("Press on, men. Just leave me here. I'll only slow you down.")

There is a photograph taped to my mirror that appears to show a couple of fat prisoners of war at the end of a death march, but it is merely myself and my colleagues, eyes aglaze, knowing in our hearts that the skull found in the cavern by earlier explorations wasn't that of an ancient bluff dweller, as advertised, but the mortal remains of the last person who had attempted to follow Alvis Owen on his breakneck rounds.

The tour was arranged by the Gazette's outdoor editor, John Fleming, an otherwise kindly man who had himself been the victim of one of Owen's marathon tours. Fleming didn't say much before leaving us at the cavern entrance, but he giggled a lot, and we should have known something was up. It was he who produced the photographic evidence that man can look dead and still be alive.

The tour now is as civilized as can be, and the lighting affords a breathtaking overall view of the formations that was only hinted at with flashlights and electric miner's lamps. It's about the only place I can think of where the hand of man hasn't screwed up nature's own breathtaking work. And as long as the bats are happy, I'm happy.

Standing Up for Bowie's Knife

Arkansas Gazette
October 1973

THE ARKANSAS Supreme Court has ruled that a butcher knife is not a Bowie knife, and I, for one, can't see how anyone could ever have contended differently.

The case at bar, as they say, was that of Ray Rowland, who happened to have a couple of butcher knives in his truck when stopped by Little Rock policemen in 1972. Rowland, who said he was carrying the weapons as a symbolic protest, was charged under an 1881 law that prohibits the carrying of "any dirk or Bowie knife, or sword or spear in a cane, brass or metal knucks, razor, blackjack, billie or sap, ice pick or any pistol of any kind whatever."

Some prosecutor had the temerity to say that Rowland's two butcher knives were the same as Bowie knives, a base calumny on the memory of James Black, the Arkansas smith who forged the first legendary blade for Colonel James Bowie, the hero of both the Alamo and a long-running TV series.

It took Associate Justice George Rose Smith of the Supreme Court to set the notion right, and I say to the judge, hurrah!

Butcher knife the same as a Bowie knife, indeed! Is Don Knotts the same as John Wayne? Is the Daisy Red Ryder model the same as the Benjamin Pump? Is Maxie's Reliable Pawn Shop like Tiffany's?

"A new country and a new generation," writes Raymond W. Thorp, the chronicler of that weapon, "were dominated by James

Bowie's knife." Furthermore, he says, the weapon "held the center of the American scene for more than two generations."

Try to imagine, if you will, any old butcher knife holding the attention of anyone's scene for a second longer than it takes to slice through baloney for a sandwich. You can't do it, can you? Well, neither could George Rose Smith.

It was 1830 when James Bowie rode into the Hempstead County town of Washington in search of James Black, whose reputation as a master craftsman of knives had spread far beyond the reaches of the Arkansas frontier. Bowie already had achieved some fame as a knife-wielder, having dispatched a number of his enemies with a conventional model in a donnybrook that began as a duel on a Mississippi River sandbar. Bowie had something special in mind for a fighting knife, however, and he knew James Black was the only man to make it.

He took Black a carved wooden model of the knife he had in mind, and Black copied the knife in steel and submitted it for Bowie's approval. He also, however, submitted another knife, which was based on Bowie's design but, unlike Bowie's single-edged model, was double-edged along the curved portion near the tip of the blade.

Bowie liked Black's design better than his own, so he took the double-edged weapon and headed back to Texas.

No sooner had he arrived than he was set upon by three brigands hired for the express purpose of doing him in. Bowie decapitated one of the attackers with a single stroke of his blade and disemboweled the second with an upward stroke. The third thug was picking them up and laying them down by this time, but Bowie overtook him and nearly bisected his skull clear down to the shoulders.

The rest, as they say, is history.

Black made other knives in different shapes, and almost all of them became known as Bowie knives, particularly the stiletto-like

Arkansas Toothpick much favored by mountain men for its accuracy in flight. But Black's original design remains the one that fires the imagination, the weapon that accompanied Jim Bowie to the Alamo and was cremated along with him.

Now, really, can you truthfully equate a knife like that with this thing that the lady at Franke's Cafeteria holds as she says, "Natural gravy on your roast beef, sir?" No, Mr. Prosecutor, it just won't wash!

No, a butcher knife is most definitely not a Bowie knife, Mr. Prosecutor, and in waging this lonely struggle, Roy Rowland's name has joined those of Miranda and Escobedo in the annals of American jurisprudence.

The only thing wrong is that Mr. Rowland also had a .38-caliber boomer in his possession when he was arrested, and Justice Smith says there ain't no way in the world he can get out of that one.

Queen of the River

Arkansas Gazette
October 1973

DES ARC—The car had barely come to a stop on the dusty bank of the White River when the door to the beached houseboat opened to disgorge five dogs, three cats, a gray goose, and Ray Dorthy, who has lived on or near the river for most of her life, making her living as best she can and sharing her quarters with a long line of husbands and abandoned animals.

She greeted the visitor with a wave and a laugh, and said sure, she'd sit and talk for a while with a reporter.

"I shoulda been wrote up a long time ago," she said, "but I never was. Got my picture in the *White River Journal* a couple of times, but that was always with a big fish."

Ray Dorthy fishes a lot along the river, and sells her catch to the folks in the area. She also does some free-lance carpentry work, a line that resulted in her new home, a houseboat proudly christened Rat's Nest.

"I done some work on a house for a lady, and I took a couple of rooms off it she didn't need and hauled 'em over here," she said. "Got a hunnerd and twenty-five barrels under there to keep her up."

The Rat's Nest is currently tied up within the Des Arc city limits, and Ray is going through a minor hassle with the city fathers over whether she should be allowed to stay there. She does not seem overly concerned with the threat of eviction.

"Oh, they can make me scrumble around a little bit," she said, "but they can't get me off the river. They've tried before. What they do is they give you twenty-four hours' notice to move, so you go a couple hunnerd yards down the river and tie up and they give you twenty-four hours' notice to move from there. After a couple of times, they usually forget you for about a month."

Ray has scrumbled around quite a bit in her life, but her scrumbling invariably seems to lead her back to the banks of the White, an unofficial base of operations for her other ventures.

Back twenty or thirty years ago, for example, it seems that some of the local preachers took it upon themselves to mention Ray's name from their pulpits as an example of earthly improprieties that should be avoided by the more Godly elements of the community. Deciding to fight fire with fire, Ray started her own church and kept at it for about four years.

Ray Dorthy
(photo by Mike Trimble)

"I built me three churches while I was preachin'," she said. "Then I just kind of give it up. It got to where it was tying me down."

Besides, she added, "The bastards wouldn't tithe."

Her knowledge of the river has saved the skins of a lot of people over the years, and Ray is especially fond of recalling one bitterly cold winter in the early 'forties when a levee broke and a detachment of soldiers sent to repair the damage got hopelessly lost on a barge one night when their craft wandered from the river into the flooded land around it.

"It was the middle of the night," she said, "and I seen this SOS signal they was flashing with their light, so I got in my little old wooden paddleboat and headed for it. I was about freezing to death. Them guys seen me and, man, they was tickled to death. Then they pulled me aboard, and this old sergeant said, 'Hell, it's a woman!' They all liked to died. I didn't weigh but ninety-five pounds in those days, and they didn't think I could do nothing to help 'em. But that old sergeant give me a quart of whiskey, and I took about three big old slurps and got up in the front of that barge with a microphone to the pilot house, and I got 'em back in the river."

Ray's animals swarmed about her as she talked, and they all seemed happy and healthy, with the possible exception of the goose, who seemed to have a shortage of feathers and a couple of busted wings. Surveying her pets, she talked wistfully of her favorite, a 420-pound hog named Porkchop that was raised in the house and ate from a plate at the table.

"I finally had to sell her," Ray said sadly. "She got me down and bit me on the belly. Got a hunnerd and something dollars."

Porkchop once treed an insurance salesman and ate his brief-case, Ray said, and the hog once caused a local sensation through her habit of riding along with Ray in the backseat of the latter's ancient Nash Rambler.

"Old Porkchop leaned over my shoulder to lick me while I was drivin'," Ray explained, "and she scrunched me down in the seat where I could just hardly see, and her front paws got tangled up on the steering wheel. Well, them people passing me couldn't see nothin' but old Porkchop, and they was drivin' all over the road. I got home and let her out and went to the beer joint for a six-pack, and there was these guys in there, and they was hollerin', 'I don't know if I'm drunk or crazy or what, but I just seen a hog drivin' a Rambler.'"

Queen of the River (Part 2)

Arkansas Gazette
October 1973

DES ARC—Yesterday in this space we met Ray Dorthy, one of the White River's more locally celebrated denizens, a woman who, in her own terminology, has "scrumbled around" for most of her life, doing a little bit of everything but whose fortunes seem ultimately to be tied as fast to the banks of the river as is the Rat's Nest, the newly completed houseboat where she now maintains her residence.

Profoundly simple, simply profound, happily profane, she lives with her husband Lester and a dizzying assortment of dogs, cats, and geese, pursuing a life that consists mostly of doing what she wants to do—running her trotlines and selling her catch to the folks at Des Arc, doing a little carpentry work, gathering a few pecans, and drinking a little beer.

Listening to Ray spin her yarns and laugh her ear-splitting laugh, there's a tendency to discount the darker ramifications of scrumbling, to discount the obvious fact that Ray Dorthy's life hasn't been all beer and catfish. Ray doesn't seem to be particularly bothered by it now, however, and talks about her past as matter-of-factly as she discusses everything else.

Her "childhood" ended for all practical purposes at age eleven, when she left a Little Rock orphanage to strike out on her own. The people at the orphanage had told her that her mother was killed in a car wreck, and it wasn't until after her first marriage that she learned that her mother was still alive.

"I was about eighteen when I got word she was still livin'," Ray said. "She lived until after me and Lester got married. Annie Gamlin raised me some after I got outta the home, and I had a aunt and some cousins, but they never done nothing for me. Mostly, I just raised myself, I guess."

Ray has a sister, Mae, who is "doing real good" in Michigan, but that seems to be about the only surviving family. She reeled off a list of names from bygone days, but it was impossible to tell if they were relatives, friends, or former husbands.

"Helen's dead, Miss Warren's dead, Alvie's dead, Eli's dead, all the people's dead," she said.

As evidence that she's not been completely immune to despondency, Ray Dorthy bears the mark of one ambitious suicide attempt, not the skinny wrist scars of a half-hearted swipe with a razor blade, but that of a bullet wound, inflicted by a rifle strapped to the end of the bed, discharging when Ray calmly lay back on her pillows and pulled the trigger with a string.

"It was a dandy," Ray recalls. "Went in the front and out the back. Through and through. Holler-point shell. This old guy found me in the bed and carried me to the hospital. I was there for eight months."

Why?

"Hell, I wanted to die," she said, as though the question was a stupid one, which it was. Since her recovery, however, she's never given another thought to taking her own life.

"That suicide business hurts like a sumbitch," she said.

Ray's gone away from Des Arc and the White River on occasion, but she always comes back, though she's not sure why. "Just seems like I can't get away from this damned old river," she said. She's fiercely chauvinistic about the White, however, and to a lesser degree, about rivers in general. Knowingly or not, all the possible alternate lifestyles she discusses involve living on or near a body of water; she doesn't seem to even consider a landlocked existence.

"Oh, I guess I could go somewheres else," she said, "but the White River is the cleanest river there is. That's why the fish taste so good. I just can't eat a lake fish. I can't even eat a Cache River fish. Tastes like cypress.

"Well, let's see, there was that man I found in a drift down there one time, and there was another I didn't get no credit for him 'cause Bob Chapman and Al Williams was in the boat, but it was me that drug him up and got him on the boat …" She keeps reeling them off matter-of-factly; they are just another part of her life on the river.

There was one, though, that was different.

He was a twelve-year-old boy, and the dragging crew couldn't find his body all during the day, and Ray had gone home after working her shift on the draglines.

But she couldn't sleep. The thought of the child, alone in the river at night, swirled around her like a pesky mosquito. A grown man can drown in a river and it is just carelessness, or stupidity, or maybe plain bad luck, but a child isn't the same somehow, and sleep didn't come.

So Ray Dorthy, who can't swim a lick, got out of bed and rejoined the dragging crew, and it was she who finally found the boy, brought him into the boat, and laid him on the shore. Then she went home and got some sleep, at peace again with her river as it slid slowly, quietly by.

Move Over, MacArthur

Arkansas Gazette
November 1973

I WASN'T GOING TO SAY anything about this, but since the governor passed up a second opportunity to make good on a solemn campaign promise, I feel duty-bound to bring up the question of why I am not adjutant general of Arkansas today.

The pledge was made during Mr. Bumpers's first primary campaign, when he was just a lawyer from Charleston trying to get people to remember his name. Since nobody gave him a chance of getting into the runoff with Orval E. Faubus, the city editor assigned me to cover him for the newspaper. (I have also covered the gubernatorial campaigns of Walter Carruth, Lester Gibbs, Bill Wells, and the late Clyde Byrd. Remember them?)

It happened at Russellville, the last stop on Mr. Bumpers's campaign tour that day. I had rented a motel room there, but the future governor planned to drive on to the next day's first stop.

Only problem was, he had to go to the bathroom something fierce, and after I graciously allowed him to use my rented facilities there at the Holiday Inn, he promised me any post in his upcoming administration. I said I'd take Adjutant General, and he said "fine," but he hasn't said a word about it since.

He'll probably try to worm out of it by saying that he forgot, but you just don't forget needing to go to the bathroom as badly as he obviously needed to go.

I'll not dwell on the fact that I voted for him in that first primary and even in the runoff against Faubus, who was by that time beginning to look fairly good in comparison with the others that the Democrats had been coming up with the last couple of elections.

All I'll say is that he's had two chances now to make good on his promise, and he's flubbed them both.

It's as though I wasn't qualified for the job. I will stand on my military record, compiled in part while a PFC with probably the best weapons platoon in the state, Company B, 153rd Infantry, Hope, Arkansas. In addition to being proficient enough at military skills to regularly embarrass the Green Beret outfit at Mena on field problems, B Company had other basic skills that caused it to be picked for a different highly vital mission—handling the beer concession for the entire battalion at summer camp.

With one 2 1/2-ton truck loaded with weapons and the other loaded with Budweiser, Company B headed out each year to make Fort Chaffee safe for democracy. In addition to handling their assigned task of selling beer while on bivouac, the men of Company B showed their initiative by setting up an outdoor casino of admirable quality, using field generators to supply the light and camouflage nets to hide the operation from enemy aircraft.

The only threat to the spirit of Company B came when some hotshot lieutenant from Texarkana was assigned as commanding officer and the men responded with admirable zeal. The first official act of the new lieutenant, who liked to wear his helmet in the armory so he could cock it to one side while talking on the phone and look like Frank Lovejoy, was to call all the officers and senior non-coms for a meeting.

"Men," he said, "we have the makings of a crack outfit here, if we can just stamp out all this drinking and gambling during duty hours. Can I count on your support?"

The group rose as one to give the reply. "No!" they said and walked out of the briefing room.

I think I am safe in asserting that my service with this fighting outfit, marred only by the time that I involuntarily squealed on the first sergeant for swiping some grenade simulators, would give me a good crack at the adjutant general's post even if it weren't for that solemn promise made so many years ago to the accompaniment of the gurgling Holiday Inn plumbing.

My administrative skills were honed to such a degree during my tenure as Company B's clerk that a battalion inspection once yielded the comment that our files were certainly secure from possible enemy pilferage, seeing as how they weren't done in English.

Now I know this probably doesn't bother the governor, now that he's hit the big time and gets to hobnob with Grover W. "Buddy" Turner, the speaker of the House from Pine Bluff, and all those guys, but the hurt is still there, and, yes, bitterness. I don't know if I'll ever get the chance to vote against Mr. Bumpers, but I'll tell you one thing—the next time he needs to go to the bathroom in Russellville, he can forget about calling on yours truly.

Chateau Ripple 1973

Arkansas Gazette
January 1974

BENTON—You may have noticed that this newspaper has been running a series on wine. It is being written by a Little Rock fellow, Kenneth J. Forrester, who is a member of Les Amis du Vin, an international society of wine lovers.

It's a pretty good series, debunking as it does a lot of the fancy notions about wine guzzling. Don't worry about what people will think, says Kenneth J. Forrester; buy something that tastes good, slop some of it in a jelly glass, and heave to.

As democratic as Mr. Forrester is, however, he hasn't quite reached the socioeconomic level of Arvin the Wino, of Benton, who seems to exist fairly well on wine, salted peanuts, and a monthly VA disability check.

Arvin admits that, strictly speaking, he'd have to be classed as a wino, but he's a little mad about it, saying that if he had a lot of dough, people would think up a nicer name for him. I didn't mention Les Amis du Vin to him; it probably would have made him madder.

Arvin is a good man to talk to about the lower echelons of wine drinking, because, living as he does in a dry county, it takes a high degree of dedication to indulge his passions.

"I try to get to the county line about twice a week," he says. Sometimes that isn't too hard, for Arvin has a buddy who possesses a pickup truck and a thirst similar to Arvin's. "He's got a wife, though, and she makes him dry out every now and then."

At such times, Arvin says, he will hitch rides up the interstate to the county line, or sometimes borrow a car.

That latter practice has gotten him in trouble a couple of times, for, according to the police, the owners of the cars didn't know they were being borrowed. Arvin relies in his defense on the explanation that he would have notified the owners if he had known who they were.

Once his transportation problem is solved, Arvin doesn't waste much time shopping around. He sticks generally to a simple Concord grape wine of Arkansas manufacture, though he isn't necessarily motivated by state pride.

"It's cheap," he says.

He has had his flings with Strawberry Hill and Zapple Apple and Cold Bear, but he always has returned to his Arkansas wine, with an occasional departure into Tiger 186.

"That stuff is too sweet," Arvin says. "Makes your chin sticky."

Serious students of wine know that different shapes of wine bottles indicate different types of wine, and Arvin takes note of bottle shapes, too, although for different reasons.

"You get more in a fifth," he says, "but I generally get me a bunch of pints and half-pints. You can roll over on a flat bottle and it won't bust as easy as a round one. I had to have six stitches in my belly once."

Arvin says he prefers wine to beer or the hard stuff, because there's no refrigeration problem and you get more for your money. "Hard whiskey makes me sick," he says, "and I can get me some wine and have plenty left to get me some peanuts or crackers."

Trying to somehow bridge the gap between Kenneth J. Forrester's world and Arvin's, I asked if he had ever had any fancy wine. He said he had—once—and that he had never wanted to try it again.

He came into a little extra money once, he recalled, and he also had a pretty good little buzz on from some afternoon celebrating, so when he and his pickup-driving buddy arrived at the county line they asked for a bottle of the best French wine in the place.

It was too sour, Arvin said, and besides, he had a devil of a time getting into the thing.

"Damn bottle had a cork in it," he said. "We like to never got it pushed down in there."

Fame Comes to Arvin the Wino

Arkansas Gazette
February 1974

BENTON—Some people just can't handle fame, and I fear that Arvin the Wino is one of them.

Arvin, who lives here and regularly commutes to the county line to dispose of his veteran's disability check, was interviewed in this space a while back, in what amounted to a poor man's guide to wine drinking.

The problem is that Arvin, who probably hadn't used a newspaper for anything but a blanket in the last ten years, squandered a dime of his VA money to read the account, and now is so enamored of seeing his own words in print that he envisions a series of articles, maybe even a book, possibly even a movie of his life, in which he would play the title role (and, not incidentally, would be flown to California, the home of Ernest and Julio Gallo).

My mistake was dropping in a few days ago to see if Arvin had read the article. Oh, my, yes, he certainly had.

"Listen," he said, "I forgot to tell you about that time when me and Jack was driving back from the Line and he had a rubber tube stuck down under his shirt down to the jug on the floorboard and he was stopped by the State Police."

Arvin was off and running, bubbling over with accounts of his bleary-eyed misadventures, and he stopped only to register a complaint about the original article and to suggest a remedy.

The problem was the "Arvin" business, he said. Since I had chosen not to use his real name in the paper, he had been unable to convince any of his friends that the article was really about him. "We got to use my real name in the next one," he said.

Overlooking for a moment my intention that there never be a "next one," I began to explain to Arvin that the libel laws prevented the use of his real name. It was tricky going, the object being to get across to Arvin that his real name couldn't be used while hiding from him the fact that he would be the benefactor in any libel judgment. I didn't care how hungry Arvin was for fame, the prospect of him interpolating a fat libel judgment into X number of cases of wine did not appeal to me.

The explanation, as it finally came out, was something along the line that if Arvin's real name appeared in the newspaper the price of wine would skyrocket, the Razorbacks would be kicked out of the Southwest Conference, and Justice Jim Johnson would never be allowed to run for public office again.

Arvin accepted that logic, but was rather sullen about it and a little defiant.

"What if I just change my name to Arvin?" he asked, and I went through the whole tortured lie again. Arvin was still adamant. He had heard some guys down at the filling station taking about how funny that guy Arvin the Wino was, and he was determined that the reading public would not be denied the privilege of hearing about him again.

In desperation then, I unleashed the final argument. I say desperation because, first of all, it probably would hurt Arvin's feelings, and, second and more important, it would reveal the most closely guarded secret of all newspaper columnists: that we are egotists, liars, and thoroughgoing fakers.

"Arvin," I said, "you didn't even say that stuff. You just sort of hinted at most of it. I was the one that put it all together and made it sound so good."

Arvin sulled up even more. "Prove it," he said.

"Good grief, Arvin, you know you didn't say all that stuff."

"That don't prove nothing. I'm a drunk. I'm always forgetting what I said. That don't mean I didn't say it."

That's when I left in a panic, and the only reason this is appearing in the paper is that today is Sunday and while Arvin might spend a dime to read about himself, I'd stake my life that he'd never spring for thirty cents.

Neighbors

Arkansas Gazette
November 1973

I GOT TO THINKING today about the Snopes family and how things have been kind of dull around my place since they moved from the apartment next door.

I never learned the family's true names. Snopes seemed to fit and Snopes it has remained in my memories of the clan. The family consisted of Miz Snopes and a bevy of kids ranging from a boy of about three to a girl of about nineteen. I think the youngest belonged to the eldest, but I was never able to find out for sure. They remained as neighbors for about eight months, a period I now recall with that bittersweet irony, something akin to most men's attitude about basic training.

The Snopeses first came rampaging into my life on a weekend and as I was nursing a cold, a hangover, and a general feeling of self-loathing. Just as I was contemplating going out to find a moor to tromp, there came a pounding on my door and the cry, "My car's on fire! My car's on fire!"

Miz Snopes had arrived and, indeed, she spoke the truth about her automobile, for heavy black smoke was pouring from under the hood of the elderly Ford parked in the street outside the apartment house.

Using an old blanket, we were able to extinguish the flames in short order, but Miz Snopes insisted, against my advice, on getting the old Ford running again. Luckily, her efforts were in vain, so the next step, she said, was to use my telephone to call her boyfriend, a crackerjack mechanic, whose name may or may not have been Carl.

Carl proved a hard man to track down by telephone so while I nursed my head and my nose and my ego, Miz Snopes dialed around town for old Carl, keeping a steady gaze all the while on a partially filled bottle of booze near the telephone.

The request wasn't long in coming, but was presented in the tactful manner that Miz Snopes thought proper when meeting a new neighbor for the first time. Her eyes still firmly planted on the bottle, she asked sweetly, "You wouldn't happen to have anything to drink around here, would you?"

Well, as a matter of fact, I replied, I thought there might be a little something left in a bottle right close to the telephone there.

"Oh, this?" she said with surprise, already pulling the cork. "I don't need no ice, hon, just a jelly glass or something."

So we waited for Carl, having finally reached him on the phone, as Miz Snopes swigged Scotch from a jelly glass and filled me in on the night shift at the Toddle House and on Carl himself, who was "a regular whizzard with cars, but he ain't been working lately 'cause he's been sick."

Carl finally put in an appearance, and I discovered that Miz Snopes's observations about his health had been as correct as those about her automobile. Carl was the sickest person I have ever seen in a vertical position.

About six feet tall, Carl may have tipped the scales at eighty-five pounds, if you counted his motorcycle boots and the half-pint of wine in his back pocket. He also possessed a four-day growth of beard and a case of halitosis that would have knocked a buzzard off a dung heap.

Seeming to limp with both feet, Carl made his way to the Ford with the avowed intention of "fixing that little mother up." I was assured that my services would no longer be needed, whereupon I repaired to my own digs and resumed breathing through my nose.

Carl apparently lost no time with that little mother, because before my nostrils were fully cleared another knock came at the door and opening it revealed that Snopes was again the knocker.

"My car's on fire! My car's on fire!"

That was how it began, and the ensuing eight months were made memorable not only by the periodic eruptions by the ancient Ford but also by interior eruptions in the form of monstro donnybrooks involving Miz Snopes and one or more of her older daughters. One historic melee, as near as I could tell through the thin wall of my living room, was caused by someone pirating a can of chili that Miz Snopes had been saving for her own midnight snack. Several cries of "You better put down that knife" had me reaching for the phone on several occasions to send for the riot squad.

No one ever seemed to sustain serious injury, however, and it was with mixed emotions that I received from Miz Snopes one day the news that she had found herself a husband (not Carl, by the way) and was moving off. Her youngest children had become my friends, coming over occasionally to listen to records and play with my typewriter, and I would miss them.

The eldest Snopes daughter elected to keep the apartment and lives there now equipped with a roommate and a never-ending stream of hirsute gentlemen callers. Where once my living room wall vibrated regularly with shrill screams and epithets, only an occasional "Yeah, man," or "Far out, man" softly penetrates the insulation.

The reverie has been broken only once, when a young lady, apparently the spurned sweetheart of one of the gentlemen callers, stood outside the door threatening at great length and volume that she was going to kill somebody, possibly herself.

For a while, it was like old times.

I Left My Heart in Bodcaw

Arkansas Gazette
November 1973

I GUESS EVERYONE knows by now that the Chamber of Commerce over at Pine Bluff shelled out a thousand smackers for an official song, and I endorse the concept, even if their particular tune didn't turn out so hot. (Love may have built their river town, but I bet it wasn't what prompted the grand jury investigation of the police department.)

A Little Rock TV station has followed Pine Bluff's lead, signing off each night with a ditty extolling the civilizing influences of Central Arkansas. Alas, it, too, is a pretty crummy song, containing such lyrics as "Looking down on the Arkansas River, what a beautiful sight" and failing entirely to mention the city's main industry—orthopedic surgery and medical testimony in whiplash lawsuits.

But, as I said, it's a good idea, and it's to be hoped that every Arkansas town eventually will have its own song. The only problem is that few of the smaller towns can spare a thousand smokes to pay a songwriting team, and that is too bad.

But did you think I'd point out the problem without providing a solution? You know me better than that! I come from a small town myself. With a little imagination, any self-respecting Chamber secretary can write his or her own song and save a pile of cash. There are just a few basic guidelines to follow.

First, try to pick a theme that fits the town, such as:

Polish, kosher, sweet or dill,
Atkins folks can fill the bill.
You've not lived until you've tried
hunks of gherkin deep-fat fried.
City life becoming hellish?
Come and try our pickle relish.
Try them once, for them you'll yearn.
Come to Atkins, get heartburn!

Here's another example:

Looking for a spot that's fun?
Come on down to Morrilton.
Join right in our frequent purges:
Throw some rocks at ol' Gene Wirges.
Morrilton is where it's at,
If you're a Democrat!

If you don't have an interesting industry or a political machine, advertise the joys of living in the country, like this:

If you're tired of playing bridge,
come and live at Vimy Ridge.
Air so pure and grass so green
in the county of Saline.
Leave that city life so grimy.
Come and see our ridge that's vimy.

Or this:

If it's cities you're despisin',
come on down and live at Rison.
We will share our ample bounty:
nicest town in Cleveland County.

As you can see, I'm strictly a lyric man and will leave the composing of melodies to someone else. There is, however, one possible town song that has a built-in melody, and I'm happy to pass it along for what it's worth.

> Some go to Lockesburg and some go to Bright Star,
> But I know a place they'll adore ya.
> I'll bet you a bundle you'll want to put your dough
> in the bonnie, bonnie bank at Ben Lomond.

Some towns, being small, feel that they have a negative image to overcome and would prefer not to be so boastful early in the game. Here's one that's not so pushy.

> It's just a place where the road gets wide,
> but, to us, it's fair Mount Ida.
> Stop and have your gas tank filled;
> we're not as dull as we are billed.

All these ideas will work for towns that are trying to attract new residents and businesses, but the truth is that a few towns like themselves just the way they are, and want little to do with so-called progress. There's a way to write a song for them, too.

> Welcome to Ivan.
> Keep drivin'.

Freeway, Moon, and the Holy Ghost

Arkansas Gazette
October 1973

HAVING BEEN ENLISTED as a teamster last weekend to deliver a dog to my attorney in Indiana, I got the chance to re-experience an old sensation: screaming down the Interstate in the dead of night, belly and brain arumble with truck-stop coffee, while great bugs smash into the windshield and radio evangelists show the Way and the Light over WWL, the voice of New Orleans.

As far as I know, no research group has ever investigated just what combination of fatigue, caffeine, diesel smoke, and Holy Writ produces this strange euphoria, and it's probably just as well. They'd probably make it illegal, create a national commission on nocturnal highway abuse, and publish pamphlets on how alert parents can spot the telltale signs of late-night cruising around on the Interstate.

I haven't done much serious thinking about the phenomenon either, except to note that it seems to manifest itself more readily in the warmer months, when the car windows are rolled down and an occasional hard-shelled bug whaps you on the elbow with the force of a Benjamin BB rifle.

It is certainly not the cheapest high in the world, what with the price of gasoline and oil, and it may not be the safest, since you're constantly dodging armadillos and being buffeted around in the wake of big Kenworths and Peterbilts, whose drivers are just as high as you are on the heady drug of the night-time freeway. But it's one of the most exhilarating, and when your radiator hose finally busts at Marion about two in the morning, you've got to stalk around the car for a while in order to come down to earth enough to go into the truck stop and order the coffee that will start the whole process all over again.

A good clear-channel radio station is a necessary ingredient, and WWL usually provides just the combination of raucous disc jockeys, country music, and fire-and-brimstone preaching needed to get the juices flowing and set you to squirming around in the car seat. Last weekend, however, some station functionary was apparently asleep at the wheel, for Billy Graham gave the same sermon three times in a row before someone replaced the tape cartridge with the Mull Family Singing Convention.

Now, Billy is still a whale of a preacher, despite the old sourpusses who think he's gotten too fancy with his visits to the White House and all, but the same sermon three times over is a little hard to take, no matter who's delivering it. You start getting hypercritical the third time around, challenging Billy to describe in detail the "immorality that has been reported taking place in the very church sanctuary during young people's services." You also feel a little uneasy when Billy talks for fifteen minutes about the nation's obsession with material wealth and then offers at the end of the program to take some of yours off your hands.

Finally—and I hesitate to take a stand here, because it's purely subjective judgment and I know it's going to make a lot of folks mad—George Beverly Shea can't sing for beans. I don't care what anybody says to the contrary. He might be all right for funerals, but for making a joyful noise, I'll take the Chuckwagon Gang or the Happy Goodman Family every time.

That's why I greeted Brother Mull and his wife with a whoop of relief. Plenty of hand-clapping gospel music and no lectures about materialism; just send in your dough and receive the Mull Family Bible, a red-letter edition complete with subject index, scriptural interpretations, and genuine photographs of the six-day Arab-Israeli war in the Holy Land.

The hands itch for the wheel just thinking about it.

Waking Up in the Middle of a Dream

Arkansas Gazette
December 1973

HOPE—It had been raining all morning, the temperature was beginning to drop, and Jimmy Porterfield was doing a little bargaining with a fellow who wanted to buy a rain suit.

The customer had come into Jim's One-Stop on state Highway 4 a few minutes earlier, and he needed the rain suit right away, because he had to go out and get his cows in. Despite his immediate need for the rain suit, the customer was reluctant to close the deal.

"They got 'em over at TG and Y for less than that," he said.

Porterfield responded by saying something about getting what you pay for, and was able to close the deal after lopping about a dollar off the price. Then he relaxed behind the counter, interrupted only occasionally by the potato-chip, Coca-Cola, and Twinkie trade.

At an age when most of his schoolmates were planning to be firemen or cowboys or railroad engineers, Jimmy Porterfield was telling people that some day he was going to own his own bait shop. It took him a little while to get around to it, but now he says he can't imagine ever doing anything else but selling his crickets and minnows and plastic worms and pumping a little Lion Oil gasoline on the side.

He graduated from Hope High School in 1958 and two and a half years later he had attended three colleges and learned enough to know that he didn't want to go to school any more. He put in a stint with a couple of pipeline companies, and then journeyed into the wilds of Austin, Texas, to work at what was to be his only real "indoor" job, as a kitchen manager for one of the city's ritziest steakhouses.

"It was a pretty good job," Porterfield recalled, "but I can't say I enjoyed it just a whole lot. Too much sitting around inside." As for Austin, it was all right—"for a city."

"Daddy called me up one day and said this place was vacant," Porterfield said, "so I hightailed it on back here." He borrowed a little money on some land he owns and after about two years of just squeaking by, he and his wife Lavern started realizing a comfortable little profit from the place.

Although he's technically a retail merchant, Porterfield considers himself more of a professional outdoorsman than a shopkeeper.

"It's not like I was sacking up groceries at the Safeway," he said. "There's a lot more conversation to it. I've got to be able to tell out-of-town folks where the fishing is good, or whether Millwood Lake is muddy or clear. Then there's a lot of regulars come in just to bat the breeze."

Since he considers it part of his job to know what's going on at the local fishing spots, Porterfield is able to justify taking off about once a week to do a little fishing. "In the wintertime, I try to give myself the full day off once a week," he said, "but I'm lucky to get half a day free in the summer."

Except for his occasional fishing trips, and an annual week off during deer season, Porterfield is in his shop about twelve hours a day on an average of six and a half days a week the year round.

It isn't a bad place to spend your time. No modern merchandising methods here; the place is haphazardly and appealingly jam-packed with plastic worms, shotgun shells, shiny fishing lures, and insulated underwear. Hats of all descriptions hang by clothespins from wires strung the length of the building, and there's an old-fashioned display case filled with hunting knives. I hesitate to say that there's a keg of nails to sit on, but I saw it and sat on it, so I know it's there.

Jimmy Porterfield regards himself as a pretty unremarkable fellow, and he seemed a little puzzled over why anybody's newspaper would waste any space on the genesis of a bait shop.

Well, I'll tell him why. When I was a child, my dream of the perfect life was to man one of those giant D-8 Caterpillar tractors of the type that piled up the bauxite ore in the mines around my hometown. I finally got my chance as a summer worker on a road-construction crew, when hours of unauthorized lunch-hour practice on the stockpile tractor qualified me—I thought—as a pinch-hit operator when the regular driver showed up one morning with a bad case of Old Mr. Boston.

The official tryout lasted about five minutes, and resulted in a broken treadpin, a bent bulldozer blade, and a yard-long rent in the side of the chief mechanic's brand-new panel truck.

My boyhood dream ended in a cloud of dust as I hightailed it off the construction site with a wrench-wielding mechanic in hot pursuit. I imagine just about everybody else's boyhood dreams went the same way at one time or another.

Jimmy Porterfield kept his dream in the back of his head while he was counting those Texas ribeyes. Now he's sitting smack in the middle of it by the side of state Highway 4.

The Woodchopper
of Fiddler's Bane

Arkansas Gazette
February 1974

FIDDLER'S BANE—Deep in the Ozarks, the old man hunkers under a tree, the little children at his feet, telling of the bygone days of Fiddler's Bane.

The settlement, according to legend, got its name in the territorial days, when a wandering musician happened by and lingered long enough to initiate a little funny business with one of the community's comely girls. The girl's father got wind of the dalliance, and his reaction resulted in the minstrel's making medical history of a sort after being transported by wagon and packet boat to the nearest doctor for surgical removal of a homemade violin.

The settlement has all but disappeared now. Only the old man remains to tell the children the quaint old folk tales.

"Twarn't no gas buggies in them days," he says. "Twarn't no talkin' machines."

"Gas buggies?" says one of the children incredulously. "Talkin' machines? Twarn't? What makes you talk like that?"

"Because this is a quaint old folk tale, gourdhead," replies the old man. "You wanna hear Ronald Colman, go watch the late movies on TV."

The old man gently illustrates his point by rapping the child smartly across the nose with a stick he has brought for that purpose, and continues with his quaint old folk tale. Today he is telling of the woodchopper of Fiddler's Bane, and this is what he says.

In the early days of Fiddler's Bane, everyone heated their homes and cooked with woodstoves, and the wealthiest man in town was the woodchopper, who had worked up a nice little business by virtue of having the only chopping axe ever seen in these parts. He also sold cookstoves, and made quite an extra bundle selling ornamental wooden torches for the townsfolk to burn in their yards at night.

Then one day the woodchopper went before the town meeting at Fiddler's Bane. There was a tree shortage, he said, and he was being forced to go farther down the mountain in search of wood. He was going to have to build a road, he said, and, in order to pay for the labor, he was going to have to charge more for firewood.

The townsfolk weren't too pleased about this, but they had to have wood with which to cook their meager diet of biscuits and gravy, so they didn't have much choice.

The woodchopper told them that he was really just working in their best interest and that he had a deal that might make things easier for them. Since everyone in Fiddler's Bane lived on biscuits and gravy, he said, and since he had never learned how to mix up an acceptable batch of biscuit batter, he would be willing to accept the extra payment in the form of biscuit dough, which he could cook up on his own stove.

The townsfolk at the meeting then voted to let the woodchopper try out his plan to see how it worked out, but it was soon clear that the women of the town, the ones who did the cooking, weren't going to go along.

"He comes in and takes half my biscuit batter," one woman said. "I don't have enough to feed my family. How can he eat so many biscuits?" She suspected the woodchopper was storing the batter away in a secret place as a hedge against inflation.

So a committee selected by the people of Fiddler's Bane went to search the woodchopper's place. And, sure enough, they found his springhouse full of unbaked biscuit batter. Another meeting was held, and while it was decided that the woodchopper was entitled to some of the batter he would have to give half of it back to the women of the town.

The old man has just about finished with his quaint old folk tale, but the most important part is still to come.

"And so, young'uns," he says, raising a finger, "that woodchopper had to give back half that batter, and that's why, to this very day, you can hear old timers say …"

Here the old man is interrupted by a bright-faced youngster who jumps to his feet and shouts proudly, "If you start messing around with the biscuit-cookers, you'll end up giving back half the dough!"

The old man pauses a long while, and nods slowly. Then, with a smile that is both wise and sad, he looks at the proud little boy, raises his gnarled old hand and pops the kid right in the mouth.

Respect for one's elders is important in Fiddler's Bane.

Giving the Devil Hell

Arkansas Gazette
December 1973

I DON'T KNOW if Uncle Purl Stockton modified his appearance and personality into the standard pattern of a rescue mission superintendent or if the pattern evolved to Uncle Purl's image, but it really doesn't matter. Whenever I think of down-and-outers and soup kitchens, I can see Purl A. Stockton Sr., head of the Union Rescue Mission in Little Rock, looking as seedy as some of his charges while doling out food and old clothes and giving the Devil hell.

Uncle Purl founded the Rescue Mission in 1946, and until he left it in 1970 to embark on a new project, he spent his time ministering to the drunks and drifters whom no one else seemed to have any time for, ministering to their bodies with a hot meal and a bed and to their souls with a nightly sermon, sometimes given by a guest preacher but more often delivered at maximum volume by Uncle Purl himself.

The rules of the place were simple. You could stay as long as you needed to, but miss one nightly service and out you went, and none too gently, according to local folklore.

I first laid eyes on Purl Stockton when I was just a child, and he came to the Bauxite Methodist Church to talk about his work and consequently squeeze a little dough out of the congregation for operational expenses.

I think it's safe to say that the pulpit in that comparatively reserved Methodist sanctuary never again got a pounding to equal the one given it that day by Purl Stockton. I had seen a little ministerial shouting in my time, but most of it was of the joyous type, praising the Lord and hollering about salvation. Paul Stockton wasn't joyous that day at Bauxite; he was mad, and what he was mad at was the Devil and the things the Devil was using to make wrecks out of men—booze and cards and dice and jazz music and fancy women. The words he used escape me now, but I recall that he expressed the fervent wish that the Devil himself would come stalking up that aisle right then so he could grab him and shake his teeth out and then throw him right back out the door.

Mightily impressed, I stole a glance toward the back of the church, but the Devil had wisely declined the challenge.

The only other time I ever saw Uncle Purl was soon after I became a newspaper reporter in Little Rock, when I was sent to talk to him and find out how a drive for food and clothing had turned out. It was a simple assignment, involving only the adding up of canned goods and hand-me-down jackets, but, being a smartypants young journalist in the best tradition, I wasn't about to let it go at that.

What bothered me, you see, was this no-sermon, no-chow policy. What right did he have, I wondered, to deny a hungry man a meal just because the man didn't want to be exposed to religion? While I was arrogant enough to raise the question, I wasn't brave enough to use the word I was thinking of, and Uncle Purl supplied it with a laugh while I was still groping for a euphemism.

"Blackmail?" he roared. "Yes, you bet I'll blackmail the Devil every day if I have to."

Again, the exact words had faded from memory, but the gist of his explanation was that the Lord had called him to do two things: preach the gospel, and give aid and comfort to the walking

273

corpses who came wandering into his mission. He offered men a deal: Let Uncle Purl answer his first calling and they could enjoy the fruits of his second. He said he didn't have any illusions about how many souls he was saving, but if he touched only one in a thousand it was worth it and it was probably as good a batting average as the big downtown churches could boast of. On the other hand, he said, those other 999 men weren't hurt much by listening to a sermon, or even by sleeping through it, and it kept them off the street just that much longer, away from the cold and the whiskey and the cards.

He was right, of course, and when he died Monday at eighty-five, there wasn't a reason in the world for his conscience to bother him. I am not so sure about the rest of us, for we let Uncle Purl handle a lot of our burden simply because he, for some reason, was willing to do it.

While we patted ourselves on the back for being concerned about the more fashionable social problems, Purl Stockton voluntarily committed himself to a world of vomit-stained clothes and midnight screams, where the inhabitants weren't appealing or responsive, or even particularly grateful, a dark world where men's fears live.

What Uncle Purl did, I guess, was run the spiritual equivalent of television's M*A*S*H, where the horribly maimed are rushed in in such numbers that the immediate concern isn't maximum eventual recovery but with simply beating death away so that the patients can be sent out to face the same thing all over again.

Uncle Purl took to his maimed patients over on Confederate Boulevard and he tried to stanch their wounds with hot food and clean beds and a little healing preaching, and if there were just too many of them to allow for a high recovery fate, then the fault was ours, not his.

Dolls Still Need a Mama

Arkansas Gazette
January 1974

HOT SPRINGS—Bettie Sharp's corporeal world is not beautiful to look at, much less to live in, consisting as it does of a ramshackle house beset by building inspectors and a standard of living closely regulated by an eighty-four-year-old widow's Social Security check.

How much more pleasant, then, to spend as much time as possible in a world of crisp, starched crinoline and little top hats, where miniature ladies and gentlemen stand in proper poses and wait for the children to come and pay their respects. That was Bettie Sharp's world once, and it is one that she dreams of inhabiting again.

Mrs. A. Bettie Sharp has been making dolls since she was a little girl at Weatherford, Texas, and until recently she had been able to make a good living from showing and selling her dolls, and repairing the dolls of others.

She once ran a doll museum on Whittington Avenue here, and then she moved it to Central Avenue over the Mayflower Restaurant. Her business was good, and she said she has clippings of newspaper articles about her exhibits.

"Oh, I was written up a lot," she said. "And everyone just loved my museum. The little children especially loved it. I charged seventy-five cents for everyone else, but the little children got in for just a quarter, and they'd just stay and stay."

She closed her museum in 1969 and in 1972 she moved to Dallas and set up a little doll hospital, where, at first, she seemed to be doing all right.

But it didn't work out. Last year, she was injured when a freezer door hit her sharply on the head, and the doctors told her the injury would never heal completely. Then, in November, she got word that there was a problem with a house that she thought she had sold at Hot Springs, so she bought a bus ticket with the last of her money and came back to see what the trouble was.

It turned out that the person to whom she had sold the house had defaulted on the payments, so it still belonged to her. The home had been vacant for a time, and vandals had all but ripped it to pieces. Having no place else to go, she moved into the place and cleaned it up as best she could.

But some things were impossible for her to fix, such as the ripped-out ceiling and the broken windows, and a water bill run up by the former tenants had caused the water to be shut off. She was told that the building was condemned and that she couldn't live there.

An article in the Hot Springs paper chronicled Bettie Sharp's troubles, and city officials, who really didn't much relish the role of Scrooge in the first place, turned on her water and more or less decided to let the condemnation notice get lost in the bureaucratic shuffle. Thanks to that newspaper article, Bettie Sharp's present world is safe, for the moment, but it's one she never wanted, and she'd rather talk to a visitor about her museum, or about the exhibit of dolls she had at the 1946 Texas State Fair, or about what she might do now if she had the opportunity.

"I've still got a lot of dolls I could show," she told her visitor. "And I could start a little doll hospital. Do you know of a little place in Little Rock where I could start a doll hospital?"

She also remembers what a nice time she had a few years ago when she visited some friends at an apartment complex for retired persons. "Oh, they loved me there," she said. "I got everybody down in the game room to sing, and I put on a tacky party like you've never seen. They wanted me to stay there all the time."

She thinks she might like to do that, but she has no money, and it is hard for her to recall the name and address of the place. "So many things have happened; there's too many things to remember."

She can't afford materials, but there is a hickory tree in her yard, and she showed her visitor how she was painting faces on the nuts and gluing them to pencils to make little dolls.

"Now look at this," she showed her visitor, picking up a foam-plastic egg carton and tearing off a section. "Most people would just throw this away, and I was about to, too, but just look."

She picked up one of the pencils with the little hickory-nut face glued to the end and placed the piece of egg carton on the nut.

"See? It's a bonnet," she said. "A bonnet for a doll!"

The Truth Revealed Unto Us

Arkansas Gazette
October 1973

IT WAS ONE of those offhand bar-room comments that should, by rights, be forgotten along with the last Beer Nut in the sack, but instead goes caroming around the brain, refusing to drop, like a pinball marble controlled by a master of the flipper button.

"I wonder," said my friend, as he contemplated the swirls in his martini, "is Frank Broyles looking more and more like Billy Graham, or is Billy Graham looking more and more like Frank Broyles?"

The question just lay there on the bar, its author, no doubt, not really expecting an answer, and the conversation slid into serious inquiries about what Marsh White had been doing lately, and guilty admissions that hearts had leapt slightly when it appeared for a moment during the Texas–Oklahoma game that the Longhorns' Roosevelt Leaks might have sustained an injury worthy of a week on the sidelines.

But the idle question stuck in the brain—in one brain, at least—through The Hour, through a Number Six with fries at the Minute Man, indeed through the evening hours, not to be dislodged even by the amorous adventures of Travis McGee, who in this episode is trying to recover a king's ransom in rare stamps.

The question keeps intruding: Who is looking like whom? Frank has a modish new haircut this year, but the resemblance is more than can be accounted for by a pair of scissors and a little

Dippity-Do. It is not just the hair or the facial features; the demeanor is the same.

I wish I could claim credit for coming up with the answer, but I can't. As with so many problems, the obvious answer abided in the mind of a person whose view of the forest wasn't obstructed by the trees.

"It's simple," she said. "Frank Broyles is Billy Graham."

Well, of course! You've never seen them together, have you? The crusade business is always a little slow in the fall, isn't it? Well, isn't it?

It explains a lot of things. The rise, for example, of the Fellowship of Christian Athletes, those fellows who grunt, maim, cripple, and accept an ill-gotten touchdown on Saturday and proselytize in behalf of the Moral Life on Sunday.

(Not to criticize, but wasn't it a little simpler back in the days when a college student didn't have to worry about the religious leanings of a football player, only about staying out of his way? To paraphrase my favorite radio show opening: "Return with us now to those bygone days, with the rumble of approaching footsteps, the vice-like grip on the shoulder, and a hearty 'Get lost, buster, I'm gon' dance with your date.' *Leslie Letsinger Rides Again!*")

Of course, the revelation of Billy Frank, as he shall henceforth be known, poses some questions, but the faithful can rest assured that they will be answered at the proper time. For instance, has Billy Frank always played this dual role, or is it the result of some transmogrification decreed by the Most High, or maybe even the White House? We will just have to wait to find out.

I can see what you're doing out there, you skeptics, you sharpshooters. You're waiting for me to get through so you can blow my answer full of holes by harkening to the '69 Arkansas–Texas game, allegedly attended by the president of the United States, Billy Graham, AND Coach Frank Broyles.

"Gotcha!" you say. "If that was Billy Frank on the sidelines directing the actions of the Razorbacks, who gave that invocation? Who was that smiling and waving and sitting up there right by the Prez?"

I'll tell you who it was. It was E. Howard Hunt in a red wig, that's who it was.

Mgwphwuglug!

Arkansas Gazette
February 1974

"WELL," BEAMS THE LADY in the front of the dentist's office, "how are we this morning?"

"We are afraid," I reply.

The lady picks up a sinister-looking instrument, and I figure the ordeal has begun. "What are you going to do with that thing?" I ask apprehensively.

"I am going to write on this card with it," she says, taking what indeed turns out to be a pencil and scribbling on an index-sized card.

I sneak a look. The card has my name on it, and the lady has written, "Sweaty palms" across the bottom.

I take a seat beside a fish bowl with no fish in it. Pretty soon, one of the dentists comes in with a bag of fish. He empties them into the bowl. Maybe he has been checking their teeth. They seem to have pretty good choppers. Then again, maybe he locks them up at night in the office safe. Maybe they have been on vacation. Maybe they have been away to school.

"Mr. Trimble."

It can't be my turn already. I haven't even got halfway through the little folder where Johnny Whitetooth clobbers mean old Mr. Tooth D-K with a toothbrush and administers the *coup de grâce* with a wad of dental floss.

It *is* my turn. Another nice lady takes my hand and puts me in the recline-o-chair. She goes over to my card and underlines the words, "Sweaty palms."

"Dr. Cloud will be with you in a moment," she says, and splits.

I check around to see if the coast is clear. Might as well go ahead; it is the only chance I will ever have to have any fun in this place. I grab the water squirter and speak into it: "Mission Control, this is Apollo 7. Pitch and yaw increasing, and manual override is negative function, repeat, negative function."

I peer into the little round basin where the water is shooshing around in a circle. "Houston, the gyros can't compensate. It's the thrusters. I'm going to have to go EVA. I don't care what von Braun says! I'm going EVA. End of transmission."

"What about the ADA?"

It is Dr. Cloud, and the mission is scrubbed. The water squirter goes back into the instrument panel.

Dr. Cloud is my favorite dentist. That means I fear him slightly less than I do the Boogie Man or nuclear war. He always says, "See you in six months," but upbraids me only mildly when I show up four years later with my teeth covered with a green, sticky substance and with a filling gone from having bit too hard into a Willy Wonka Goo-Goo Cluster. He is very reassuring, eschewing those antiseptic-looking green coats. He wears civvies and a welder's mask.

He picks up The Needle, and I whimper. He puts it down, goes over to my card and draws another line under "Sweaty palms." This time, he discreetly turns his back as he prepares The Needle.

"This will hurt a little bit," he says. Dr. Cloud certainly knows his business. He has called it right on the button. He's nice enough to say nothing about the tears running down my cheeks and fouling up his equipment.

Proceeding apace, now. Thank God, the drilling's over. Wait a minute! What's that he's putting on the drill bit? THE SAND-PAPER DISC!! NO, DOC, NOT THE SANDPAPER DISC!

It's too late. BZZZZZRAP BZZZZZZRAP. My toenails claw their way past the socks and into the shoe leather. Why does he always have to use the sandpaper disc?

"All done," he says triumphantly, and whips out a mirror. "Take a look. Got a little surprise for you."

Great Scott! What's he done to my busted front tooth? That tooth has been sliding off at a 45-degree angle since I whacked it on the monkey bars in the second grade. I'm used to it, and now it's gone. Dr. Cloud has put a whole tooth in there without so much as a by-your-leave. The man has taken liberties!

"It was so shot through with decay that that was the simplest way to repair it," he explains. "Besides, see how much nicer that smile is?" I am not aware that I am smiling or that I will ever smile again.

"See you in six months," says Dr. Cloud.

Fat chance, Doc. Four years, soonest.

Cow Shopping

Arkansas Gazette
January 1974

DES ARC—The man hefted his glass and stared intently at the polar bear in Johnny Prislovsky's living room. The bear, being stuffed, made no response, but the man, being in a similar condition, didn't seem to mind.

"Mighty nice-looking animal," the man said as he glanced down to his drink. "Have me a few more of these and I might just bid on the booger."

The man was in a kidding mood, but he had spent that afternoon at the second annual polled Hereford auction at Prislovsky's Circle P. Ranch. Seven bulls and fifty cows had been auctioned for a total of $81,000 at Johnny's place.

The recipe for a successful auction seems to be about 50 percent beef cattle and 50 percent bourbon whiskey. The night before the sale, Prislovsky and his wife, Flo, had entertained almost 150 prospective buyers at a steak dinner held at the Brinkley National Guard Armory. Next day at the sale, the rueful grins and comments about large headaches testified to the fact that a good time had been had by all.

Now, the process was being more or less repeated at the post-sale party: a busy bar in the kitchen and a lavish buffet in the dining room featuring great hunks of beef.

"I got to be careful this year," one guest said, declining another drink. "Last year, I had to drive all the way home with one eye closed."

The sale itself had a festive air, as folks greeted friends they hadn't seen since the last sale, and the Des Arc Jaycees dished up catfish and hushpuppies before the bidding got under way.

To the uninitiated, the sale seems about as organized as your basic prison riot, but the appearance is deceiving. The auctioneer's assistants, who are spread around the outside of the show ring, seem to be doing nothing but hopping up and down and hollering, but they are in reality transmitting the bids from the prospective buyers to the auctioneer on the platform. They have eyeballed the crowd before the sale and have separated the high rollers from the window shoppers, so they know who to keep an eye on.

The first cow offered turned out to be the star of the sale. She brought $4,200, the top price of the day. Some of the other cows brought less than $1,000, and a slicker there just to watch couldn't tell that there was a $3,000 difference in any of them, so he asked a stranger who obviously knew what he was doing: "Excuse me, but if you were me and didn't know anything about cows, what would you look for when they're brought out?"

The stranger obviously didn't think much of being interrupted, but he was too polite to say so, and he pondered the question for a moment.

"If I were you, and I didn't know anything about cattle," he finally said, "I wouldn't be lookin'."

Wayne Barger, the manager of the Circle P.'s cattle operation, was more helpful. You want your cows to be wide across the rear end, he said, and built high off the ground, two qualities that make for easy births. Then, he said, you look for a lot of length between the cow's rear and the front of her hips. "That's where the steaks are," he explained.

Probably the most serene fellow at the sale was CMR Rollotrend 187, who is called "Ears" by the Prislovskys and is the Circle P's head honcho breeding sire.

Ears wasn't for sale, but since twenty-four of the heifers offered for sale had been bred to him, he was on hand so prospective buyers could look him over and see what their new grandchildren might look like.

Ears is, to coin a phrase, a lot of bull, but Flo Prislovsky said he's as friendly as a big old dog, and that the kids ride around on him a lot. Indeed, Ears has none of that menacing look that slickers usually associate with bulls. He's got a great disposition and about the only danger involved in standing close to him is that of being licked by a tongue about the size of a rolled-up Sunday *New York Times*.

The visitor looked at Ears for a long time, and although he tried to coax a moo, or whatever it is that bulls do, old Ears didn't have anything to say.

But then why should he? He's got it made, and the only message you'll get from him is when you gaze into those big dark eyes that look as wise as a tree full of owls and seem to be smug in the knowledge that their owner has the only job in the world where a fellow hates to take an occasional day off.

Oh, the Ravages of Age!

Arkansas Gazette
November 1973

ON MY WAY to the liquor store, I stopped at Little Rock's
Junior Deputy Field and watched the Teeny League footballers
work out while their adult coaches barked orders and walked
around in their baseball caps looking for all the world like
Frank Broyles.

Aha, you say, here's where we get that message about how kids
are oversupervised by adults who act out their childhood fantasies,
and so on and so forth.

Well, you're wrong. All that may very well be true, and I made
a meager attempt while watching the practice session to work up
a little indignation about it, but that really wasn't what was on my
mind. What I was really thinking about was how the Norton Town
Nightmares could have used some of that equipment.

Norton Town was a neighborhood in Bauxite inhabited by employees of the Norton Abrasives Company, and the Nightmares
were a sandlot team made up of the neighborhood kids. Their
season consisted of about 150 games against the Holly Street
Hoodlums, the only other team in town. I was a Nightmare, not
because I lived in Norton Town but because I lived closer to
Norton Town than I did to Holly Street. Also, the Nightmares
were pretty hard up for material and therefore accepted players
from outside the neighborhood boundaries.

The rivalry between the Hoodlums and the Nightmares continued through the summer, when the football teams transformed themselves into baseball teams. Between sports seasons, the Hoodlums and the Nightmares contented themselves with having pinecone fights or just beating each other up.

The Hoodlums were a tough outfit, led by Jiggs and Sonny Bono, Barrel Burrow, and Bobby Joe Harrell, who made life miserable for Nightmare tacklers by wearing his older brother's souvenir German infantry helmet in all the ball games.

Just about the only hope for the Nightmares in their daily gridiron encounters with the Hoodlums was the passing game, which was dependent on two of the team's female players, Jayme Smith, a pinpoint passer who could scramble when necessary, and my sister Pat, a tight end with good hands and moves that would do credit to Raymond Berry.

That battery, along with Lawton, Zachie, and Mary Ann Higgs providing protection in the interior line, put the Nightmares on more or less an even footing with the more physical Hoodlums, whose offense revolved mainly around Bobby Joe Harrell and his cast-iron helmet.

I still recall with sadness the Nightmares' last season, when what had developed into a fairly cohesive ball club was decimated at midseason by the ravages of age. We had been holding our own pretty well that year with the Hoodlums, with Jayme throwing those long bombs to nullify those long Hoodlum drives that left our defensive linemen with sick headaches. As I recall, our won-lost record at midseason was about 30–30, the best we had ever been able to manage, and we were looking forward to our first winning season.

Then disaster struck. Pat's, Jayme's, and Mary Ann's parents got together and decided the girls were too old to be playing tackle football with a bunch of boys, and jerked them from the team, thereby tearing the heart out of what was, at best, a rather shaky offense.

288

The girls, as I recall, were of two minds about the decision. They were pretty pleased about growing up and becoming ladies, but they were still loyal to the team, and they realized, probably better than we did, that they were the best players we had.

As for us—the male members of the squad—we had never heard of anything so ridiculous in our young lives. Mary Ann was the only one on the team, male or female, who could handle Barrel Burrow in a one-on-one situation, and, without her and our passing battery, we were sunk.

We also did a lot of conjecturing about the reason for such an arbitrary decree on the part of the parents involved but were never able to figure it out to our satisfaction. Lawton Higgs, one of the older members of the squad, and Mary Ann's brother, said he had talked it over with his mother, and as near as he could figure out it had something to do with bosoms.

That didn't make any sense to us then—truth to tell, it doesn't make a whole lot of sense to me now. All I know is that the Hoodlums whipped us regularly for the rest of the season, and we didn't get revenge until the baseball season rolled around. The girls were allowed to rejoin the team for that noncontact sport, and we more than held our own, because Jayme was the only kid in town who could throw a knuckleball, and Pat was the only one who could catch it.

Snapping a Disgusting Habit

Arkansas Gazette
December 1973

THEY LURK BACK THERE in the darkest recesses of the mind, then dart out unexpectedly, taking control of your conscious actions, sometimes for only a moment, and then they slink away, leaving only that feeling of self-loathing, that realization that you have once again succumbed.

Probably everyone is possessed of these demons—these dark, dirty little habits that we keep secret at all costs. In extreme cases, they may involve narcotics or alcohol, but, major or minor, they are alike in their sinister nature, alike in that we are shamed by them and at the same time powerless to break free from the hold they have on us.

I am no exception. For years, I have recognized the vile habit for what it is, but only to myself, never indicating to anyone else the sordid details of my degrading obsession. It has finally reached the point where the soul must be cleansed, where I must shout out the truth to the world at large in hope of starting on the long road back, and possibly even encouraging others suffering from the same addiction.

I read *Nancy*.

There! I've said it! I read the stupidest, most asinine, unfunniest comic strip in the nation and read it every day. It is not so bad when I am alone; then I am spared the furtive page flipping, the pretense that I am really looking through the want ads for a used car. So far, I have never been caught, although there have been some close calls. It is the prospect of discovery as much as anything else that prompts me to bring the whole thing out in the open. It is not so bad, somehow, to voluntarily admit to reading *Nancy*, but the prospect of being discovered in the act, of being publicly branded by peers as a *Nancy* reader, is just too much to bear.

I can't really remember when it began, or if, like most addictions, there was any pleasure in it at first. I don't think so. For as long as I can remember, Nancy has been a crumbum strip. It has never elicited so much as a faint smile, only groans, and not the kind of admiring groans that follow a clever pun, but real groans, indicative of genuine pain—pain and indignation that a man can make a good living turning out such tripe.

But, like a moth to a flame, I am drawn to the want-ad section of the paper every day. Usually, I lie to myself along the way. "Just going to check out what Dick Tracy is doing," I say under my breath. But I always end up at the same place, without really knowing how I get there, and there is Sluggo, with spaghetti all over his head.

There are days when I vow that it's over; I'm going cold turkey starting with the morning paper. The knot begins to form as I peruse the front page, and the fist in the gut tightens as I move back through the sports section.

By the time I get to the lost-and-founds my hands are shaking, and there is a thin film of sweat on my upper lip. It is getting close now. I have checked out *The Family Circus* and *Belvedere*; I'm almost through. I can see it over there, over on the corner of the page, but I'm not going to look. I'm not going to …

Aaaaaaaagh! Sluggo's bought a bag of peanuts and he's waited until he sees a sign saying "Loading Zone" before pouring them all down his throat.

It is on days such as that that the guilt is the worst, and I stumble unseeing through the day, going home to bed only to be tormented by nightmares peopled by Fritzi, Ritz, Irma, and Rollo the Rich Kid.

It has been a long way down, but with no way to go but up, the day seems a little brighter somehow, the air a little clearer, now that I've made the admission.

All I can do now is urge the rest of you out there to do the same. I know you're out there; I can tell by the empty stares I see every morning downtown. *Come out of the closet!* Together, we can lick this thing. When you get back in the classified ads and feel that knot in your stomach, give me a call. We'll talk it over. Maybe I'll come over and we can have some coffee.

The important thing to remember is that no one can be expected to kick the habit on his own, and we're just going to have to take it one day at a time.

Be Thankful You Aren't Virgil

Arkansas Gazette
January 1974

IF YOU ARE MOPING AROUND the house this morning thinking you have nothing in the world to be thankful for, I suggest you be thankful that you are not Virgil Hampton, for I am about to do the blighter in with a few deft strokes of the old Underwood upright.

(Libel laws being what they are, Virgil's last name has been changed, but you know who you are, Virgil, and this is for you!)

Virgil, you see, has written me a letter, in which he opines that I am to column writing what the Houston Oilers are to professional football! Noting that I put the bad mouth on a certain comic strip a couple of days ago, Mr. Hampton writes: "While I must agree that the comic strip 'Nancy' is utterly devoid of humor, I find it surprising that it should be you who raises the protest, for compared to the scribbling that bears your name, the inane adventures of Nancy and Sluggo seem to have been written by James Thurber himself."

Virge then goes on to say some pretty ungentlemanly things about my dog Pearl, who has been mentioned here from time to time, and he ends by saying he has read about a nationwide shortage of newsprint, and why don't I do my patriotic part by shutting the hell up and giving this valuable space over to obituaries or stock-market quotations, both of which, he thinks, would elicit more chuckles than do my feeble efforts.

293

Well, Virgil, I am a pretty reasonable man, and nobody realizes better than I that one man's yuck is another man's yawn. I have a friend whose idea of a real fun joke is to rent a wheelchair, place an empty picnic basket in the seat and wheel the contraption around town, pausing occasionally to open the top of the basket a little and say solicitously: "You doing okay in there, Arvin?" That is a little ripe for me. I generally go in for milder stuff, such as going into a record store and slipping a few Loretta Lynn albums into the opera stack, although I must admit to having given some boffo performances in the past with my dribble glass and my whoopee cushion. I personally draw the line at joy buzzers and exploding cigars, but I have never been intolerant of those who prefer them.

So you see, Virgil, I am pretty much a live-and-let-live man when it comes to funny stuff. Like I said, a reasonable man.

But, Virgil, that stuff you said about Pearl was pretty nasty, considering she can't even respond, and I'm afraid I'm just going to have to give you to know that you're not dealing with small potatoes here. I am plenty big-time, Virgil, and when you take on the biggies, you've got to be prepared to take the consequences.

Now, I suppose I could be reasonable about this, Virgil, and relate in logical and measured tones just exactly why you are full of grits. I could, I guess, relate how it is generally conceded that I am probably the best daily newspaper columnist ever to come out of the 1961 graduating class of Bauxite High School.

Or, I could tell you about the reactions of my college English professor when asked to comment on my success: "Who? Oh, him. I think he dropped out at semester."

Yes, I could do all that, Virgil, but I don't think it would do any good. I know your kind, and being a nice guy just doesn't cut it when dealing with your ilk.

No, Virgil, what is called for here is nothing less than the heaviest artillery in the arsenal of us big-time columnists. The razor-sharp putdown, the rapier-like thrust of words that will reduce you to a sniveling pile of Jell-O. It may sound cruel, but it's probably more merciful in the long run. You will learn your lesson once and for all, and will be spared future embarrassment at the hands of other, less compassionate, masters of the perfect squelch. So, get ready, Virgil, here it comes: NYAAAAAAH!!!

I'm sorry I had to do that, Virgil, but when you engage in a battle of wits with an acknowledged master, you can't expect to escape unscathed.

Testing the Thoroughbreds

Arkansas Gazette
March 1974

HOT SPRINGS—If horse racing is indeed the sport of kings, a lot of snooty people might be inclined to assign Orville Terrell, Vernon Myers, and Jerry Magie the social status generally reserved for the Spook, that hairy unfortunate who spends much of his time suspended upside down in the comic-strip dungeons of Id.

But they are wrong. Orville, Vernon and Jerry are at the very least dukes of the sport of kings, possibly even princes, and they constitute as agreeable a trio as ever second-guessed a horse race.

Orville, Vernon, and Jerry work for the state Racing Commission in its Oaklawn Park testing barn, a brisk walk from the amenities of the Park's betting windows and beer concessions. The Commission is there to see that there's no hanky-panky such as doping up the horses and, to that end, the winner of each race—and often an extra "spot check" horse—is subjected to urine tests just after it runs a race. That is where our three friends come in, for it is they—armed with a long-handled cup and the patience of Job—who accompany the horses into a private stall to collect the goods.

The idea of talking to the fellows at the test barn came from a friend of mine who writes newspaper editorials for a living. Not only did he think it would make an interesting piece, he said, but he had always felt there was a certain spiritual kinship between his job and theirs, and he'd like to know a little more about them—compare professional notes, so to speak.

So there I was at the test barn, where Orville, Vernon, and Jerry were swapping yarns with Dr. Don Burrows, the Racing Commission's vet for that day's activities. Vernon, who lives at Perryville, and Jerry, who comes from Bigelow, were expounding at length on the past grandeur of Little Italy, a community near the Pulaski-Perry county line. Jerry had got just about halfway through a colorful account of an Italian wedding when word came that the two horses from the seventh race—No Advance, the winner, and To the Rescue, the "spot check" horse—had been washed down, walked and watered, and it was time for the team to spring into action.

Vernon took the winner, and not wanting to be associated with an also-ran, I went with him. As No Advance was being led into the stall, Vernon explained the tricks of the trade. There weren't many.

"'Bout the only thing you got to make sure of," he said, "is whether you got a filly or a gelding. It makes a difference. You'd be surprised at how many folks would forget to check."

Other than that, he said, the only other requirement for the job is patience. "It's all pretty much up to the horse," he said. "They're supposed to be trained to go when you whistle at 'em after a workout, but sometimes they do and sometimes they don't."

We went in the stall, and the door was closed behind us, and No Advance, a beautiful gelding with Arkansas Derby hopes, proceeded to prove Vernon's theory that you can lead a horse to drink, but you can't make him water.

Vernon began the short, low whistles designed to produce results, and from the next stall, we could hear the same technique being applied to To the Rescue. In a matter of moments, we heard the door to the next stall open and To the Rescue was led out.

"See there?" Vernon said. "Sometimes you're in and out in a minute. Looks like this is gonna be a bad 'un."

Vernon continued his patient whistling as horses from subsequent races came and went. The pattern was the same. The stall next door would open, there would be a few short whistles, and the door would open again to let the horse out. Jerry and Orville began to rag Vernon a little.

"Hey, Vernon, you gonna get chapped lips, all that whistlin'."

Vernon remained patient, but he was beginning to frown through his pucker.

Another horse went in and out next door. "Just got to have that touch, Vernon. Heh, heh."

"Phooey," said Vernon. "Let's walk him around some more." No Advance was taken from the stall.

While the horse was being walked and watered some more, Vernon's colleagues commiserated. "Now, we kid him and everything," said Orville, "but it happens to all of us. You should have been here last year. Remember Jovial John? We'd have to stay up with him pretty near all night sometimes. That rascal was hard to catch."

The additional walk was apparently just what No Advance needed. Back in the stall, a few short whistles, and then: "Bingo," Vernon said quietly, quickly leaning forward with his cup, not unlike a fencer thrusting at a very small opponent.

We emerged from the stall, Vernon proudly bearing the fruits of his labor, accepting the accolades of his fellow workers.

The wait with No Advance had consumed the rest of the racing day, so Vernon had some time to relax. He is a welder by trade, but he takes off each year to work for the Racing Commission for the full season.

Why?

"Well," Vernon said, slowly shifting a chew of tobacco about the size of a golf ball, "the money ain't all that great, and it's not real exciting. I guess I just love racing."

A Trust Betrayed

Arkansas Gazette
October 1973

SPIRO AGNEW, the natural enemy of all us newspaper types, has bitten the dust, admitting to being a tax chiseler in return for not being proved an extortionist, and I've been sitting here all day wondering why, as one who howled as loudly as anyone about him, I still feel lousy about the whole thing.

I think I got my answer this afternoon, in a telephone conversation with a friend in North Arkansas, a retired professional man with whom I had enjoyed several fist-pounding arguments via the mails about the vice president. An unstinting conservative, my friend has been unable to go along with the oiliness of Reagan and the Snopesian appeal to prejudice of George Wallace, and with Goldwater seemingly relegated to a back burner he had found in Spiro Agnew a person who eloquently outlined what he believed was wrong with the country.

"I feel like I've been gut-punched," he said. "I respected the office of the presidency, but Nixon didn't speak for me. Ted Agnew spoke for me. Now, it doesn't mean anything."

That, I think, was what had bothered me all day and had finally prompted me to pick up the phone and make what was startlingly like a condolence call to a friend who had lost a close relative. All those poor ladies in California who stood on the tables and cheered as the president pledged to fight on and prove his innocence, and the man who had paid for that sadly ironic billboard in Baltimore—"Keep Punchin', Ted!"

Given the self-imposed isolation of the White House, those people naturally gravitated to the man who was chosen to do the gut fighting for Nixon. Agnew said it as they would have, but with an alliterative flourish that made them chuckle and roar for more. When those first leaks revealed that Spiro was in trouble, there weren't any bland statements by press secretaries; he met reporters head-on and called the reports "damned lies." Then he worked out a deal, quit, and stood before the judge—with "trembling hands," press reports said—and said he didn't want to contest a government charge that he cheated on his income taxes, that he had failed to report money that he had received from Maryland contractors who later had obtained fat state jobs under him.

A few of his supporters, of course, will be able to forge right ahead believing that the vice president was the victim of a colossal frame, blaming once again the Eastern establishment media. Others will be able to forget the whole thing rather quickly, shrugging it off with a "That's politics" and "Everybody does it."

But my friend won't and neither will a lot of other people who believed in the vice president.

"If what he said back then was right," my friend said, "it's still right, and it shouldn't make any difference what he did. But it will to all those people like you who put him down, and it does to me, too."

"You know what got me?" he continued. "All that evidence they submitted, that forty pages of stuff he never bothered to deny. It said he kept on getting that money after he left the governor's office in Maryland and became vice president, and he took it in the vice president's office."

My friend's voice was rising now with that mixture of anger and sadness that is indicative of a trust betrayed.

"Right there in the office of the vice president of the United States of America!"

There was a pause on the line, and then he spoke again, softly. "I guess it'll all turn out for the best," he said. "They'll probably be able to get better men on both sides now. I'm just glad I'm getting old, so I won't have to care about it any more."

He said goodbye and hung up, and I got a cup of coffee and sat for a while, thinking that of all the reasons to welcome old age, that is about the saddest one I had ever heard.

The Secrets of Weather Science

Arkansas Gazette
November 1973

I AM IN RECEIPT of a rather soggy letter from a lady at Augusta who wants to know "when the hell all this rain is going to stop." We have had, of course, a couple of days of brilliant sunny weather since she sloshed to the mailbox to post the letter, but I think her question is still relevant. After all, this two days of sunshine might be a trick to lull us into a false sense of security, to let us get our hip boots put back up in the upstairs closet before the next deluge.

In answer to the lady's question, I have to admit that I don't know when the hell all this rain is going to stop, unless day before yesterday really was the end of it, which would mean that the rain is going to stop two days ago.

The people at Augusta are concerned, of course, because they've got crops in the fields, or at least they had crops in the fields the last time they looked. The lady from Augusta says no one is exactly sure what's under all that water now.

City folks have had their problems, too, with National Guardsmen and residents teaming up over in Argenta to fight what appears to be an only moderately successful battle against the Arkansas River.

I have felt a little guilty during all the hubbub, since I don't have any crops out, and since I live on fairly high ground. I have tried to come up with some personal privation that would make me a kindred spirit to the farmers and the hardy North Little Rock folks, but about the only thing I could think of was the fact that my dog Pearl refuses to set foot outside the house when it's raining.

There is a little sense of sacrifice there. While others are gamely attempting to get combines unstuck or are filling sandbags twenty-four hours a day, I am manning the scoop in the living room of my apartment and hollering, "On the PAPER, dammit Pearl, on the PAPER!"

The lady from Augusta, as sort of an afterthought to her letter, has a few things to say about the TV weather shows. "I am not blaming the weathermen on the television," she writes. "They just get it from the Weather Bureau. But they are saying we are twenty-one inches above normal in rainfall for the year. We are in water up to our bellybuttons over here, and that seems a lot more than twenty-one inches above normal to me. Does somebody in Washington sit up there and decide what is normal rainfall for Arkansas?"

I think I can be of more help on this question. The answer to the question is this: Yes, somebody in Washington sits up there and decides what is normal rainfall for Arkansas, and through diligent research and communication with the *Gazette*'s Washington Bureau, I have found out who that somebody is.

The bureaucrat's name is Aqueous P. Waterlevel, and he is in charge of determining not only Arkansas's normal rainfall, but also that of the Florida Everglades. He was assigned to Arkansas only this year, receiving the added assignment because he had done so well on the Everglades job.

This information wasn't easy to ferret out, and I must give credit to the lady from Augusta, who gave the major clue when she reported that the water on her place was at bellybutton level. Using this data as my inspiration, I pressed for all the information I could on Mr. Waterlevel, and was able to unlock the mystery. Here is how he works.

As everyone knows, everything is normal as long as the water stays below the ground, where it belongs. When it starts sloshing into your shoes, it is "above normal," to use the Weather Bureau's technical phraseology.

Once or twice each year, Mr. Waterlevel makes a trip to Arkansas and stands out in a field. If no water gets in his shoes, he figures that the rainfall has been, at most, "normal." Then he pokes in the ground with a stick to see how much, if any, the state is "below normal."

That second step, of course, is omitted if he finds during Step One that the water is indeed higher than ground level. If that is the case, he checks his special government-issue trousers, which have been calibrated in inches along the seam, to see how much "above normal" the water is.

Now, here is the interesting part. As we all know, thanks to the lady from Augusta, the water is bellybutton high, which would seem to indicate an "above-normal" figure of more than twenty-one inches. That seeming contradiction is cleared up with this vital statistic, gleaned only through painstaking research and dogged determination. Aqueous P. Waterlevel is four feet tall, and his bellybutton is exactly twenty-one inches from the ground.

I hope that clears everything up.

Let's Talk About the Weather

Arkansas Gazette
January 1974

COLD ENOUGH for you?

We columnists always like to begin each effort with something really clever and original. It grabs your attention and lets you know how wonderfully funny the rest of the piece is going to be. Wait a minute! Come back! I was only kidding. You people don't give a fellow much leeway, do you?

Okay. If you're going to be that way, I'll answer my own question. Yes, it IS cold enough for me. It is also cold enough to freeze all the pipes in my dignified but elderly apartment building. I was fortunate enough to have a few out-of-town friends stranded at a Little Rock hotel, and, by a little harmless defrauding of an innkeeper, was able to wangle a shower and a shave. But it is hard to explain frozen pipes to a dog that has never seen an empty water dish. The selection of other prepared beverages being limited, the dog was left to make do for the day with a small bowl of beer, while her master crept downtown to earn her another day's ration of puppy chow.

I am anxious to get back home, for my apartment, located as it is at the top of a steep hill, provides one of the finer vantage points from which to observe the thin veneer of civilization being stripped away from drivers who find that they can't go up or down, only sideways.

In past years when the hill iced over, it was my custom to go outside and invite the stranded motorists in for coffee, but I soon found that most folks resent having their rage interrupted by an act of humanity, and were happier being left to cuss their errant machinery. Now I just hide and watch.

The action thus far has been only fair; I would not honestly give it more than two and a half stars. The Wednesday evening traffic was spectacular enough—plenty of Oldsmobiles, sitting sideways in the street as their owners looked wistfully at Volkswagens putt-putting effortlessly to the top of the hill. But there wasn't much going Thursday morning, possibly because a lot of folks stayed home, but more probably because there is some screwy natural law that decrees that most people drive smart in the morning and dumb in the afternoon.

It is a popular fiction that Southerners just don't know how to drive on ice, and that if this was Chicago we'd all be zipping around town as though it were the middle of May. Well, I recently returned from up North, where they were supposedly used to this sort of thing, and I can report firsthand that their traffic gets just as balled up as ours. About the only difference I could see was that you could hear the Rs when they were cursing.

Another misconception that each of us labors under is that everything would be all right if all those other meatballs would just stay off the streets and leave the driving to those of us who really know how to navigate when the streets are icy. Unfortunately, this theory almost always goes down the drain sooner or later, usually after you have passed some other poor clown in the ditch and have deposed to your passengers how the mutt could have avoided his predicament. About thirty seconds later, you are in the same ditch, and your passengers (there are ALWAYS passengers when you slide in the ditch; the car is always empty when you masterfully avoid every pitfall) are (1) giving you the old hee-haw, or (2) cussing you for stranding them a mile away from their nearest martini.

Possibly the saddest fall from icy-street expertise I ever saw took place on my hill a year or so ago. A big black Buick made it almost to the top, but just couldn't make it over the crest. The driver wasn't frustrated in the least, however, and he confidently declined my offer of coffee and a telephone.

"I'm prepared for this kind of stuff," he said.

Indeed he was. Assuring his passengers that they would be on their way in a jiffy, he strode to the back of his car, opened the trunk, took off his expensive-looking overcoat, folded it carefully, placed it in the trunk, and donned a pair of overalls over his Hickey-Freeman suit.

He then extracted a set of tire chains from the trunk and installed them in short order, doffed his coveralls, slammed the trunk, walked to the car door, and reached for his keys. Which were in his overcoat, which was in the trunk.

Spring will come, I promise, spring will come.

My Cup Runneth Over

Arkansas Gazette
November 1973

THANKSGIVING has always been my favorite holiday, not only because of the chow and the family gatherings that always seem to end in a debate on whether Justice William O. Douglas should be impeached, but also because it's about the only holiday I know of that can be truly therapeutic, if used correctly.

My observance of Christmas usually begins on December 24, when I start my shopping, and ends in a blue funk about midnight, when the last piece of wrapping paper rips down the middle as I am trying to wrap a unicycle. By the end of that annual ritual, I am generally qualified for a visit from the Spirit of Christmas Past and yearn only for the hour on Christmas morning when my brother-in-law breaks out the eggnog.

Easter I can usually ignore, although I am sometimes haunted by the childhood memory of the most evil, diabolical, and traumatic ritual ever devised by adults and inflicted upon their unsuspecting young: the egg hunt.

But Thanksgiving, if observed in the true spirit of the day, can always leave you feeling a little better than you felt before, aside from the heartburn. If an outright declaration of thanks is distasteful to the most secular minded, the same result can be achieved by just thinking about the things that make you feel good, or even a little less bad.

I, for instance, am thankful that a few prominent members of the state's legal profession have assured us that it's okay to cheat on our income taxes. Everybody's been feeling the pinch lately, and this will be a good way to get a little ahead. Granted, tax cheating isn't exactly new, but now that the lawyers tell us that it isn't nearly as evil as, say, stealing a $32 welfare check from a mailbox, that nagging little pall of guilt will be lifted and we can all deduct, deduct, deduct.

I am thankful that it wasn't an American-made tape recorder that messed up in the president's office. We have stood too long in awe of those crafty Asians, and the failure of Mr. Nixon's Sony recorder on the White House tapes rekindles that comfortable old suspicion that everything they turn out over there is really made from old beer cans.

I am grateful that Mr. Nixon has assured us that there are no more skeletons to be dragged from the closet in the Oval Office, as the country is already hip deep in bones.

I am grateful that three years isn't such a long time.

I am grateful for Bud Wilkinson, who sometimes manages to shut Chris Schenkel up for a few minutes on the Saturday football games, and I am thankful for Frank Gifford and (to a lesser degree) Don Meredith with Howard Cosell on Monday nights.

I am thankful for Dickey Morton.

I am thankful that I lucked out and bought a four-cylinder automobile before gasoline rationing started, and I am thankful I haven't broken it yet. I am grateful for the phrase "middle-distillate fuels," for although I don't know what it means, it trips happily from tongue and typewriter, and I am having a great time using it in as many conversations as I can.

I am thankful for the Fouke Monster, the White River Monster, the Ghostlike Bearded Creature at The College of the Ozarks, the two fellows at Bono who dressed up in tinfoil, and the man at Fort Smith who climbed up in a tree and hooted like an owl.

I am grateful for the Cache River, as long as we have it, and for the National Guard, so long as I'm no longer in it.

I am thankful for Fisher's Barbecue, fried okra, banana pudding, condensed-milk lemon pie, Jimmy Jones's mushroom sauce, and gin.

I am also thankful for Cletus Slim Jones, Martha Mitchell, Garner Ted Armstrong, Napoleon B. "Nap" Murphy, and the Downtown Officers Club.

This may look like a pretty low-rent collection of blessings to you, but I value them every one, and they have also jogged my brain about the real ones, the important ones that I'll keep to myself and savor later today, along with the turkey.

The Egg and I

Arkansas Gazette
October 1973

IN CASE YOU MAY have missed the news article, Serious Misconduct, aged seventy-four, of Welwyn, England, died last week.

Mr. Misconduct had not always borne that name. He was christened Malcolm MacTaggart, according to the brief account in the paper, and he carried that name until he was forty.

At age forty, MacTaggart was fired by the London Midland and Scottish Railway for what the company called "serious misconduct," and MacTaggart was so embittered that he had his name legally changed to be the spurious charges against him.

The saga of Mr. Misconduct might be considered a sad one by some, but I prefer to consider it one of those examples that prove it's more fun to be a human being—and thus to be able to watch other human beings—than to be, say, a turtle or a salamander.

It was no surprise that Mr. Misconduct was an Englishman; they have always been a lot more original with that kind of stuff than Americans, and I think we might do well to follow the late Mr. Misconduct's example. Probably half of us aren't too pleased with the names our parents stuck us with in the first place, and it would be therapeutic as well as interesting if we all dredged our memories for the worst injustice ever perpetrated on us and took that as our first names. It would do us all good to get those things off our chests, of course, and it also would make a nice icebreaker at parties: everybody giving the gory details of their first names.

My own name, for example, would be I Was Forcibly Dragged to Easter Egg Hunts Until I Was Ten Years Old and I Never Found a Single Crummy Egg Trimble. For legal purposes, the full name would be used, but my friends would call me Egg. A casual introduction at a party as Egg Trimble would naturally elicit a request for the full name, and that would be followed by a request to explain the injustice. I would then be able to unburden myself of all the bitter memories of standing in the middle of the picnic grounds in my little white short pants, screaming at the top of my lungs to be taken home, holding all the while a silly-looking and always-empty Easter basket.

I would then inquire in turn about my new acquaintance's name, and by the time we had both explained our names—and therefore our traumas—we would be fast friends.

The country would be led by President Eastern Establishment Press Nixon, and the immediate-past vice president would be Nolo Contendere Agnew.

Locally, our state government would include such officials as state Senators Duck Dinner Howell and Income Tax Fraud Jones, and the Capitol grounds would be kept spotless by Secretary of State New Decade Banquet Bryant.

The coach of the Arkansas Razorback football team would be known as We Couldn't Find a Fullback Who Could Block Broyles, and his counterpart at Iowa State would be They Had Twelve Guys on the Field Bruce.

Meanwhile, back at the Capitol, there would be state Transportation Commissioner I Was Tired of Being Winthrop Rockefeller's Bagman Tyler, and just across the Arkansas River, now in comfortable retirement, would be Federal Grand Jury Laman, taking life easy while enjoying reading about the tribulations of his successor, Mayor Riding Around On the Firetruck and Whipping Up on Aldermen Rosamond.

With a custom such as this, everyone could enjoy the pleasure of being bitter about their own personal bum raps each time they signed a check or introduced themselves, and we would owe it all to Mr. Misconduct, the man who first advanced the theory of constant ventilation of the spleen.

May he rest in anger.

Respectfully Submitted ...

Arkansas Gazette
March 1974

CAVE CITY—The Cave City Lions Club met Monday night at the Modern Cafe. Present were President Jim Musick and Lions Jack Patterson, Leonard Lewsaw, and Elisha Jackson.

Everyone wore his white Lions Club jacket with the purple-and-gold piping and the big Lions Club emblem.

Dinner was served promptly at 6:30. Lions Musick, Jackson, and Patterson had the chicken-fried steak. Lion Lewsaw had some cottage cheese with fruit on top. Lion Patterson finished up with some deep-dish cherry pie with ice cream. Lion Jackson had two scoops of vanilla.

Just as everyone was about to finish eating, a stranger approached the membership. The stranger had been sitting at the adjoining table, and had just finished eating a dinner of catfish, hush puppies, blackeyed peas, applesauce, and coffee for a buck and a quarter.

The stranger said he was a newspaper reporter from Little Rock and that he couldn't help noticing that this was a Lions Club meeting, what with the jackets and all, that his daddy was a Lion, and that he thought a club so small as this one was interesting, and could he sit in on the meeting and put something in the paper at Little Rock about it?

The membership said the stranger was surely welcome and they invited him to bring his coffee over and sit down, which he did, and the meeting continued.

314

President Musick brought up the subject of the club's annual light-bulb sale. He had a couple of offers for wholesale light bulbs and one offer seemed better than the other. Lion Jackson said the membership should make sure that the bulbs in the better offer were good bulbs. President Musick said he was pretty sure they were good bulbs.

Lion Lewsaw suggested that the Lions Club go on record as supporting the Cave City Jaycees in their campaign to do something about the parking situation. Lion Jackson noted that a bunch of cars were double-parked outside the Modern that very minute and that getting back on the highway from an inside slot was like trying to get toothpaste back in the tube. Lion Patterson said it was really bad when the Baptist Church had a funeral. Lion Lewsaw said the problem was that most of the members of the Town Council were downtown merchants and that they didn't want to make anybody mad.

President Musick reminded Lion Lewsaw that the membership had voted a couple of meetings ago to support the Jaycees' parking campaign and Lion Lewsaw said he must have been absent.

President Musick said he wanted to get back to those light bulbs for a minute, and he asked the membership what he ought to do. Lion Patterson moved that the matter be tabled until the next meeting, and the motion passed 3 to 0. (The president votes only in case of a tie.)

The stranger asked if this was the usual attendance, and President Musick noted that the stranger had caught the Club at a bad time, when a lot of Lions were sick or out of town. He noted that the Club had a membership of about fourteen and that the average attendance was eight or nine.

Lion Lewsaw asked that while activities were limited there were many ways that a small Club could be of service and that everyone was proud of the Club. The membership echoed this statement.

Lion Lewsaw, who noted that he was a charter member of the Cave City Lions, noted that the club contributed to the eight conservation programs of the Lions International by such things as the light-bulb sale and further noted that Lions sold tickets at Cave City High School basketball games, for which the Club received $7.50 a game.

Lion Patterson further noted that much of the $7.50 went back to the school in Club contributions to school activities.

President Musick noted that Cave City had an active Jaycees chapter of about thirty members and that the Lions often supported the Jaycees' worthwhile projects and that there was no rivalry or bitterness between the two organizations.

President Musick noted, however, that he was a bit disappointed in the attendance at Monday's meeting and assigned each member present some absentee members to call and remind about the next meeting at 6:30 p.m. March 18 at the Modern.

The stranger offered to print the names of the absentees in the newspaper so maybe they wouldn't miss any more. Everyone had a good laugh at that, but President Musick said it probably wouldn't be too good an idea and, besides, he didn't want to embarrass anybody.

There being no further business to conduct, the meeting was adjourned and everybody had another cup of coffee.

No Holiday Inn

Arkansas Gazette
November 1973

CAVE CITY—"Cave Courts," the sign says. "Modern." Well, maybe so, but they're not fanatics about it.

The place was built in 1930 by a fellow named Prince Matlock, who built it for Hubert Carpenter, the original owner. Matlock sold it six years ago to Dewey Buffington, and Mrs. Jewell Street now runs the place for the latter gentleman.

Matlock took a lot of stones from the nearby Strawberry River, some quartz from down at Hot Springs, some old Indian relics from the Crystal River Cave under the motel site, and mixed them all up. Then he apparently got drunk as a lord and went to work.

The result is a little grotto of cottages that appears to have sprung from the rocky ground where it sits, to be heavily frosted with a glittering icing and left to dry rock-hard in the sun. The chimneys aren't chimneys, but spires, with curling points around the tops as though had they had been shaped by a baker's frosting knife. Some of the cottages have small concrete porches out front, with ornamental concrete molding around the edges.

The cottages are arranged in a semicircle around the entrance to the cave, which visitors can enter by paying a fee at the office. The guest has to walk down steep concrete steps to get to the little park that has been built around the cave entrance. The park is cool and dark, and smells of wet leaves. The small space is crowded with trees: oak, pignut, mulberry, walnut, and one big sassafras. A massive rock archway has been built at the entrance of the cave.

Back up the steps to the cottage area, the guest discovers that Mrs. Street keeps a few chickens in a little coop off to the side of her cottage. A homemade chickenwire-and-wood cage next to the guest's cabin looks as though it may have once held a large bird. It is empty now.

The guest opens the door to cottage Number 3. No Holiday Inn here: The floors are of linoleum and the walls and ceiling are of wood. No strip of paper across the toilet seat; no color television; no radio; no telephone; no room service (but the Modern Cafe is just down the street).

The white chenille bedspread is turned back to reveal dazzling white stiff-starched sheets and two monster pillows that weigh about five pounds apiece. The bedsprings (not box springs—bedsprings) creak hospitably as the guest gingerly tests the bed.

A hotplate sits in the corner, along with a coffeepot, coffee, and the necessary condiments and hardware. In the hallway leading to the bathroom is an old refrigerator with a horn-of-plenty decal on the door. The bathroom is spartan but has all the necessary stuff. A degree of self-sufficiency is encouraged: A plumber's friend stands by the john and a broom is in the corner.

Back in the bedroom, the guest hangs his coat on the back of a ladderback rocker and surveys the room again.

There is a stone fireplace, inoperable now—you can't have everything—and in front of it is a big gas heater. The *Gideon Bible* is on the mantle. On the wood dresser is an October 1971 issue of *Esquire* and a 1968–69 *Photoplay TV Star Annual* with Carol Burnett and Rowan and Martin on the cover.

Under the glass on the dresser are posted the House Rules, of which there are three: Terms are cash in advance, checkout time is 10 a.m., and anyone making a nuisance of himself will be summarily ejected from the premises.

318

The guest sets up his portable and does a little typing, pausing occasionally to warily contemplate his roommate, a wasp that makes intermittent passes at the room's bare light bulb.

The guest considers taking some sort of preventive offensive action against the creature, but decides against it after observing that the wasp seems mainly intent on snoozing near the top of a wall, only occasionally making short forays to bump his head against the bulb before returning to the wall to cool off.

The guest retires early, as does the wasp, and he listens in vain for the usual motel sounds—the drunks or TV sets next door, the ice machines down the corridor, the sound of shuffling feet. All he hears are the chirping of the birds as they, too, bed down in the little park, and the sound of a brief but gusty rainshower just before he says goodnight to the wasp and goes to sleep.

Passing It On

Arkansas Gazette
February 1974

PINE BLUFF—The gray-haired man is scraping the griddle in the burger place and making life miserable for the two teen-aged boys who are his employees.

"When you gonna get that GI can out, Ralph?" he barks, and one of the helpers, a small boy dressed in a limp, dingy, short-sleeved white dress shirt and a clip-on bow tie, begins to wrestle with a brimful garbage can in the corner.

For his efforts, the boy is rewarded with a shirt front full of mustard, chili, root-beer syrup, and melted ice cream as the top layer of garbage cascades to the floor.

The man laughs, but cuts the laugh short when it appears that the boy is about to exit with the can, leaving the mess on the floor.

"Get that crap cleaned up!" he yells, and both boys fall to their knees and start rummaging through the goo on top of the overflowing garbage can. Each takes a handle and together they carry the can outside.

The man is upset at being left without a helper, and he voices his disapproval when the boys return: "How many people it take to carry one little old garbage can, for God's sake?"

The boys share a look, but say nothing.

A couple comes in with their child. The woman is dressed in red slacks and a tan raincoat, and her head is covered with tight, black, beauty-parlor curls. She is slender and pretty, as is the boy she carries, who looks to be about three.

The man has on a hunting cap, plaid wool shirt, work shoes, and blue jeans, not Levis but the kind made of cheap denim, with bright orange stitching and a pocket on the leg for a folding carpenter's rule. He is obviously just off from work, and he is dirty and tired. His hands are grimy, and one knuckle is bleeding. In his back pocket is a shiny, expensive-looking walkie-talkie of the type used by police officers.

The woman and the baby sit down at a table, and the man waits at the counter to place his order. One of the boys saunters over, and the man orders a couple of cheeseburgers, fries and Cokes.

"What kinda cheeseburgers?" the boy asks with a bored expression. The man doesn't understand.

"Look at the sign, will ya?" The boy points to a sign filled with exotic burger names such as Cheese-O-Burger and Whammo-Cheese and Whatta-Cheese.

"I'll take whatever's the plainest," the man says.

The two boys behind the counter share another look, and the man can feel the contempt. His ears redden a little, but he says nothing, and sits down to await his dinner.

The man's back pocket clears its throat suddenly, and he whips out the radio, unfurling the telescoping antenna with a practiced, fluid motion. He answers the racket with his call letters, and it is the first time he has looked pleased since he walked into the place.

"Nothin' much shakin', Cecil," he says into the walkie-talkie. "Our ten-twenty is The Whopper; Lou burned the dinner so we're eatin' here."

While the man is talking, his wife gazes at the electronic instrument with obvious loathing, seeing perhaps a washing machine or a refrigerator. She also glances outside at the pickup truck, which sports a whip antenna full of stick-on letters and numerals.

321

"I wish you would leave that thing in the truck every once in a while," she says during a break in the radio conversation.

The man looks at her briefly. "Shut up," he says without expression, and goes back to the radio.

"Is anybody gonna pick up this food?" It is one of the counter boys. The man motions to his wife, who gets up and brings the tray back to the table. The man continues to talk as he eats his cheeseburger.

The little boy at the table grabs a fried potato and waves it around happily a couple of times before thrusting it into his mouth. It is too hot, and he spits it out with a wail. He hasn't quite made up his mind yet whether to cry, so he looks at his mother entreatingly and gives a tentative whine.

She looks down at him and her eyes are mean.

"Shut up!" she says.

Where Are Our Blockades?

Arkansas Gazette
December 1973

ANY DYED-IN-THE-WOOL Arkansas booster couldn't have helped being a little disappointed Thursday upon reading that while about 1,500 trucks turned out to block a bridge in Delaware, the best that Arkansas could do was a measly three over near Brinkley.

I don't mean to criticize the truck drivers—I realize that fads are always slow getting to Arkansas—but Jeez, fellas, three crummy trucks? Here we are trying to live down a backward image, and all we can come up with is three lousy trucks. What good does it do for Governor Bumpers to have his hair styled and go around to other states talking about the "New South" if one sheriff can single-handedly dismantle a truckers' highway blockade?

Seeing all those pictures from Ohio and Delaware showing the Interstate choked with big trucks, one had to be grateful that no photographers were on hand to record the embarrassing affair over at Brinkley. The only way it could have been worse was if no trucks had shown up and the protesters had been forced to carry a big cardboard cutout with "Truck" printed on the side.

The state can take pride, however, in one thing—that an Arkie, Lloyd Whitman of Springdale, was one of the head honchos in the Ohio tie-up, parking a semi full of ice cream bars to melt by the side of the road as he provided copy for the media scribes in attendance.

(It would have been a little better, PR-wise, if Whitman had been loaded with something other than ice cream bars. One can picture the children of America crying for their Dilly Bars or Sidewalk Sundaes while a hastily formed convention of cats lays up the goods by the side of an Ohio highway. Since Whitman is from Springdale, it would have been great if he had been loaded to the gills with some of those North Arkansas broilers, thus giving the state exposure on two fronts.)

Whitman said he was going to just let them by-God Dilly Bars melt by the side of the road until somebody showed a little more appreciation for truck drivers.

Well, Mr. Whitman, it's hard to show all that much appreciation for an occupational group that can't do any better than a three-truck blockade over at Brinkley, but I hereby go on record as appreciating truck drivers.

I don't appreciate truck drivers because of the potholes, feathers, cow flops, and old tires all over the roads, nor because they make driving so interesting by blowing you off the road when you're in your little Chevy and trying to, as the president says, keep it down to fifty.

No, I appreciate truck drivers because, if it weren't for them, there would be no truck stops. I could do without a lot of things, but a nation without truck stops would be a dreary place.

Aside from the fact that you can get chow and (until the embargo) gasoline there, truck stops are the best entertainment value in the country. Nearly every one of them has a jukebox packed with George Jones, Loretta Lynn, and Charley Pride, and if you tire of listening to the music you can sneak off and leaf through the latest copy of *Overdrive* magazine, which once devoted three whole pages to a scathing exposé of waitresses who don't wipe the table off properly, or maybe go in the men's room and peruse the exotic vending machines.

Once back at your table with your breaded-veal cutlet and fries, the passing parade continues, for as a general rule dull folks just don't go to truck stops.

I once saw a truck driver walk into a truck strop, ask for a glass, fill it with the contents of the Tabasco Sauce bottle on his table, drink the whole mess and depart, all without saying a word.

I also saw a table full of truckers pass the hat for a young couple stranded at midnight in a broken-down car bursting with hungry kids. The spokesman for the drivers emptied the cap full of money on the table where the couple was trying to convince their children that crackers and milk constituted a meal, and he walked out before they could thank him.

The preceding examples shouldn't give anyone the impression that truckers are a taciturn bunch. They talk a lot, and laugh out loud a lot, and if the syntax is sometimes a little tortured, there usually is a thread of strange logic to their conversations and opinions.

My all-time favorite *non sequitur* was heard in a truck stop near Carlisle, where a bunch of drivers were discussing Watergate. "Nixon ain't much," said one of the drivers, "but he's a hell of an improvement over what we've got."

Keep these truck stops open, gentlemen, and I'm for letting you drive just as fast as you please.

Where's the Real
Orphan Annie?

Arkansas Gazette
January 1974

I AM NOT at all sure about the propriety of bringing this up, but someone needs to get to the bottom of it, and no one else seems to have picked up the gauntlet.

I want to know what happened to Little Orphan Annie.

Now, I am aware of the fact that Annie is not featured in this newspaper, but I have followed her adventures closely in another local publication for many years. Annie has always been one of those things that you could depend upon. The artwork (two eyeballs), the story lines (commie rats trying to take over America), and the political viewpoint (a little to the right of Attila the Hun) have been as reassuringly unvarying as the faces on Mount Rushmore.

Even when the creator of Annie—a man named Gray, as I recall—died some years back, his successor retained the original flavor of the strip, with Punjab and The Asp always arriving just in time to save Annie and Sandy from a cruel fate at the hands of abductors planning to bring Oliver Warbucks—and thus the nation—to his knees.

Why, only a couple of months ago Annie and Punjab enlisted the help of the ghosts of our founding fathers to thwart a scheme of world domination hatched by a Nazi U-boat commander in league with the international Communist conspiracy.

But then something began to happen. Annie became involved in a struggle with a little old lady who lived in a house full of pets and a big university that wanted to condemn her home to make room for a cancer research building. Now, the lady eventually got to keep her house, and the university eventually got its building, but the disturbing thing was that Annie herself was confused for a time about the moral implications of the thing.

One of the beauties of Little Orphan Annie—indeed of all good comic strips—is that everyone skillfully avoided the possibility that there might be two sides to a question. There were good guys—Daddy Warbucks, The Asp, Punjab, and anyone Annie might befriend—and there were the bad guys, who were hippies, peace creeps, spies, do-gooders, and liberal judges. It was disturbing to see Annie even conjecture that the other side might be right.

We should have been warned by that episode, but then again probably no amount of warning could have prepared us for what came next. In the current episode, in case you don't follow the strip, Annie is traveling with a van full of illiterate actors—nay, more: HIPPIE actors—and they are the good guys. I mean, they haven't kidnapped Annie or anything. She's there of her own free will, and everybody's just living in that van, boys and girls alike, and, well, it's just the damnedest thing I've ever heard of.

Townspeople who object to having the scruffy band in their midst are portrayed as mean, nasty people, and the actors themselves are shown going about doing good and ignoring caustic remarks about their long hair. It's as though Dick Tracy had come out in favor of a civilian police review board.

What's worse, the artwork has gone to hell. Where once we had those wonderful empty-eyed people who could bend only at the waist and thus looked like a company of zombies, we now are confronted with little round people who look as though they once were tall but have been squashed to fit inside the cartoon panel. They are "cute" in the worst sense of the word, and Annie is the worst of all; she looks as though she is now being drawn by Ernie Bushmiller.

Now, I want to know just what's going on. Perhaps there's been some kind of announcement about a new guy doing Little Orphan Annie, but if there has, I've missed it. What seems more likely to me is that the Red Menace finally tired of fooling around, has seized control of the strip, and is using it to chip away at the moral fiber of the country.

At this very minute, the bona-fide Annie cartoonist is probably bound and gagged in the back of a seemingly abandoned warehouse, while bomb-throwing anarchists turn out strips endorsing gun control, the nationalization of General Motors, and the busing of school children to achieve racial balance.

If something is not done, and done quickly, we can soon expect to see Judge Parker letting criminals off on technicalities and Mary Worth burning her bra in front of the White House.

Daddy Warbucks, where are you now that we need you?

Fan Mail and All That Stuff

Arkansas Gazette
October 1973

I HOPE that no one will mind if I use today's space under the Book Excerpts to catch up on my mail, but the letters have been pouring in at the rate of about one every two weeks and some of them contain questions that require immediate answers.

Also, it is getting late, and the remains of about fourteen leads lie strewn about me on the floor, so Mailbag City it is, with my compliments to the nice folks who came up with the questions.

Q—"I see you are hot for pigs. [I wouldn't have put it quite that way.] What do you think of the theory that pigs are the smartest of animals?"

A—I really don't know. I used to accept without question the assertions that pigs were the smartest of animals, but lately a few chinks have appeared in the theory. I used to like to cite a report from a newsroom buddy about an outfit called Uncle Heavy and his Porkchop Revue, in which Uncle Heavy put his talented porkers through all manner of intricate maneuvers. The pigs were dressed in ballet costumes, I was told, and they followed Uncle Heavy's every command without hesitation. Lately, however, evidence has come to light that tends to show that my friend made up the whole thing. More seriously, *Gazette* farm columnist Leland DuVall, who has raised a few pigs in his day, swears they are dumb, ill tempered and generally unfit for anything except bacon. He says he has only found two men who have ever trained pigs, and both of them used a club as the main training aid.

• • •

Q—"Who the hell are you to criticize the vice president of the United States, Spiro Agnew?"

A—At this point in time, as they say, there is no vice president of the United States. There used to be a vice president of the United States, but he copped a plea for income-tax evasion. I am told there will soon be another vice president of the United States.

• • •

Q—"Why haven't you taken out after the telephone company?"

A—The telephone company and I have gotten along pretty well, considering the fact that I'm one of the most deserving of the company's 'Class D' credit ratings, a designation reserved only for the deadest of deadbeats. For a time, I was on a first-name basis with a Miss Ballew, who would call each month to tell me that my phone would be disconnected if the company's dough wasn't in the office five minutes before I hung up. She got transferred or something.

• • •

Q—"If you are such a buddy of that communist, Grant Cooper, why don't you both move to Russia?"

A—I am not a buddy of that communist Grant Cooper. I have met him a couple of times, and about the only thing I can recall about the meetings is that I once took violent exception to his contention that Oscar Peterson couldn't play the piano for sour apples. I respect Dr. Cooper's right to have a negative opinion of Oscar Peterson, but if he ever starts propounding it in the classroom, I'm going to demand equal time.

A Lady With a Past

Arkansas Gazette
January 1974

HOT SPRINGS—It's been an uneventful but pleasant day here, and I've been doing a little idle wondering about what makes Central Avenue the most interesting main drag among Arkansas's larger cities.

Nobody else's main street is close, really. Texarkana has some interesting old buildings along State Line Avenue, but, technically speaking, State Line isn't that city's main street. Broad Street is, and Broad Street—like the main drags of Little Rock, Fort Smith, Pine Bluff, and the rest—has about as much charm and character as your basic federal office building.

(In all fairness, Texarkana also possesses one of the few really classy movie theaters still in existence—the Paramount—but it's not on either Broad or State Line, and it's on the Texas side to boot.)

One thing that sets Central Avenue apart from other main streets in the state is that it's a street of shops, of small businesses with no stockholders and no board of directors. Suburban shopping centers have made small shopkeepers just about extinct in most of the state's downtowns, but for some reason small businesses survive along Central Avenue, although I have no way of knowing if they actually thrive.

Several good restaurants line the avenue and people, not corporations, run them. There are curio shops and those marvelous "art galleries" filled to overflowing with little cloth figurines that play "Somewhere, My Love" when you wind them up. There is a hat store, as far as I know the only store in the state that sells nothing but hats ("Buy Your Hat From A Hat Store," says a sign in the window), and a knife shop with a show window chock full of hunting knives, kitchen knives, whetstones, and those mouth-watering Swiss Army pocket knives with seventeen blades, four screwdrivers, a leather punch, and a compartment to keep the butter fresh.

And, of course, there is the Arlington Hotel, that slightly shopworn but still magnificent old dowager, with her potted palms, wicker chairs, and bingo nights.

The folks at the Arlington and those all up and down Central Avenue seem somehow to have become immune to that mentality that defines progress as the art of throwing out anything made of wood or leather and replacing it with plastic, stainless steel, or Naugahyde.

No one could claim, of course, that Central Avenue is the epitome of good taste. The street has its share of tacky little places, and certainly more than its share of tawdry little nightclubs featuring down-at-the-heels go-go dancers. That tawdriness, however, has a permanence about it, a sense of belonging. Walk down Main Street in Little Rock and you won't come across one place in ten that couldn't be stripped to the walls overnight, leaving not a trace, not an inkling, of what had been there before.

The physical aspects of Central Avenue aside, there is something else, something intangible, that makes a stroll down its sidewalks more than just a means of getting from Point A to Point B.

The casinos may be gone forever, the mobster bosses may be long-departed to their Sicilian hideaways, and the alligator farm may still be the hottest thing in town, but—to a Saline County ap-pleknocker, at least—there remains a faint trace of that exotic aura not unlike that which might surround an elegant lady with a slightly shady past.

It doesn't really matter that nothing exciting happens during a walk down Central Avenue. The important thing is the feeling that it *could* happen. A woman in black *could* grab your arm on the street and say, "Please, act as though we're together!" A squat little man with a moustache *might* run up, thrust an attaché case into your arms, and disappear. A man in a tuxedo just *may* be looking at you from behind a potted palm in the lobby of the Arlington.

What I'm saying is that Central Avenue is the only place I know of where I wouldn't feel funny wearing a trench coat.

The Ghost Who Walks

Arkansas Gazette
October 1973

CLARKSVILLE—The paper said Tuesday morning that a "ghost-like bearded creature" was stalking the grounds of the College of the Ozarks here, and after a whirlwind tour of the campus I have only two facts to add to the mysterious report.

Fact No. 1—The ghost doesn't come out in the mornings, at least not on Tuesday mornings. A brisk walk across the campus revealed not a single ghost-like bearded creature.

Fact No. 2—Student Union coffee is about the same everywhere.

My intensive investigation of the phenomenon began by collaring a student and asking: "What do you think of the ghost-like bearded creature?"

The answer—"Not much"—indicated a revision of the question was needed, so subsequent subjects were asked if they had any ideas about the identity of the creature. The responses indicated only that today's college students simply don't have the proper respect for ghost-like bearded creatures.

Three people said they thought it was Spiro Agnew, a couple said it was the Fouke Monster, and the rest said they hadn't thought much about it. The only glimmer of originality came from a student who advanced the theory that it might be the ghost of Gabby Hayes.

The way I see it, the only way we're ever going to identify the ghost-like bearded creature is to work backward, eliminating fallacious theories as we go along.

First, the ghost-like bearded creature is NOT the Fouke Monster. Everyone who has seen the ghost-like bearded creature has described him as being fully dressed and wearing a coat, and we all know that the Fouke Monster is naked as a jaybird. The only possible connection here is that the ghost-like bearded creature might be an educated cousin of the Fouke Monster who has taken to dressing up and hanging around institutions of higher learning.

The ghost-like bearded creature is NOT Spiro Agnew. In none of the confirmed sightings has it said a word about the Eastern Establishment Press. In fact, it hasn't said a word about anything.

One admirer of the late Ernie Kovacs has suggested that the ghost-like bearded creature might be a member of the famed Nairobi Trio, those talented orangutans who used to whap each other over the heads with their drumsticks on TV. Logic dictates against this, for there have been no reports so far of drumstick wounds among the faculty or the student body. Still, the Trio has not been heard from in recent years, and authorities might do well to run a check on their whereabouts.

Finally, there are two theories that I hesitate to mention, for they are too farfetched to merit serious consideration. The first is that the ghost-like bearded creature is nothing more than a puckish student in a ghost-like, bearded-creature suit who is relieving the tedium of the academic world by trying to scare the pants off his fellow students. This contention will be rejected out of hand, of course, by anyone familiar with the serious nature of your basic College of the Ozarks student.

The second theory, prompted perhaps by several descriptions of the ghost-like bearded creature as "an old man with long gray hair," is that the ghost-like bearded creature might be an old man with long gray hair. While this is the wildest of all the theories, it is also the one portending the most danger. If gray-haired old men—nay, *more* longhaired, grayhaired old men—are to be allowed to enjoy a nocturnal stroll on a college campus, then we are all in big trouble.

A Mishmash of Minor Chores

Arkansas Gazette
November 1973

WELL, here we all are, still full from Thursday, just starting to get tired of turkey sandwiches and football games and wondering where that nice long weekend went. You are lethargic; I am lethargic. You don't want to spend a lot of time reading a long collection of bucolic homilies any more than I want to spend a lot of time writing one, so what we are going to do have today is a tying up of loose ends—a mishmash of minor chores that I've needed to tend to for some time.

(Before going any further, I've got to confess something. See that first sentence up there, the one about turkey sandwiches and football games? Makes you think I'm writing it after finishing a Thanksgiving feast, doesn't it? Well, it's a big lie. This isn't being written on Saturday, or Friday, or even on Thanksgiving Day. It's being written on Tuesday—last Tuesday is the correct phraseology, I guess—and it isn't even Thanksgiving yet. It's just another one of those sneaky tricks that the President keeps telling you about, written on the unlikely assumption that you people might believe I crept down here early Sunday morning and pasted this column on every copy of the paper as it comes off the press. I'm really sorry about it. Really.)

Okay, now that that's off my chest, we can get down to business. Let's just thumb through this stack of stuff on the desk here, and see what we can get out of the way.

First is a public apology. In this space a while back, I made reference to a friend of mine and his stories of a trained animal act called Uncle Heavy and His Porkchop Revue, an outfit supposedly comprising the aforementioned Uncle Heavy and a bevy of talented pigs that jumped through hoops, turned somersaults and danced the mazurka, or something like that. Partly because I could find no one else who had heard of this aggregation and partly because of my friend's marked propensity for stretching the truth, I conjectured in print that Uncle Heavy and his Porkchop Revue was merely a product of my friend's fertile imagination. Well, I was wrong. Uncle Heavy lives, and I have a photograph clipped from a New Orleans newspaper to prove it. The picture shows Uncle Heavy himself, posing with some of his more talented performers, all of them dressed in tutus (except for Uncle Heavy, of course; he was in overalls).

In addition, there is a giant postcard from Mrs. Arnold Maley, whose husband is the treasurer of the Clyde Beatty–Cole Brothers Circus. Mrs. Maley deposes that Uncle Heavy and his Porkchop Revue have been with the Beatty Circus for four years now and that Uncle Heavy is a real nice fellow.

In the face of this overwhelming evidence, I hereby offer my apologies to Uncle Heavy and also to my friend.

Next item in the pile on my desk is a rather yellowed newspaper clipping bearing the headline: "Gnostic Bible Views Snake as a Hero."

The article goes on to say that Bible scholars in California have translated a version of the Old Testament in which the snake in the Garden of Eden is the good guy. The article says that the old Bible gives your conventional account of the snake conning Eve into eating the forbidden fruit, but then remarks approvingly that "the light of knowledge shone upon them."

I looked up Gnosticism in the encyclopedia, and about the only thing I was able to understand was that it came right before Gno. There was one fairly coherent passage, however, saying that

Gnostics believed in the "redemptive nature of knowledge," thereby buttressing the discovery of the Snake-in-the-White-Hat version of the Bible.

The phrase "redemptive nature of knowledge" has a deceptively nice ring to it, and I suppose that knowledge is redemptive to a certain degree. Over the long haul, however, I must admit to being a What-You-Don't-Know-Won't-Hurt-You man, generally going along with the philosophic theory of Larry Obsitnik, who once opined to a cocktail-hour group at the Downtown Officer's Club: "You know, it sure would have been nice if Eve hadn't messed with that apple. I mean, here we'd be, sitting round this bar, drinking our drinks and having a good time just like now, but we'd all be naked."

I'll drink to that, and, as I recall, we did.

The Judge and the Cons

Scared to Death

Arkansas Gazette
December 1971

JOE LEWIS, twenty-six, a tower guard at Cummins Prison Farm, testified Thursday in federal District Court at Little Rock that he was ordered to shoot his rifle at the feet of Willie Stewart as the Black youngster entered the prison yard to begin a one-day sentence for burglary. Lewis said he was ordered to fire the shot "to scare him a little bit" before he was sent to the field for hard labor.

Stewart, who was seventeen, became ill and died en route to a Pine Bluff hospital.

Dr. Rodney Carlton, the state medical examiner, testified that Stewart died from "a first-cousin to sickle-cell disease," a blood ailment that affects mainly Blacks, but that extreme fear and exertion could have aggravated the condition enough to cause sudden death.

The testimony came in federal court hearings that are being held to assess the progress that the prisons have made in meeting constitutional standards. Federal Judge J. Smith Henley, who is presiding, ruled in February 1970 that conditions at the state's prisons made confinement there cruel and unusual punishment in violation of the Constitution.

Although the incident involving Stewart occurred after the hearings were under way, attorneys for the inmate petitioners have produced testimony about it, and the hearings have become what amounts to a public inquest into Stewart's death. Governor Dale

Bumpers, who was told about the shot and Stewart's death later in the day, was visibly upset. He said he was told that the boy was only five feet three inches tall and weighed 112 pounds. The court and the prison should not have sent the boy to labor at the farm, especially with his medical condition, and no one should fire shots to scare new prisoners, Bumpers said.

Lewis, who said he had been hired at the prison about three weeks earlier, testified that he was on duty in the tower about 5:10 a.m. when he received a telephone call from the main gate, saying that "we've got a one-day wonder coming in and make some noise and scare him a little bit."

A few minutes later, Lewis said, he saw Stewart running toward the tower, illuminated by the headlights of a car that was following close behind. He said the car was driven by Reggie Fletcher, a security guard, but he didn't know who had made the telephone call and ordered him to fire his rifle.

"I don't question it, I just do it," Lewis said.

Lewis said that as soon as Stewart stopped by the tower he fired a bullet close to Stewart's feet. Lewis said the area was well lighted, and he was not afraid that he would hit Stewart, even in the early-morning darkness. He said Stewart jumped and then cringed against a nearby chain-link fence. "He would'a gone through it if he could've," Lewis said.

Lewis said he then pushed the electrical switch that opened the gate to the inner prison compound, "and Fletcher pushed him through."

Stewart was wearing a white sweatshirt and green trousers when he arrived at the prison, Lewis said. As he was going off duty about an hour later, he saw Stewart again. His hair had been cut and he was wearing a white prison uniform. Two inmates were forcing the youth to do pushups on the floor near the chaplain's office. He said one inmate had hold of Stewart's ankles, and each time Stewart would do an unsatisfactory pushup the inmate would yank the youth's feet backward, forcing him to fall on his stomach, Lewis said. Fletcher, the security guard, was again standing nearby.

On cross-examination, Lewis said that Stewart was the first inmate serving a one-day sentence that he had been ordered to shoot at, but that when he had first received the job, "Carter [Cummins officer Bill Carter] told me when those one-day wonders come in, then shoot at their feet and scare them." He said that all one-day prisoners were shot at in the same manner.

Lewis was asked why he didn't report the practice to Correction Commissioner Terrell Don Hutto, and he replied: "Why tell a man something he already knows?" He later said he wasn't sure that Hutto knew about the practice of shooting to scare the one-day inmates, but that Cummins Superintendent A. J. Lockhart, Associate Superintendent Cecil Boren, and the entire Cummins staff knew about it.

[It was later testified that Circuit Judge Maupin Cummings of Fayetteville and Paul Wolfe of Fort Smith started the practice of sending youthful first offenders to prison for a day of hard labor in 1969 and then other judges around the state adopted the practice. Faulkner County Circuit Judge Russell C. Roberts sentenced Stewart to a day at Cummins. Former Corrections Commissioner C. Robert Sarver said more than a hundred youths had undergone the one-day incarcerations at the state prison farms.]

Lewis was asked if it wasn't his job to look out for an inmate's safety, and why he didn't stop the pushups.

"There was a captain standing there and I was off-duty," Lewis replied. "If an inmate jumps on an inmate, I'll stop it, but when a lieutenant jumps on an inmate I am not going to get into it." He described himself as "on the bottom of the pole" on the staff chain of command.

Reverend Elton F. Ballentine, coordinator of special services at Cummins, had testified earlier in the hearing on Stewart's death that he had observed two guards drag Stewart unconscious through the hall of the prison administration building after the work day had ended. Lewis said he had received orders not to let Reverend Ballentine into the inner compound if he arrived during the night.

Boren, the associate superintendent, testified that he had given an order that Ballentine was not to be allowed inside Cummins unless he, Boren, was there because prison inmates were "worked up" over Ballentine's testimony. Lewis said he was not going back to work at the prison farm because of the way Ballentine had been treated.

Robert Oliver of Little Rock, who was released from Cummins Tuesday after serving seven and a half months for a parole violation, testified that while he was working in the prison laundry the day Stewart arrived, he saw the boy being forced to stand in a shallow pond near the laundry building and duck his head under the water. Oliver said he had seen many one-day inmates forced to stand in the pond or run barefoot down a drainage ditch that emptied into the pond.

Oliver said prisoners at the farm were "going to begin to start something" Monday night after they had heard of Stewart's death, but that when they heard that the boy was to be released the next morning "every one of them, Black and White, came by my bunk and told me to come to this court and tell what had happened to him." Oliver is Black.

One-legged Inmate Put in Fields

Arkansas Gazette
December 1971

ROGER OLLEN, twenty-three, of Jacksonville, an inmate at the Pulaski County Penal Farm, testified Thursday in federal District Court in Little Rock that he was placed on the farm's "long line" even though he has only one leg.

Ollen, whose right leg has been amputated above the knee, said he worked for two days on the long line before buying a job in the kitchen by giving five dollars to a free-world warden. He said the warden, who has since been fired, also offered to help him escape for a hundred dollars.

Ollen was one of eight witnesses who testified Thursday as the plaintiffs rested their case in a suit that seeks to have conditions at the farm declared unconstitutional. Two inmates, Julius Foster and Jimmy Little, filed the suit in May against County Judge Frank Mackey and farm superintendent Marshal L. Cherry.

At the close of testimony, Chief Deputy Prosecuting Attorney Robert J. Brown, attorney for Cherry and Mackey, asked Judge J. Smith Henley, who is presiding in the hearing, to tour the farm, and Judge Henley agreed to do so at 9 a.m. today. The defense testimony will commence after the tour, and Judge Henley said the hearing would be completed this afternoon.

Ollen, who is serving a one-year sentence for possession of narcotics, testified that when he first arrived on the farm he was told he was being put on the long line "to sweat the dope out of me." (The long line is the group of inmates who work in the fields. It is the lowest classification of inmates.) Ollen said that after two days on the long line he had rubbed a blister on the stump of his right leg. He said that Loyd Dyson, who was a free-world guard at the time, offered to get him a job in the farm's kitchen for five dollars, and that he was transferred soon after he gave Dyson the money.

"Seeing as how I couldn't run," Ollen said, "he told me then that for a hundred dollars he'd drive me home."

Ollen said that he had lost weight while at the farm and, as a result, his artificial leg didn't fit any more. He said he had been refused permission to have the limb refitted.

Steve Herman, an attorney for the inmate plaintiffs, asked Ollen to describe the kitchen, and he responded that it was "filthy, with grease and grime all over the place." He said the kitchen had a large meat slicer, but the only time he saw it washed was two weeks ago "when a rat used the bathroom on it."

Cherry testified that Dyson had been fired several weeks ago after he brought a large quantity of wine and whiskey to the farm and then wrecked a county-owned truck while going back to buy more. Cherry said Dyson had passed out the wine and the liquor to several inmate trusties but that he had not punished the trusties, because "it wouldn't have happened except for the actions of that free-world man."

Several inmates testified that long-line workers at the farm had held a sit-down strike November 22 and that, as a result, they received no meals for three days. They were offered bread and water during the three-day period but they refused it. They said, however, that they were allowed to buy candy bars and soft drinks from a commissary operated by Assistant Superintendent Clayborn McDonald.

348

Cherry said the inmates had contended that it was too cold to work but that it was only 46 degrees. He said snow fell on November 23 and several inmates wrote a note to him saying that they were ready to go back to work. He said he didn't feed them that day because they wouldn't have had to go to work anyway because of the snow. On the third day, Cherry said he asked the inmates at noon if they were willing to work and they said they were.

He said McDonald bought candy and resold it at the commissary "at a very slight margin." He doubted that McDonald made very much money from the operation. Cherry said he stocked the soft-drink vending machine from his own pocket and took the receipts himself. He said the profits from the machine were used to buy sports equipment for the farm. On cross-examination, Cherry said it had been about a year since there had been any sports activities at the farm because "militants" had used the games as an opportunity to escape.

During the November 19 session of the hearing, Cherry had testified that a large percentage of the farm's inmates were alcoholics, and that when an inmate was stricken with an attack of *delirium tremens*, he was placed in one of the farm's isolation cells—a small shed with a concrete floor equipped only with a bucket and a mattress.

Thursday, Dr. Ronald W. McNichol, head of the State Hospital's alcoholic-treatment unit at Benton, called such a procedure "the greatest departure from treatment—or lack of treatment—that I've ever heard of."

Dr. McNichol said that a person suffering from an attack of DTs needed constant observation and also such treatment as immediate sedation, massive vitamin injections, and physical restraints. Even at the State Hospital, where such care is available, he said, the mortality rate from DT attacks was about 2 percent. At other institutions, he said, the rate is as high as 25 percent.

Persons suffering from delirium tremens, Dr. McNichol said, are in danger of dying from such complications as pneumonia or withdrawal convulsions, also known as "rum fits." A few patients, he said, have died from "sheer exhaustion."

On cross-examination, Brown noted that the State Hospital had a 2 percent mortality rate for DT victims, and he asked Dr. McNichols how he would react to a statement that no inmate confined in isolation at the farm for the DTs had ever died.

"I'd say it's a damned lie," Dr. McNichols replied.

Dr. McNichols also described a fairly new practice whereby chronic offenders with alcohol problems were being offered the opportunity by a few judges to choose between a stiff sentence at the County Farm or participation in a program in which they receive periodic doses of antabuse, a drug that produces violent but non-fatal illness if followed by a drink of alcohol. Almost all persons given such a choice choose the antabuse, he said, and the program has been successful.

On cross-examination, Brown tried to elicit testimony from Dr. McNichol that poor conditions at the farm actually were an asset to the antabuse program, because they made the choice to take the drug an easy one. Judge Henley interrupted. "This argument is not particularly impressive to the court," he said.

The testimony of two inmate witnesses prompted Henley to question whether the men were being held legally at the farm. Herman and Al Daniel, another attorney for the plaintiffs, hurriedly began the process of trying to get the inmates released.

Victor Bogart, seventeen, serving a sixty-day sentence for involuntary manslaughter stemming from an automobile accident, testified that he was scheduled to be released Thursday but that Cherry had added two days to his sentence because he had participated in last month's strike. The judge doubted that any statute would allow a prison administrator to add time to a prisoner's maximum sentence.

Curtis Lee "Cannonball" Turner, seventeen, testified that he had been sentenced to forty days at the farm and fined $363 for a series of unpaid traffic tickets. He said he had not been given an opportunity at his trial to arrange for payment of the fine and was now working it out on the farm, his forty-day sentence having been completed. Judge Henley asked Brown if he thought Turner was being held illegally, and Brown said it appeared that he was.

Daniel began preparing writs of habeas corpus late Thursday afternoon, asking that Turner and Bogart be freed, but he didn't have time to file them before the court recessed. Herman and Daniel didn't say if they would ask the judge to void the two-day extensions placed on the sentences of other inmates who had participated in the strike.

• • •

Two Leaves Join Worm as Evidence

A worm was introduced as evidence Thursday in the federal District Court lawsuit concerning conditions at the Pulaski County Penal Farm.

Calvin Canley, twenty-four, an inmate at the farm, testified that he had found the worm Wednesday afternoon in his turnip greens. Accompanying the worm into the record were two leaves, which Canley said he also found in his greens. The worm, which was dead, was on one of the leaves. Federal Judge J. Smith Henley, who is presiding at the hearing, examined the leaves carefully.

"I guess that's a worm," Judge Henley said. "It certainly is something foreign." Concerning the leaves, he said: "The court cannot say what kind of leaves these are, because it doesn't know, but they do not appear to be from a turnip plant."

351

The leaves were brought into court wrapped in a piece of torn Sunday newspaper comic strip. Steve Herman, as attorney for the inmate plaintiffs, handed the paper to Canley and said: "I hand you this newspaper and ask you if you can identify it for the court."

Canley replied that it was the paper in which he had wrapped the worm and the leaves.

Down on the Old Penal Farm

Arkansas Gazette
December 1971

PRISONERS at the Pulaski County Penal Farm are whipped with switches for severe disciplinary infractions, farm superintendent Marshall L. Cherry said Friday in federal District Court.

Cherry said he had delivered two such whippings in the last two months.

Cherry testified Friday in the trial of a lawsuit that contends conditions at the farm violate constitutional provisions prohibiting cruel and unusual punishment. Cherry—along with Pulaski County Judge Frank Mackey—is the defendant in the suit, but he was called to testify as a witness for the inmate plaintiffs.

Under questioning by Philip E. Kaplan, an attorney for the plaintiffs, Cherry said the switches were used in "extreme cases" of disciplinary violations.

Cherry said he had whipped an inmate named Olin Harper two months ago after the latter had attempted to escape. About two days ago, he said, he whipped an inmate named Hatfield because "he called me a lot of foul names."

Concerning the beating of Hatfield, Kaplan asked Cherry if any kind of hearing had been held before the punishment was meted out.

"No," Cherry said.

"You just took him in there and hit him?" Kaplan asked.

"That's right," Cherry replied.

Cherry said the whippings were administered to inmates as they lay face down on the floor. He said inmates were fully clothed when whipped. Asked what portion of the body was whipped, Cherry replied: "right where your mama would whip you."

Kaplan introduced into evidence a photograph of a thin sapling limb with the end shredded and asked Cherry if that was one of the switches used at the farm. Cherry said he couldn't tell if it was or not but that it might be.

Cherry also testified that he kicked inmate Calvin Hutchinson in the presence of Steve Herman and Al Daniel, two other attorneys for the plaintiffs. Cherry said Hutchinson had been ordered to go outside the farm office to a police van that was waiting to take him to the Pulaski County jail, and that Hutchinson had stopped to talk to Daniel and Herman in violation of Cherry's order. Cherry said he kicked Hutchinson in the buttocks to make him go through the door. He called Hutchinson, who has been a trusty shotgun guard at the farm, a "troublemaker."

Kaplan asked Cherry about the farm's isolation cells, which are eight-foot-square cinder-block structures with concrete floors. Cherry said the cells had no lighting, heat, furniture, or plumbing, but that there was ventilation through a small window in the door of the cell. He denied that the isolation cells were used for punishment.

"When a man refuses to go to work and you put him in there," Cherry said, "he's still not working."

Cherry said inmates entering isolation were given a bucket in which to urinate and defecate, a mattress, and a blanket. He said he couldn't recall anyone's being confined in isolation for more than three days.

Many of the inmates at the farm are there for crimes related to alcoholism, Cherry said, and the isolation cells were used to house prisoners who were experiencing delirium traumas. Inmates with DTs can't be kept in the barracks, he said, because they are a danger to themselves and others, and they keep the other prisoners awake.

Cherry said that, as of Friday, fifty-six inmates were at the farm, and they were supervised by four "free-world" employees, including himself. He identified the other three employees as Clayborn McDonald, the farm manager and assistant superintendent, a man named Dyson, who works as a warden and sleeps in the barracks, and Harry Moore, who runs the farm's mechanical harvester and doubles as a warden. Cherry said Moore had been on sick leave for the last ten days with "an alcoholic problem." Dyson, he said, is a former inmate at the farm. Former inmates frequently are hired as wardens, he said.

"We like to give a man a chance. It doesn't always work out, but we like to try."

Cherry maintained at first that separate barracks was the only practice of racial segregation at the farm, but confirmed when asked by Kaplan that whites and Blacks ate in separate dining areas. He explained that by describing the living areas, saying that the dining hall was in the center of the building and was bisected by the kitchen. A door from the white barracks leads to one section of the dining hall and a door from the Blacks' section leads to another.

Within the barracks, inmates sleep inside an enclosure called "the bullpen" that is locked at night. Trusties in the white barracks are allowed to sleep inside the bullpen, but Black trusties must sleep inside the bullpen in the Black barracks. Asked why Black trusties weren't allowed to use the same sleeping arrangements as their white counterparts, Cherry replied, "It's just not our policy."

Seven of the eighteen trusties at the farm are Black, Cherry said, and they are given such duties as raking leaves in the compound yard. Black trusties are not assigned to shotgun-guard duty, in the kitchen, or to duty on the sight-security desk. He said he assigned two Blacks to kitchen duty in 1960 "and they ran off." He admitted that many white trusties also had run off from the kitchen but said that more Blacks ran off than whites.

Shotguns used by the trusty guards are kept in an unlocked cabinet in the front office of the building that houses the barracks, Cherry said, and the trusties keep their shotgun shells in their pockets at all times when the guns are in the rack.

Kaplan asked Cherry if a doctor had come to the farm during the last two years.

"Doctors don't make house calls anymore," Cherry replied.

Asked if the suit angered him, Cherry said he was "not displeased by it. I think it has long-range good."

Hutchinson, the inmate Cherry said he had kicked, testified that he was being transferred to the county jail to await trial on an assault-and-battery charge when the kicking occurred. He said Daniel and Herman had interviewed him earlier in the day with Cherry's permission, and as he walked through the office he stopped to ask Herman if one of the two lawyers would act as his attorney in the forthcoming trial. "Mr. Cherry grabbed me and kicked me through the door," Hutchinson said. He said the kick landed at the base of his spine and "it still hurts."

Hutchinson said he frequently had seen McDonald hit inmates with a hickory stick without warning when he thought they were not working fast enough.

None of the prisoners at the farm, he said, had sheets on their beds and that the mattresses and blankets were dirty and torn.

He was asked how he liked being a shotgun guard and replied that he didn't. "Actually, I don't think I should guard them," he said.

Deputy Prosecuting Attorney Robert J. Brown, who is representing Cherry and Mackey in the suit, enlarged on that subject while cross-examining Hutchinson.

"You don't want to shoot anyone, do you?" he asked.

"No, sir," Hutchinson replied.

"Have you told the other prisoners that?"

"Some of them."

"You're not a very good guard, are you?"

"No, sir."

Hutchinson served a six-month sentence at Tucker Intermediate Reformatory in 1970 for escaping from the farm, and Brown asked him if the farm wasn't a better place to be confined than Tucker.

"Isn't the farm a pretty easygoing place?" he asked.

"I don't see it that way," Hutchinson replied.

Johnny Mensie, nineteen, of North Little Rock, an inmate at the farm, said that it was a simple matter to escape by bribing a trusty shotgun guard or currying his friendship.

"Catch a wino on shotgun, you flip him a quarter, and he'll tell you to get gettin'," Mensie said.

Steve Branch, another inmate, said he had walked off the farm before, and Brown asked where he had gone to prevent capture.

Branch paused before answering: "Well, I might want to go there again."

He was instructed to answer, and he paused again before saying: "I, uh, went to my mother's."

"The Smell of Death"

Arkansas Gazette
December 1971

PULASKI JUDGE J. Smith Henley ruled Friday that conditions at the Pulaski County Penal Farm were unconstitutional and ordered county authorities to upgrade the facilities or close it.

Judge Henley made his oral ruling after touring the farm briefly during the morning. He said improvements in the farm's physical plant must begin immediately if the county wished to keep the farm open, and, although he didn't set a deadline for completion of the improvements, he said minimum compliance should be reached within thirty days.

He noted that Pulaski County voters this week approved the construction of a $3.2 million county penal facility that would replace the county penal farm and the county jail, and for that reason he said he would not order remodeling of all the farm buildings.

"If the county had not made plans to replace the facility in the near future," Judge Henley said, "the court would know what to do. It would order its replacement with all deliberate speed."

Most of Judge Henley's ruling dealt with the physical conditions at the farm and with sanitation. He also ruled that the farm illegally segregated inmates by race, that Black inmates were systematically excluded from responsible trusty positions, and that whipping inmates with tree branches must cease.

In February 1970, Judge Henley ruled that conditions at the state prisons violated the Constitution, and one of the practices he cited was the control by inmate trusties of almost every facet of prison life. In Friday's ruling on the county farm, however, he ruled that the trusty system there, including the use of armed trusties to guard other inmates, was not unconstitutional. The difference, he said, was in the day-to-day power that the state prison trusty inmates had wielded over rank prisoners. At the county farm, he said, there was no indication that trusties "have the power to extort, threaten, or otherwise dominate the existence of other inmates."

In the way of physical improvements, Judge Henley ruled that the roofing must be replaced immediately on the farm's main building, which houses the farm office, the inmate barracks, and the dining hall. "The main building is a disgrace," he said, "whether it is constitutional or not." He counted twenty to twenty-five leaks to the ceiling during his visit there Friday morning.

Many windows in the barracks were broken when he toured the farm, and he said they must be replaced "immediately" if the farm is to meet constitutional standards. He said the wood stoves in the barracks seemed to furnish adequate, although inconsistent, heat, but he said officials should check to make sure that the temperature in the barracks was at a "livable and comfortable level" at all times.

"If it takes another stove, put it in!" he ordered.

Sanitation, especially in the dining hall and kitchen, was below a tolerable level, and he ruled that officials must act immediately to "bring them to the highest state of repair and cleanliness possible."

The judge spoke at length about the odor that pervaded the main farm building but added that "it probably couldn't be eliminated with fifty men scrubbing it ten times a day." He characterized the odor as a mixture of sewage, human perspiration, cooked food, and rotting timbers from the building itself.

"The novel *For Whom the Bell Tolls* contains a description of what it calls 'the smell of death,'" Judge Henley said. "I believe it comes as close as anything else to describing the smell of the Pulaski County Penal Farm."

Inmate witnesses had testified before Judge Henley that there were not enough showers or toilets in the inmate barracks, but the judge decided that those facilities weren't constitutionally inadequate, although they were "relatively primitive." He directed officials to repair the existing toilets and shower and keep them in good condition.

He ruled that the farm's staff, which currently is composed of Superintendent Marshall L. Cherry and Assistant Superintendent Clayborn McDonald, was "woefully inadequate" in number. He said county officials must hire enough personnel to insure that at least one free-world person would be on duty in the inmate barracks at all times.

The farm normally has two more free-world wardens, but Cherry fired one of them, Lloyd Dyson, because he said Dyson got drunk, wrecked a county truck, and brought wine and whiskey back to inmate trusties at the farm. The fourth employee, Harry Moore, did not return to work after taking extended sick leave for what Cherry described as "an alcoholic problem." Cherry testified Friday that while he and McDonald were off duty this weekend there would be no free-world personnel to supervise the inmates.

In enlarging the staff at the farm, Judge Henley said, officials should try to employ a trained person who could give preliminary examinations to inmates with medical complaints. Several inmates testified that they were refused permission to see a doctor when they were sick.

Inmates currently occupy racially segregated barracks and dining halls, and Judge Henley said that practice had to be ended immediately.

360

Cherry also had testified that his policy was never to appoint a Black inmate as a trusty in a supervisory position, and that while white trusties were allowed to sleep outside the inmate "bullpen" area in the barracks, Black trusties were made to sleep in the Black inmates' bullpen with the other rank inmates. Henley said those practices had been rendered illegal when he made his decision on the state prisons, and ordered complete racial desegregation of all prison facilities.

Corporal punishment, which at the farm took the form of whippings with heavy switches, also was ruled unconstitutional. Whippings took place in a side office, where the offending inmate was forced to lie face down on the floor while being whipped on the legs and buttocks. Cherry testified to having administered three such whippings recently.

In his tour during the morning, Henley observed the farm laundry, which consisted of one washing machine with a malfunctioning pump, and he ruled in the afternoon that the laundry was inadequate. He said he would not order that the farm have a laundry but that if the officials didn't choose to update the equipment they should arrange for some type of laundry service for the inmates.

In addition to his formal ruling, Judge Henley had some advice to prison officials on matters he did not deem worthy of official notice. He told the attorneys that testimony that a large cat population at the farm had created a sanitation problem in the barracks, the kitchen, and dining areas was aggravating but that he was "not about to declare cats unconstitutional." He proposed that officials keep the cats away from the kitchen and dining areas and provide litter boxes throughout the main prison building.

Cherry had testified that he had discovered weevils in the corn meal in the farm's kitchen, and Judge Henley had a remedy. Store the meal in metal cans, he said, and place an open bottle of "High Life" about halfway down in the can. Henley said they could keep meal for as long as two years without any worries about weevils. "Those helpful hints don't cost anything extra," he said.

Judge Henley's tour of the farm began soon after 9 a.m. and lasted a little less than an hour. Accompanied by Cherry, Sheriff Mackey, court officials, attorneys for both sides, and reporters, the judge inspected the main building, the isolation cells, and several storage sheds.

Leaks abounded in the ceiling of the main building and Thursday's rains caused steady drips of water during the tour. Much of the flooring in the Black inmates' bullpen was wet and in several spots water was coming through the ceiling in an almost steady stream.

None of the three toilets in the Black inmates' area worked, but Cherry said two of them had been in good working order earlier in the morning. He suspected a few inmates had broken the toilets on purpose. Henley agreed. He did not comment while at the farm and spoke to only one inmate, a man with cuts on his face who asked if a doctor was coming to the farm Friday.

"Do you need a doctor?" Henley asked. The man's reply wasn't audible. Cherry said the only thing wrong with the inmate was "a little old age."

Henley's ruling means that both county prisons now have been declared unconstitutional. In February, in a lawsuit filed by five inmates, Judge G. Thomas Eisele ruled that the county jail failed to meet constitutional standards.

7.

MUSINGS FROM
FARTHER SOUTH

*Prize-winning editorials by Trimble
from the* Denton Record-Chronicle

The Air Force addresses
the squeezebox gap

Denton Record-Chronicle
July 2004

OF THE ALMOST 500,000 active-duty soldiers in the Army, only one has the job of playing the accordion. That seems about right to us.

We will admit that there might at some point be a military need for an accordion player. There may exist somewhere in the world a fortification with a construction defect that would cause it to crumble like the fabled walls of Jericho at the first eight bars of "The Pennsylvania Polka." We would even go so far as to bet money that a couple of uninterrupted hours of "Lady of Spain" would extract valuable military secrets out of the most recalcitrant enemy commander, although we fear that it might violate the Geneva Conventions.

So we are OK with Sergeant Major Manuel Bobenrieth, first chair accordion player in the United States Army Band, the only accordion player in the entire United States Armed Forces. We hope he will never be needed, but we are willing for him to sit there between the French horns and the double-bell euphoniums, giving the country an accordion first-strike capability should it ever be needed, heaven forfend. But one Weapon of Musical Destruction is enough. It is not as though there aren't already enough bagpipes out there to destroy musical civilization as we know it four times over. Adding another accordion player to the American musical arsenal is madness—*madness!*

But that's what the United States Air Force is doing. At this very moment, undercover Air Force operatives are cruising wedding receptions and polka fests looking to add an accordion player to the Strolling Strings ensemble. The Strolling Strings has been without an accordion player since its last one retired two years ago. We had hoped that the retirement was a welcome sign of musical disarmament, but apparently not.

Apparently, we are on the dangerous path of accordion proliferation once more, and it is 11:45 p.m. on the B flat Doomsday Clock. Sergeant Major Jane Bockenek, the music director of the Strolling Strings, is the Dr. Strangelove behind this plot of Musically Assured Destruction, and she told The Associated Press she was having a tough time finding this new accordionist, for which we can only say we are grateful. She indicated that it is hard to find an accordion player who is anxious to go through basic training. (Accordion players may be musical malefactors, but they are not idiots.)

Bockenek speaks of the need for another accordionist in soothing terms, sort of like Paul Wolfowitz predicting showers of roses for the liberators of Iraq. The Strolling Strings, she says, entertain at White House functions and are "important from a diplomatic standpoint."

Well, wise diplomatic decisions aren't made by dyspeptic diplomats, and about the surest way we know of to ratchet up a surly envoy's bile duct is to subject him to an evening of the "Saber Dance" cranked out by some Air Force accordion player wearing a humongo pinky ring.

Bockenek also tries to get us to believe that the Strolling Strings have an important role entertaining our troops in wartime. *Right.*

366

We can just hear it now: "All right men, as you know, Bob Hope is no longer with us, and we weren't able to book Tim McGraw, Li'l Kim, or the Playmate of the Year for this USO show, but we've still got a real treat for you: The Air Force Strolling Strings, featuring Corporal Milo "Fingers" Mapes playing the soldiers' all-time favorite, the "Pizzicato Polka!" Take it away, Milo!"

We have only one word at this point: mutiny.

And that is where the whole scenario falls apart. The last image we see is of Slim Pickens falling from the bomb bay of a B–52. He has a Hohner accordion—a Gola model—strapped to his chest, and he is laughing maniacally as he hurtles to the earth, while playing "Flight of the Bumblebee."

Protesting accordion players serenading Trimble in the newspaper offices the day after the offending editorial appeared.

Big Brother moves in down the street

Denton (Texas) Record-Chronicle
May 2005

WE PROBABLY shouldn't worry about the Code Rangers, but we do, a little bit. The Code Rangers, if you didn't see the paper the other day, are a corps of volunteers who are going to keep their eyes on how often we cut our grass and how high we stack our garbage.

When we don't measure up, the Code Rangers will send us a little reminder in the mail. If we don't straighten up and fly right after that warning, our friendly neighborhood Code Ranger calls in the heavy artillery, the "city code officers."

We shudder to think what that might mean: the knock on the door in the dead of night; the endless interrogations ("Are you saying this isn't your rotten two-by-four, MIS-ter Anderson?"), landscaping miscreants being herded into the backs of city trucks, which will take them for "re-education" at Frenchy's Lawn Care and Gulag, or, if the offense is particularly heinous, to a device hidden in the city Service Center on Texas Street, a device known only as "The Big Chipper."

You see? We're working ourselves into a lather over this for no reason at all. All the City Council has asked residents to do is what good citizens do anyway: Keep an eye on things and drop a dime—er, a reminder—on a neighbor if something isn't quite up to snuff. The council came up with the idea last year when it approved some stricter requirements concerning grass cutting, tree trimming, junk-car displaying, and the like. Because we assume the council acts only with the best of motives, we assume it believed it was simply tapping Denton's renowned well of volunteer spirit in recruiting residents to keep an eye out for their neighbors' Johnson grass and garbage piles.

We wish we could think of it in the same way, but we can't.

At best, we think of it as an amusing annoyance, in which the neighborhood Barney Fifes patrol the streets, secretly yearning for a uniform and a whistle, on the lookout for high grass and old washing-machine parts. Gotta nip it, nip it, nip it in the bud, Andy.

At worst, we can see neighborhood grudges escalating into blizzards of warning letters and the use of official power to settle personal business. We can see suspicion blooming with the azaleas, ill feeling piling up along with old newspapers.

We think it is revealing that the city's two existing Rangers declined to comment on their activities for the story in the paper the other day. What would they say? What *could* they say? Would they have to appear wearing a ski mask?

Yes, we all have a stake in clean, healthy neighborhoods, and there needs to be a way to help an overtaxed code-enforcement staff find out about the most egregious violations.

But it seems to us there already is a way. Anyone who sees an overgrown lawn or a clapped-out Henry J in somebody's front yard already has the power—and, we believe the obligation—to report them to the proper city officials.

Of course, the possibility of abuse exists with individuals just as it does with the Code Rangers, but a complaint that comes from a private resident is just that—a complaint to be looked at with no prejudgment of guilt or innocence. A complaint from a Code

Ranger has the imprimatur of the city government right from the get-go. If the Code Ranger says your back yard's a mess it's up to you to prove that it isn't.

If it's all the same to the City Council, we like our neighbors just fine like they are, and would rather not see any of them turned into the law Gestapo. We had just as soon skip this side trip to the brave new world.

Governor closes the borders

Denton Record-Chronicle
June 20, 2005

GOVERNOR RICK PERRY has invited homosexual war veterans from Texas to move elsewhere, a statement so breathtaking in its bigotry that we thought at first that reports of it had to be incorrect.

Sadly, they were not. A quick check in newspapers and wire-service web sites confirmed that the governor had uttered the 21st-century equivalent of "Send 'em all back to Africa," and, even sadder, that he did it before an approving audience at a private Christian academy in Fort Worth. A couple of circumstances might tend to mitigate the governor's vile pronouncement:

One: It was in response to an obviously hostile question, and,

Two: Perry may simply be too dumb to realize just how vile his answer sounded.

Perry had orchestrated a big campaign photo op at the Calvary Christian Academy in Fort Worth over the weekend to watch him sign legislation requiring minors to get parental permission for abortions and a proclamation putting a constitutional amendment banning gay marriage on the Texas ballot. Several protesters on hand objected to one or both of the measures Perry was signing, and to what they perceived as an unhealthy melding of church and state. At some point in the proceedings, someone asked Perry what he would say to a returning veteran of the Iraq war who wished to marry someone of the same sex, the unfriendly but not unreasonable implication being that a Texan who has fought for his or her country has pretty much earned the right to marry whomever he or she damn well pleases.

Perry answered thus:

"Texans have made a decision about marriage, and if there is some other state that has a more lenient view than Texas, then maybe that's a better place for them to live."

Setting aside for a moment the technicality that the people of Texas have not yet voted on this proposed amendment, let us examine the malign prejudice that is implicit in Perry's words.

Plenty of intellectual arguments can be made for and against constitutionally defining marriage as a union between one man and one woman. They involve custom, sociology, child welfare, economics, individual liberty, and a raft of other issues. Perry addressed none of them; he simply implied, strongly, that gay and lesbian people are not welcome in "his" Texas. Because the question was couched in terms of returning war veterans, that's the way he answered it, but his "invitation" seemed pretty general in nature: If you are gay or lesbian, don't let the door hit you on the way out.

Some people in Texas, and everywhere else, believe that way, and Perry seemed to be pandering to that constituency. He may well win their votes with such statements, but they do him no credit among people of good will, no matter how they feel about same-sex marriage. We do not want our governor to be a bigot. We fervently hope he just said something stupid again. We can live with stupid.

Bye bye, American pie; hello, whipped topping

Denton Record-Chronicle
July 6, 2005

"These are the times that try men's souls. The summer soldier and the sunshine patriot will, in this crisis, shrink from the service of their country; but he that stands by it now, deserves the thanks of man and woman."

—Thomas Paine, "The Crisis," 1776

"Here I stand; I can do no other. God help me. Amen."

—Martin Luther, 95 Theses of Contention, 1517

"The pie-eating contest, really a whipped-topping-eating contest, was the biggest dish served up in the city's rain-soaked Fourth of July Jubilee."

—Cliff Despres, *Denton Record-Chronicle*, 2005

THESE ARE indeed trying times. When a city government can plop a dollop of whipped "topping" on a paper plate and call it a "pie," when these "pies" are then used in a "pie"-eating "contest" in which no one eats more than one "pie;" and when this "contest" is held on the Fourth of July, a day revered by all as being as American as "apple pie," well, our endurance is exhausted, as are our typing fingers, and our supply of quotation marks. For those who missed the account in Tuesday's newspaper, here is the grave situation.

373

As is the custom in this good town, the city government scheduled a wingding on Monday to celebrate Independence Day. It rained, forcing cancellation of the big parade and the horseshoe-pitching tournament, but spirits were still high for the pie-eating contest.

Imagine our shock upon reading our correspondent's account of the contest in Tuesday's paper and learning that contestants were asked to eat only one pie, and that winners were determined by timing the contestants, shortest time winning.

Worst of all was what passed for pie.

Let us ponder for a moment the entire concept of a pie-eating contest: It must involve a pie. A fruit pie is best, and cherry is the best of all, given its arresting, attractive color. Banana cream is OK, too, but meringue pies should be avoided, as they contain too much air, and lead to falsely impressive eating totals.

At its very least, a competition-worthy pie includes a metal pie tin, crust, and a substantial filling that requires some chewing. That is to say, the pies in a pie-eating contest must be pies, not "pies."

The "pies" used Monday in the city of Denton's Fourth of July pie-eating contest were not pies at all; they were plain old plates onto which were splashed some kind of whipped "topping" that we can only assume was suitable for human consumption.

And what, may we ask, is the idea behind timing the eating of just one pie? For children, maybe this is the way to go, but a Fourth of July pie-eating contest for grownups should be an exercise in good old American gluttony, with moaning and eye rolling and the threat of projectile vomiting. It is the American way!

This newspaper has never avoided controversial editorial positions before, and it doesn't intend to begin now. It is with faith in the right, as we see the right, that we hereby declare that if the city of Denton is going to throw a pie-eating contest, it should supply the contestants with real, honest-to-God pies. Moreover, the winners should be determined by the amount of pie they eat, not the time in which they eat it.

If the city cannot afford to buy pies, it should encourage someone to donate them. We nominate Ken Willis, the proprietor of Ruby's Diner on the Square. Willis would no doubt be more than happy to donate a couple of hundred pies to avoid being branded a cheapskate.

That is our position. Here we stand; we can do no other. God help us. Amen.

We modestly await the thanks of man and woman.

Ernest Wayne Dallas Jr.: Two pictures, one life

Denton Record-Chronicle
July 29, 2005

THAT PICTURE of Ernie Dallas Jr. in Thursday's paper, the one that shows him as a child in his baseball uniform, is what being an American boy is all about.

In that picture, replicated a million times each summer across the land, you can tell the young Ernie Dallas is already rehearsing how he'll pose for his rookie baseball card. He's got the stance down pat, and his uniform is perfect, from the gentle major-league roll on the bill of his cap to the batting glove on the left hand.

One senses that he is doing his best to affect a menacing batsman's stare for the camera, but he can't quite pull it off. The moment is just too perfect: The sun is shining, school is out, and Ernie Dallas is playing baseball. A smile threatens to break out at any moment.

You can see that threat of a smile in the other picture of Ernie Dallas that appeared in Thursday's paper. In that one, he is in desert camo and the black beret of a United States infantryman. He is a man now, there is no doubt of that, but the young baseball player is in that picture, too—in the clear eyes and the determined set of the jaw. Just as he had been in that earlier photo, Ernie Dallas was at home in the uniform. We know that about him if we know nothing else.

It is a source of both pride and sadness in this country that children in baseball uniforms grow up to be young men and women in military uniforms, and the physical stamina, enthusiasm, and team spirit they learned on the playing fields is spent on battlefields and carrier decks, and cockpits, and control rooms in lonely outposts that the rest of us cannot pronounce.

When any of these young men and women falls in battle, we are overcome by both sadness and pride. When it is one of our own, the loss and the pride are doubly strong.

The fog of war still surrounds his death, but we do know that Ernie Dallas died Sunday in Baghdad when the Bradley fighting vehicle he was riding in struck an explosive device. He was one of ours, the first of Denton's sons and daughters to die in that far place, and suddenly this war is brought home to us as it has not been before.

We have all formed our opinions about this war—the politics of it, or the economics—but this is not about politics or economics today; this is about one of our sons.

When members of his family spoke of him in Thursday's paper, we all became a part of that family. We went with them to baseball games, and to activities at Fred Moore High School.

We shared his parents' pride, and, we would guess, their quiet, unspoken fears, when he announced in high school that he wanted to be a police officer and enrolled in the Denton Police Department's Citizen Youth Academy.

We shared both emotions again upon reading of how he joined the Army in 2003, itching to help avenge the terrorist attacks on the United States in September of 2001. His anger made us proud again, and afraid again, afraid for him and all the young men and women whose anger, skill, strength, and confidence are necessary to survive the deadly business of war.

And on Thursday, when we read that he had died, our fear became ineffable sadness, though our pride was undiminished.

Ernie Dallas Jr. had dreamed of a life in uniform, his family said, a life of service. He fulfilled that dream, and it is our prayer that knowing this brings a measure of peace to those who loved him, and who miss him so today.

The Manchurian televangelist

Denton Record-Chronicle
November 14, 2005

THE PUBLIC pronouncements of the Reverend Pat Robertson have become so bizarre that responsible conservatives don't even bother to defend them anymore. Instead, they chide the press for paying any attention whatsoever to anything Robertson says, and we are forced to concede they have just about convinced us.

Robertson's latest outrage was to warn the people of Dover, Pennsylvania, that they had better not expect any help from the Almighty should they be beset in the future by fires, floods, pestilence, or any other disasters of an apocalyptic nature. Should they do so, Robertson predicted, God would simply tell them to go fish.

The sin of the Doverines, a sin that surely ranks up there with those of the Sodomites and the Gomorrahs was to vote from office a school board that had approved the inclusion of Intelligent Design in their schools' curricula. Spake Robertson on his television show, *The 700 Club*: "I'd like to say to the good citizens of Dover, if there is a disaster in your area, don't turn to God. You just rejected him in your city."

This, you will remember, is the man who twice claimed to have prayed hurricanes away from the Virginia coastline and nodded like a bobblehead doll at fellow parson Jerry Falwell's assertion that September 11 was God's retribution against an apostate United States, a view that happened to coincide perfectly with that of al-Qaida.

Robertson has also suggested in the past that an atomic bomb be dropped on the American State Department, that the U.S. government assassinate a leftist South American dictator, and that feminism urges women to "kill their children, practice witchcraft, destroy capitalism, and become lesbians."

Let us leave aside the merits of the Intelligent Design theory, which, simply put, argues that the universe is just too complicated a structure to have come about by chance. There are arguments to be made about it pro and con, but that is not our purpose here today.

Our purpose is to (1) ask who made Pat Robertson the arbiter of whom God will save and whom He will condemn, and (2) point out that he shot the Intelligent Design argument square in the knee with his pronouncement.

Second point first: The proponents of Intelligent Design know that they must present their theory on a purely secular basis. Intelligent Design, they argue over and over, is not about God. It is about science! Now comes the Reverend Robertson to proclaim that God Himself is supremely cheesed off at the people of Dover for rejecting this allegedly secular educational approach.

Does God take sides in these secular matters? What ever happened to rendering unto Caesar? How does God feel about cold fusion? How about the Designated Hitter Rule? Surely there should be some divine retribution for that.

First point: Pat Robertson's insistence that he speaks for God has at long last ceased to enrage us and has put him firmly in the tinfoil-hat section of the Peanut Gallery.

We knew it as soon as we heard clear-headed conservative commentators horse-laughing his Intelligent Design dithyramb along with everyone else. Some conservatives even speculated facetiously that he might be under the diabolical control of the lefties, a Manchurian preacher programmed to spout crazy stuff that makes the right look bad.

When your own side brands you a crackpot, you have pretty well slipped into the slough of irrelevance for good and all, and we don't envision commenting much about Pat Robertson in the future. He has passed into the realm of the truly whacked-out, where space flight is faked and pro wrestling is real.

Out there be dragons.

A younger Mike Trimble hiding in the Arkansas House of Representatives

Index

CPSIA information can be obtained
at www.ICGtesting.com
Printed in the USA
LVHW071509050523
746028LV00004B/6/J